Living Devotions

Princeton Theological Monograph Series

K. C. Hanson and Charles M. Collier, Series Editors

Living Devotions:

Reflections on Immigration, Identity, and Religious Imagination

Mary Clark Moschella

PICKWICK *Publications* · Eugene, Oregon

LIVING DEVOTIONS
Reflections on Immigration, Identity, and Religious Imagination

Princeton Theological Monograph Series 78

ISBN 13: 978-1-55635-288-1

Grateful acknowledgment is made for permission to reprint a stanza from "The Headcutters" by Edith Summers Kelly in *Cannery Women, Cannery Lives: Mexican Women, Unionization, and the California Food Processing Industry, 1930–1950,* by Vicki L. Ruiz, copyright © 1987 by University of New Mexico Press.

All scripture passages quoted are from the New Revised Standard Version Bible, copyright © 1989, Division of Christian Education of the National Council of the Churches of Christ in the United States of America. Used by permission. All rights reserved.

Cataloging-in-Publication data:

Moschella, Mary Clark

Living devotions : reflections on immigration, identity, and religious imagination / Mary Clark Moschella.

Princeton Theological Monograph Series 78
xiv + 230 p. ; 23 cm.
Eugene, Ore.: Pickwick Publications

Includes bibliography.
ISBN 13: 978-1-55635-288-1

1. Mary, Blessed Virgin, Saint—Devotion to—California—Los Angeles 2. Italian Americans—California—Los Angeles—Religion 3. San Pedro (Los Angeles, Calif.)—Religion 4. Catholic Church—California—Los Angeles—Customs and practices 5. Pastoral theology—United States—Case Studies I. Title. II. Series.

BT652 .L7 M67 2008

Contents

Photographs

View these photographs online at: http://www.MaryMoschella.net/LivingDevotions.

The page numbers indicate where references are made in the text to each photograph.

Acknowledgments

I T is a joy to acknowledge the many people and institutions that have made this book possible. Because this work began over eight years ago as a dissertation, before undergoing numerous rounds of revision and expansion, my debts of gratitude are many. I am grateful, first, to my research associates in San Pedro, California, who graciously shared their faith and their stories with me. Monsignor Patrick Gallagher and many of the people of Mary Star of the Sea church generously opened their doors to me, offering me their time, their thoughts, and their prayers. In particular, I would like to thank Mrs. Josephine Vrka for her extraordinary hospitality and trust. Grazie a tutie! I also acknowledge Ann Hansford and Al Bitonio of the San Pedro Bay Historical Society and thank them for their kind assistance.

This work began while I was a graduate student at the Claremont School of Theology, a unique and vibrant institution. Claremont's unparalleled Pastoral Care and Counseling Program opened up broad vistas of learning to me, not least through its ties to Claremont Graduate University. In particular, I thank Kathleen Greider, my primary advisor and mentor, for her careful guidance and stimulating reflection on this work. I have treasured also her personal support and encouragement along the way. I also thank William Clements, in particular for his corroboration of my interdisciplinary inclinations. Historians Ann Taves and Hal Barron helped me more than they knew. I am also grateful to the Louisville Institute for the Dissertation Fellowship that supported me in a full year of work on this project.

Wesley Theological Seminary took a chance on hiring me even before I was fully minted. In the seven years that I have been teaching at Wesley, I have experienced the hospitality and collegial support of an extraordinary faculty. I am grateful to all of you, for welcoming me into such a warm and caring community of scholars. I especially thank Dean Bruce Birch, whose firm optimism helped me push this work forward. I also thank Craig Hill, my faculty mentor, and acknowledge the late Sue Zabel, for her unconditional friendship and support. I am grateful to President David McAllister-Wilson and the Board of Governors for a sabbatical leave in the spring of 2004 that afforded me time to revise and re-imagine the work. In the library, Howertine Duncan helped me track down resources with speed and precision. Raymond Washington assisted me with printing, mailings, and his unflagging good will. Jeffrey Prothro worked on the bibliography. I thank my students at Wesley for their intelligence, interest, and enthusiasm.

I am grateful to the Society of Pastoral Theology for allowing me to share my work in progress. Charles Scalise and Roslyn Karaban invited me to present a paper to the Church and Christian Formation study group. I also thank the Society's Steering Committee for the generous time allotted to me to present my work in a plenary session in Denver in 2002. The Society's valuable attention and critical feedback helped me enormously. My thanks also go to the Person, Culture, and Religion group of the American Academy of Religion, for allowing me to present a portion of this work.

My thanks go to many teachers, colleagues, counselors, and friends, too numerous to mention, who have bolstered and sustained me in this work. In California, my long-time friend Lee Lassetter listened patiently as the research and the writing unfolded. My friend and colleague, Janet Schaller, was there with me in this project from the start. My friend and colleague, Michael Koppel, has helped imagine this work into being through his meditation practice during the last three years. For the last four years, Bethesda United Church of Christ has been my spirit's home, and Allison Smith, pastor extraordinaire. I thank Deborah Sokolove and Beverly Mitchell of the Wesley faculty as well as Father John Crossin (of the Washington Theological Consortium) for reading and commenting on individual chapters. I am grateful to Beverly Mitchell, not only for her comments, but also for her amazing friendship, and the inspiring play dates that we have concocted together. I am grateful to Jane Maynard and Leonard Hummel for our extensive conversations about "lived religion" and pastoral theology. Thanks also to Duane Bidwell and the other members of my on-line writer's group, for providing a gentle form of accountability for the hard work and numerous hours that writing a book entails. I am grateful to Charles Collier, my editor at Wipf and Stock, for his thoughtful reflections on the content of the book as well as for his patient work with me on the technical aspects of the manuscript. Thanks also to Chris Spinks and Kristen Bareman.

Finally, I thank my family and I dedicate this book to them. My grandparents, parents, siblings, nieces, and nephews all inspired me in some way. Julia and John, Mike and Annie, Matthew and Isabelle, thanks for being yourselves. My children, Ethan and Abbey Clark-Moschella, have grown up with this book in the background their lives, and endured our family's migrations from coast to coast. Ethan, besides accompanying me to San Pedro many times, helped with the photographs and the website. Abbey helped me with computer technology and general inspiration. Thank you, dear ones. Seeing you gives me strength and hope every day. My husband, Douglas Clark, read the entire manuscript too many times, offered insightful comments, and added much-needed precision, Thank you, Doug, not only for your intelligent assistance, but also for your love and loyalty, in every kind of weather.

1

Introduction: Ties That Bind

> What is finally at stake is at once honoring our individual dis-
> tinctions and birthing life-giving connection to one another, to all
> mortal and earthly creation, to the glory of God.
>
> —Melanie May, *A Body Knows*

> It's history that matters, what keeps you together in the tight ball
> of nerves and flesh that you are, and makes you you and not some-
> one else.
>
> —Brett Lott, *Jewel*

THIS is a book about religious connections, ties, and binds, and how
they are creatively negotiated when people immigrate. This book is
also about the sustaining and transforming potential of faith in the face
of hardship and change. I do not believe that these matters can be studied
in the abstract. Religion is not something separate from the economic,
social, or psychological dimensions of life, but rather something integrally
interwoven into all of these, shaping people and taking shape through
historical life.

In order to get at the interplay of these interrelated experiences, we
have to study them *in situ*, in a particular time and place. Therefore, I offer
a case study, basing my reflections on immigration, identity, and religious
imagination on my ethnographic encounter with a particular faith community and their religious practices. This book tells the story of what I
learned *about* and *from* a group of Italian and Sicilian Catholic immigrants
to San Pedro, California, and their devotional practices.[1] These folks were

---

1. Charles Hallisey draws attention to the distinction between learning about and
learning from religious practices. Hallisey, "In Defense," 121–62.

kind enough to allow me to get to know them, to tell me their stories of immigration and transition, and to share their families and their faith with me. Their devotional practices reveal complex interconnections—ties and binds—linking the sacred and the mundane. In the particular prayers and the particular lives of the devout, we can see ties between faith and fishing, between saints and relatives, between prayers and places.

The binding or rending of religious ties, the immigrant experience of displacement, and the ongoing project of identity formation in a new land are braided together into the family histories of numerous North Americans and woven into the larger tapestry of North American cultural memory as well. For many descendants of immigrants to North America, historical memories of cultural roots are blurred or hazy. I believe that this amnesia is due, in some cases, to the passage of time, but also in part, to a kind of selective forgetting of the painful parts of the stories. Immigration involves momentous change, loss, and grief. Given the scope of this dislocation, and the economic hardships that often go with it, the tendency to forget is not surprising. Both pride and shame–perhaps two sides of the same coin—can get lodged into family and group stories. Members of the second immigrant generation, the first born in a new land, bear the brunt of the transition and may not wish to dwell on the past. Back in 1937, immigration historian Marcus Lee Hanson observed that ". . . what the son wishes to forget, the grandson wishes to remember."[2] Members of the third immigrant generation, with the advantage of more secure footing in the new land, tend to become curious about cultural roots and family history.

But what do family history and cultural memory have to do with pastoral theology and practice? This is one of the questions that motivated me to begin this study. Historically, of course, North American churches and synagogues have been places of refuge for immigrants, places in which to gather with others from the same homelands, to speak native languages, to band together for mutual aid, and to seek the aid of a transcendent God. Because of this, religious and ethnic aspects of identity may be linked or even merged for many immigrants and their descendants.[3] While this tight association between religious and ethnic identity often gradually becomes unbound in later generations, echoes of this historical pairing may remain potent in family stories and traditions. How and why do the

2. Hanson, "Problem of the Third Generation Immigrant," 15.

3. See for example, Kim, *Women Struggling for a New Life*.

grandchildren of immigrants hold onto their ancestors' ethnic and religious bonds, or let go of them, and/or find themselves mysteriously still
held by sensibilities, images, or inclinations that they thought no longer
mattered? And how do imaginative religious ideas and pastoral practices
sustain and empower people moving through such enormous changes? I
turned to a group of Italian Catholic immigrants in San Pedro, California
and their children and grandchildren, in order to study what I call their
living devotions,[4] through which I could explore and try to untangle such
strands of identity-in-the-making.[5]

The Case Study

Mary Star of the Sea Church in San Pedro, California, is home to one of the
largest Catholic parishes in the Diocese of Los Angeles. The stained-glass
windows, statuary, mosaics, and paintings in the current church sanctuary
attest to the presence and participation of numerous groups of immigrants
from Europe, Asia, and Central America. In the center of the chancel is an
imposing marble statue of Mary, the mother of Jesus, treading on a wave.
In her left arm she cradles, not the Christ child, but a purse seiner—a
tuna boat! This statue towers over the church's central altar (Figure 1 and
Figure 2), dwarfing a crucifix standing off to the right.

The earliest members of Mary Star of the Sea parish came to San
Pedro to fish the bay. Between 1889, when the church was first established,
and 1950, when the fishing, canning, and boatworks industries peaked,
the fishing enterprise in San Pedro and nearby Terminal Island achieved
wild success. For a time, San Pedro boasted that it was the paramount
tuna fishing and canning center in the world. Yet the occupation of fishing
here always was, and still is, extremely dangerous. The two largest stained
glass windows, flanking Mary on either side of the sanctuary, suggest the
twin prayers of local fishermen and their families: prayers for an abundant
catch, and prayers for safety at sea. The window on the left depicts Jesus'
disciples hauling in their nets overflowing with fish (Figure 3); the one on
the right shows Jesus standing upright in a boat, stilling the Galilean storm
(Figure 4). Perhaps because of these two compelling phenomena—the

---

4. The term "living devotions" is based on the term "lived religion," as defined by
contemporary historians of religion. For explanations of the lived religion paradigm and
exemplary essays, see Hall, *Lived Religion in America*; and Maffley-Kipp et al., *Practicing
Protestants*.

5. The term "identity-in-the-making" is from Cooey, *Religious Imagination and the Body*.

success and the danger of fishing—many immigrants' religious practices became profoundly tied to their fishing occupation, their livelihood.

Though the once booming fishing industry in San Pedro has declined precipitously and all but ended in recent years, religious devotions to Mary and various saints remain robust in this congregation. This is still an immigrant church, conscious of its place on the shore and of the tentative feel of life on a boat. Representations of diverse patron saints, brought here from other shores, now line the interior walls of the sanctuary, holding memories of life and loss, and bridging distances in time and space.

In this research I set out to describe the piety of a group of these immigrants—from Italy and Sicily—and their descendants in San Pedro. Given that the process of immigration from one country to another involves the rending and forging of bonds, I wanted to explore the ways in which people negotiate the complex choices and emotions that tug at them in the course of this transition. So I invited members of three immigrant generations from Italy and Sicily to describe their experiences of immigration, their practices of devotional piety, and their related family stories. Listening to these stories, and observing the actual practices of the devout—what people do, what they look at and what they say, how they move their bodies, and how they spend their money—gave me a place to start.

One of my greatest teachers, Richard Niebuhr, brought to my attention one of the etymologies of the word, "religion," which is *religare*, "to bind." Related words include ligature, ligament, and obligation. Religion has been defined as, "Devotion to some principle; strict fidelity or faithfulness; conscientiousness; pious affection and attachment."[6] Religion binds or holds persons in relationship, relationship with the divine and with one another. In San Pedro, I encountered a multiplicity of religious ties and bonds of affection and attachment. These bonds seem to be working in different directions all at once. They include visual bonds to religious art and artifacts; moral and ethical bonds, such as bonds to care for the poor; bonds of memory—memories of homelands, of relatives, of the dead; bonds of marriage and family, bonds of affection for particular saints, financial bonds to the church and religious societies, and ethnic bonds, to name just a few. All of these bonds are interconnected, fluid, and shifting.

6. *Oxford English Dictionary*, 2nd ed., s.v. "religion."

It seems to me that through the practice of their devotions to Mary, Jesus, the angels, and saints, the devout have held on to, or experienced themselves as held by, bonds of memory, faith, and belonging. These religious bonds helped sustain the early immigrants, many of whom were fishermen or members of fishermen's families, through times of economic crisis, through losses of loved ones at sea or fears of such losses, and through the long periods of separation that fishing trips required. Because these experiences were often emotionally charged or traumatic, the peoples' devotional practices came to carry some of these memories and emotions. Through habits and stories, passed on to children and grandchildren, these ties and binds are continually reproduced and renegotiated. Children raised in these families take in not only the stories that are told, but also the bodily knowledges of faith, emotions, values, and aesthetic sensibilities that are experienced in this setting. Embodied knowledge is the more recondite for its unquestioned quality, the way in which it is accepted as just part of life. "It's just the way it always was," as one woman put it.[7] Such shared experiences, attitudes, skills, and habits function to preserve religious structures; they help keep the church, the people, and the devotions going.[8]

Narrative, Nerves, and Flesh

This is an ethnographic narrative, told in a pastoral theological voice. In Brett Lott's novel, *Jewel*, the protagonist declares, "But it's history that matters, what keeps you together in the tight ball of nerves and flesh that you are and makes you you and not someone else."[9] As a pastoral theologian, I am intrigued by the complex interplay of history, nerves, and flesh. I want to explore the role of history and religion in shaping our identities and imaginations, and vice-versa. In this writing, I juxtapose psychological, socio-historical, and theological perspectives on the story. I do this intentionally because I believe that in real life we experience all of these realities, all of these levels of life, at once. In this narrative I explore the confluence of faith, fishing, immigration, and identity in Italian Catholic devotions in San Pedro. Throughout the writing, and more directly in part two, I lift up some of the theological, spiritual, and pastoral questions that

7. Interview #27.

8. Bourdieu, *Outline of a Theory of Practice*, 83–84.

9. Lott, *Jewel*, 5.

I find in the story. These questions are rooted in particular practices, and yet they are broader religious questions, broader human questions as well.

I first got interested in this kind of study at the start of my graduate school education in Religion and Human Personality at Claremont School of Theology. There, for the purpose of taking a matriculation exam in religious history, I read Robert Orsi's *Madonna of 115th Street*. I found myself surprisingly moved by this study of Italian immigrant faith in East Harlem, from 1880-1950.[10] It was not that the community that Orsi described was my own. I grew up in a New Jersey suburb, in the 1950s and 1960s, the granddaughter of four immigrants from various towns in central and Southern Italy. Though Orsi does not tell my story, exactly, in reading his book, I experienced the intriguing and slightly uneasy feeling of being *known*. How could this author know me, and know me at a fairly deep level, a level that others had missed? It felt as though my own "history, nerves, and flesh" were implicated. As a student of human personality, I was curious about this. How was it, I wondered, that an historical study of religion could resonate so deeply in me? This got me thinking about the interplay between social history and the psychological and spiritual aspects of human identity.

This interplay gradually became the locus of my approach to pastoral theology and practice. I now teach pastoral theology and congregational care at a United Methodist seminary in Washington, DC. I work at the interface between contextual theology and what has historically been called "the cure of souls" tradition. If there is a theme that runs through my work, it is an emphasis on paying attention—looking at and listening to—the persons, congregations, and communities that pastors would seek to care for. In my teaching, I strive to enable students preparing for the ministry to comprehend the cultural as well as the theological and psychological complexity of the people and the congregations that they will be serving. Thus we consider the role of cultural expression in liturgy, prayer, visual environments, and food. How do all of these things influence the shape of spiritual care in a given community? What kinds of pastoral practice can enhance or limit the possibilities for social transformation? I have come to

10. Orsi, *Madonna of 115th Street.*

believe that congregational studies, ethnographic research, and historical study are vital means to these pastoral theological ends.[11]

From a pastoral and spiritual perspective, cultural identity matters. History matters in the stories we tell ourselves about ourselves. We yearn to make sense out of the past, to know how we got to be the particular bundles of nerves and flesh that we are. The historical and current phenomena of immigration play a role in the cultural identities of numerous pastors, parishioners, and diverse congregations in North America. Immigration has gone largely unexplored in the pastoral-theological literature, at least among so-called whites or Americans of European descent. It is as if we are playing along with the dominant cultural mythology that claims that only blacks or people of color are "ethnic," and thereby preserves the normative status of whiteness. With this book, I want to encourage all pastors and other religious professionals to think about their cultural roots, and the ways in which their familial, religious, and ethnic histories matter in the present. In this age of cultural and religious hybridity, people of diverse backgrounds and customs migrate, combine, clash, and/or blend with increasing frequency and fluidity. Reflecting in an intentional way on our own histories and identities-in-the-making can free us to move more grace-fully in the mix. There is a certain spiritual clarity that comes from understanding ourselves as fully historical beings, both shaped by and shapers of the religious worlds we inhabit.

Sources

I gathered the data for this case study through participant observation, qualitative interviewing, and the examination of historical documents.[12] During the course of a year and a half, I regularly traveled from my home in Riverside, California to San Pedro, on the coast. I observed, interviewed, participated, scanned documents at the local public library and the San Pedro Bay Historical Society, sat in churches, and/or walked the beach. I met and spoke with several persons in the wider community, including the

11. Authors in pastoral theology who have called for descriptive and contextual approaches include: Browning, *Fundamental Practical Theology*; Patton, *Pastoral Care in Context*, 43–45; DeMarinis, *Critical Caring*; and Lartey, *Pastoral Theology in an Intercultural World*, among others.

12. As a novice ethnographer, I relied heavily upon Hammersley and Atkinson's guidance in conducting the research. Hammersley and Atkinson, *Ethnography: Principles in Practice*.

staff and volunteers at the San Pedro Bay Historical Society.[13] In the ensu-
ing years, I have made several trips back to San Pedro. I have also brought
copies of preliminary drafts of my writing to the folks I interviewed for
their review and comment. More recently, I made a trip to Ischia, the
particular island off the coast of Naples from whence many of the families
in my study hail. I saw with my own eyes the famed resemblance of this
coastal landscape to Southern California. In conversations with returned
immigrants from San Pedro, I learned more about the beauty and powerful pull of that particular homeland.

   The thirty-two taped interviews I conducted with the devout and
their families constitute the centerpiece of the research for the first half
of the book. Because I was interested in learning something about how
the devotions transmit information, habits, and faith from one generation to the next, I chose a research model known as the snowball sample.
This is a way of selecting persons to interview who are connected to one
another, either through kinship, friendship, religious, or professional association. In San Pedro, I soon learned, many residents seem to think of
the Italian and Sicilian population as one big snowball. People are thickly
connected—they know or know of each other fairly frequently and well.
When I use the term "community," however, I am not referring to the
mass of residents of Italian or Sicilian descent, but to the smaller and more
particular group of people whom I got to know. Recognizing that my
sample is small, I am not attempting to generalize beyond it.

   I gained access to this community largely through the connection I
formed with one woman, whom I have named "Rosa" in this narrative.
Rosa questioned me intently when I first met her, asking me over and over
again, "Why? Why are you doing this?" When I finally thought it through
enough to offer her a satisfactory answer, she opened wide the gate of
friendship, both personally and in the community. I am aware that Rosa
also functioned as a "gatekeeper," steering me toward and away from interviews with various individuals. In order to compensate for the limitations
this imposed, I also sought out interviews on my own, as well as through
the recommendations and connections of each interviewee or "research
associate." Though I began by interviewing members of the Mary Star of
the Sea parish, in the end the sample was not limited to this particular
congregation. As time went by, my interviewees informed me about the

---

13. For more details on the research, see Appendix A.

existence of several additional Catholic churches in the San Pedro Bay area—totaling five by my last count.[14] My sample included some members or relatives of members of each of these five faith communities. Most of the people I interviewed were quite devout. Some might be called religious virtuosos. Some were suggested to me as good representatives of the Italian Catholic community in San Pedro. Though I tried to find them and set up interviews, the less devout members of these families were generally less interested in speaking with me. The sample does include a number of infrequent churchgoers, one immigrant who is an atheist, one self-described "fallen-away Catholic," and one second-generation woman who converted to a Protestant theology.

The persons I interviewed ranged in age from twenty-four to ninety-one. They were mostly bi-lingual; five of the interviews were conducted partly in Italian. Most of the interviews took place in peoples' homes, at kitchen or dining room tables, often overlooking the sea. In most cases, I was permitted to photograph religious art and home shrines. In some cases, family members or friends stopped by during the interview and contributed to the conversation. I was frequently the recipient of great hospitality on these visits. Italian coffee and homemade cookies—often with a plate to take home—were generously offered and gratefully consumed.

In these semi-structured interviews, I tried to strike a balance between asking my questions and allowing people to talk freely, following their sense about what was most important.[15] Using this approach often led, as I hoped it would, to the sharing of deep personal stories. I felt, at times, torn between my role as an ethnographer probing for understanding and my pastoral inclination to offer support or comfort in these moments. I felt an ethical obligation to tend this balance, not wanting to unwittingly move into a counseling role, nor to go so deep that interviewees were left feeling unraveled. At the same time, I did not imagine my proper role as one devoid of compassion or genuine connection. When I listen to the tapes, I still feel honored by all that was entrusted to me.

14. These include: Saint Margaret-Mary, Saint Peter's, Holy Trinity, Little Sisters of the Poor, and Mission Stella Maris.

15. See Appendix A and B.

Reflexivity

It seems important to say something about my place in the research for the case study as well as in the writing of this narrative. Of course a social science kind of Heisenberg Uncertainty Principle applies—the practices I studied were undoubtedly affected by my presence and my attempts to study them. Furthermore, even though I attempted to conduct the interviews in a flexible and open fashion, my questions shape the narrative. The issues and images that I observed, noticed, and commented upon are inevitably selective. I made an attempt to approach the study "with open hands," to borrow from the language of Henri Nouwen.[16] I made an effort to come to the research without judgment, to see what was going on in and though the practice of the devotions, rather than to gather evidence to support a theory. Nevertheless, it is my view of the devotions and not the devotions themselves that the reader will find described here.[17]

Knowing that this is so, I want to be as transparent as possible in my descriptions of my interactions in San Pedro, and as clear as possible about the lenses, motivations, and meanings I bring to this study. When "Rosa" pushed me hard to say why it was I wanted to do this research, I came to realize that alongside my scholarly interests, a very personal motivation was right beneath the surface. It was, quite simply, that I missed my grandmother.

Assunta Turdo Caivano was my maternal grandmother, a woman who left her home in the farming village of Picerno, Italy, at age twenty-two, to board a boat that brought her to New York's Ellis Island in 1920. Two years later she married my grandfather, Saverio Caivano. Assunta lived to be ninety-eight years old. In their home in Millburn, New Jersey, my grandmother displayed numerous colorful pictures and statues of saints. For me, as a child, going to visit there felt a little bit like going to church, though the aromas of cooking made it smell a good deal better. The statues of saints on my grandparents' bedroom dresser were beautiful, untouchable porcelain dolls. They wore shiny satin clothes that could thrill a child's heart. There was a perpetual candle burning in front of these saints, adding a bit of drama and danger. (If I reached up and touched one of these

---

16. Nouwen, *With Open Hands.*

17. Of course, there is a distance between the practices studied and my interpretations of them. For an excellent explanation of reflexivity, see Bourdieu and Wacquant, *Invitation to Reflexive Sociology.*

forbidden saints, would the clothes catch fire?) My grandmother also had a backyard shrine to Mary in the middle of the garden. On warm summer days I would help tend the blue and white plaster Virgin, bringing her bouquets of fresh flowers in glass vases. These objects seemed magical and mystical to me. They are connected to my memories of my grandmother, the unceasing clicking of her rosary beads, and the similarly persistent quality of her love for me.

This personal story reveals something about my own religious sensibilities, what Geertz might call my moods and motivations, and others might call my biases.[18] My view of the devout in San Pedro is likely to be tinged with nostalgic feelings for my grandmother as well as other feelings I may have about my Italian Catholic background. There is also the risk that I will at times over-identify with the people here, and obfuscate their West-coast experiences of immigration and faith with my third-generation East-coast experiences. The danger is that my practical knowledge of Italian Catholic faith—the same knowledge that motivates my interest and helps me gain access to the Italian Catholic community in San Pedro—can get in the way of my ability to see and appreciate the distinct experiences of the devout in this setting, or to assess them critically.

An example of this dynamic occurred during an interview with a third-generation woman who has stopped attending Mass. The woman waited until after I had finished the interview and turned off the tape-recorder before she looked at me meaningfully, and, resting her head on her hands, asked, "Do you have *the guilt?*"[19] Drawn in, I found myself compelled to utter a hasty and hearty "Yes!" The problem with this response, of course, is that it was based on my experience and my sense of identification with the woman. While I knew that a complex combination of factors may have constituted or contributed to the guilt of which the woman spoke, I did not actually know what particular guilt she was referring to. Was it Catholic guilt for leaving the church? Was it female guilt for working outside the home? Was it ethnic guilt for marrying a non-Italian? Was it a more generalized guilt for the sin of self-definition or for the good fortune of wealth and healthy children? Was it some other kind of guilt that I knew nothing about? Eventually, after I recovered enough from the question, I did query the woman about the specific sources of her guilt.

18. Geertz, *Interpretation of Cultures.*
19. Interview #21.

But my inclination in the moment she asked the question was not to be curious, but to go with a gut feeling of identification. This feeling led me at least momentarily to assume that I knew exactly what she meant. Even now, I do not feel entirely sure that I did not.

Nevertheless, I do not hold an essentialist view of Italian-American culture or identity. There is too much variety and constantly changing experience within any ethnic or cultural group to view people in this way.[20] For example, Italian immigrants to the West Coast have historically met with very different circumstances and fortunes than those who made their home in the Northeastern states, as my grandparents did. The timing of immigration, economic pull factors, and the ethnic make-up of the existing labor force, in which other groups such as Mexican and Chinese immigrants filled the lowest rungs of employment, created very different economic chances for Italians on the West Coast.[21] Factors such as climate, geography, and available occupations also make for very different kinds of historical experiences and narratives. While there are some Catholic teachings and practices and some cultural markers, such as language, that create commonalities in diverse immigration stories, it is clear that ethnic, regional, and religious practices are always complex and evolving rather than uniform or fixed.

My clinical training in pastoral counseling and "interpathic" listening has also impressed upon me the duty to hear the differences as well as commonalities between a speaker's story and my own story. In ethnographic interviewing as in counseling, listening carefully and perceiving accurately are critical constraints. Bonding with another person is tempting, but it is likely to get in the way of genuine understanding. I know this, occasional lapses notwithstanding.

One significant difference between my experience and that of the folks I interviewed has to do with my religious identity. Though I was raised and educated a Catholic, during my teenage years I had a conversion experience. Much to my parents' chagrin, I left the Catholic Church in favor of a rather extreme brand of Protestant fundamentalism. In adulthood, I eventually found my way to a broader worldview, to Harvard Divinity School, and to ordination in the United Church of Christ, a progressive Protestant denomination. I have had held ministerial standing

20. Conzen et al., "Invention of Ethnicity," 3–41.

21. Micaela di Leonardo, in her study of Italian-Americans in Northern California, notes some of the reasons for these differences. di Leonardo, *Varieties of Ethnic Experience.*

in the UCC for more than twenty-three years, and served as a pastor in two Massachusetts congregations for thirteen of those years. While I have taken issue with Catholic institutions and ideas over the years, disagreeing with popes and bishops with some frequency, I do not come to this writing with a chip on my shoulder or out of a personal need to criticize the ecclesiastical hierarchy. In fact, in many ways, I still feel myself to be a Catholic, at least a cultural one, and so my sense of affection for the church or nostalgia for what I miss about it is probably the greater bias.

Some of the devout with whom I spoke in San Pedro were troubled, I think, when I told them that I belong to the United Church of Christ. One immigrant refused an interview outright when she asked about my religious affiliation and I used the word "Protestant." (I suspect that she thought that I was going to try to convert her.) Many of the people I interviewed told me that they were praying for me. Some prayed I would get an "A" on the dissertation. Others had my soul in mind: they were praying that this research might lead me to convert back to Catholicism. In the course of the research, there were times when I entertained this possibility myself. I often sought the chance to spend time in the Mary Star of the Sea church alone. Perhaps I was experiencing the ethnographer's oft-cited inclination to "go native." Though this impulse did not result in a religious conversion, I was still touched by it. I remain grateful to the devout for all of their help and for all of their prayers.

As researcher Lynn Davidman notes, "the telling of lives always changes those lives."[22] This observation will not surprise therapists, pastoral counselors, or other practitioners. Rather than fearing that the subjectivity of human emotions will somehow compromise the validity of ethnographic research, Davidman suggests that the emotional healing or growth that the interview experience can generate for both the interviewer and the interviewee should be noted, examined, and valued. Through interviews, knowledge that is new and helpful to both parties can be accessed. In my interviews and my subsequent reflections upon them, I have tried to remain open to this transformative dimension. In my relationships with the devout in San Pedro, I was privileged to witness people constructing their life stories. These stories were told with enthusiasm, with sadness

22. Lynn Davidman, author of *Motherloss*, an ethnographic study of the impact of motherloss on the subsequent lives of surviving children, later broaches the subject of the transformative potential of the research process itself in "Truth, Subjectivity, and Ethnographic Research," 17–26.

sometimes, and often with great joy. In my own process of constructing this narrative, I have tried to make room for these emotions and for the enlivening influence of the human connections that were so generously opened to me.

In the process of writing and revising this story, I have become acutely aware of the complicated ethical issues involved in ethnography. As a novice ethnographer with a limited amount of training, I stumbled into some of these. The most difficult issue for me by far is the issue of *author*ity and power. The author of any story asserts her power to construct knowledge. However carefully one strives for accuracy and insight into the story, she is, nevertheless, likely to misconstrue, disconcert, or disappoint some of those who have trusted her with their stories and deeply held religious faith. Indeed, even when the story an author tells is perceptive, it holds the power to disturb. Perhaps we are all ambivalent about wanting to see and be seen.

Throughout the research and writing process, I have tried to address these concerns with care and with due ethical accountability. [23] I secured written permissions from those who told me their stories and allowed me to tape them. I changed the names and some identifying details in the stories in order to protect the privacy of these individuals and their families. Further, in this writing, I omit some personal information that I imagine might prove embarrassing or stressful to the persons involved. In order to improve the accuracy of my observations and to share authorial power, I also sent early drafts of the writing to many of the folks in San Pedro for their review and feedback, which I then tried to incorporate into the story. Finally, in order to push my work in the direction of "giving voice to" rather than "speaking for" my research associates, I draw upon their ideas, metaphors, and theological formulations as often as possible.

While ethnographic narratives may disturb, they also have the potential to lift up and magnify the voices of those whose religious ways are not well understood. Karen McCarthy Brown's pivotal study of Mama Lola, a Vodou priestess in Brooklyn, is perhaps the best example of this. Brown's volume helps build a bridge of understanding between uninformed read-

---

23. For a good discussion of the ethics of ethnographic research and publication, see Hammersley and Atkinson, *Ethnography*, 263–87. Also see Madison, *Critical Ethnography*, 79–129.

ers and the much-maligned practice of Vodou, through what Brown calls "an intimate spiritual biography."[24]

While the devout in my study do not suffer the same kind of racist stereotyping or rancor that practitioners of Vodou still experience in this country, it is also the case that the devotional practices are not generally well understood in America. Catholic devotions are frequently denigrated as superstitious, "primitive," or at best considered "popular religion," implying that they are holdovers from a pre-modern world.[25] It has been suggested that a liberal form of anti-Catholic sentiment has helped feed a sense of Catholic embarrassment over the devotional practices with their key cultural markers—such as food and attire—that set Catholics apart from Protestant Americans.[26] Beyond this, those who practice devotions are often marginalized not only by Protestants, but also by mainstream American Catholics, influenced by the sweeping theological and aesthetic changes that have been made in Catholic liturgies and sanctuaries since Vatican II.[27] Devotion to Mary, in particular, has been downplayed because of the liturgical emphasis on the participatory Mass, with its Eucharistic center.

It seems fair to say that Catholic devotional practices are not generally well understood or respected. I can illustrate this point by relating a story recently told to me by a colleague and friend. My colleague is a pastoral theologian and a member of the clergy in a mainline Protestant denomination. She had just visited the home of a Filipino immigrant woman. In the living room of this woman's small home was a large statue of Mary—so large that it took up a good portion of the room. My friend said she simply could not understand why someone would have such a thing in her home. "That space could be *used*," she said intensely; "I don't get it." This comment makes me think of Pierre Bourdieu's famous claim: "Practice has a logic which is not that of the logician."[28] In the logic of the immigrant's faith practice, the space in the woman's house *is* being used. It is being used to provide a place for the divine, perhaps as a focus for prayer, perhaps as a sign of blessing or protection. But the statue is being used in a way that isn't apparent to my colleague, whose God images take up less space. I

24. Brown, *Mama Lola*, ix. In her pivotal study, Brown offers students of religion a glimpse into the logic of Vodou, as practiced by a Haitian immigrant priestess in Brooklyn.

25. For a broader view of popular religion, see Espín, *Faith of the People*.

26. Jenkins, *New Anti-Catholicism*, 47–66.

27. McDannell, *Material Christianity*, 174–96.

28. Bourdieu, *Logic of Practice*, 86.

hope that this study will help open up the logic of immigrant Catholic devotional practices to my friend as well as to other colleagues and students in pastoral theology, particularly, and to disparate readers as well.

Many times in the course of my interviews, someone would confide a story to me with a preface such as, "Anyone but you would think I was crazy, but this is what happened." These stories usually had some sense of wonder to them, some hint of the miraculous if not a direct claim of supernatural intervention. I want to relay these faith stories in such a way that the reader will not think the persons telling them crazy at all, but will come to understand the way that this faith and these stories *work* for people.

At the same time, the meanings and uses of the devotions are by no means uncontested, even in my small sample that is skewed toward the most devout. For example, one immigrant clearly stated that he thinks the devotions are delusions. I do not take a side on this issue. My position is generally one of advocacy for the devout; I advocate for respect for the persons involved and try to "lift up" their voices and interpret the wisdom I see in their practices. I hope that my research partners in San Pedro will recognize themselves in this story and feel that their trust was merited and their voices heard, even though they may disagree with me on some points. This advocacy stance is not, in my view, a hindrance to some so-called objective truth about these practices.[29] Nor does it mean that my analysis is uncritical. It is more a recognition that, like every one who tells a story, I do stand somewhere, and I can only describe what I can see from where I stand.[30] I am trying to stand *with* the devout in this conversation. I care about them and I don't think that they are crazy.

Interpretive Models and Lenses

I am using and recommending a contextual theological model that owes much to Elaine Graham's "critical phenomenology of Christian practice."[31] I think of this approach as a way of paying attention to what people and

29. For a thoughtful discussion of issues of truth and objectivity in social analysis, see Rosaldo, *Culture and Truth*. Also see, Naples, *Feminism and Method*, and Madison, *Critical Ethnography*.

30. Thomas Tweed's reflections on sightings and sites help illuminate the limitations of historical narratives. Tweed, *Retelling U.S. Religious History*, 6–10.

31. Graham calls for the study of ". . . a living and acting faith-community in order to excavate and examine the norms which inhabit pastoral praxis." Graham, *Transforming Practice*, 140.

communities actually do when practicing their faith. In this model, theological analysis involves attentiveness, description, and reflection on religious and pastoral practices, in order to "excavate" and critically examine the values and theologies implicit it them. This approach is interpretative rather than prescriptive. My aim is to promote respectful encounter and theological exchange.[32]

This approach arises out of a broad trend toward contextual and narrative models in pastoral theology as well as in other theological disciplines. In the twentieth century, the dominant model of pastoral theology in North America correlated biblical and theological concepts with insights from the social sciences, most notably psychology. This method held sway in North American divinity schools and seminaries, both Catholic and Protestant, at least from mid-century through the 1970s.[33] In the last thirty years, however, many pastoral theologians have been striving to move beyond clinical and individualistic paradigms of care toward more "communal and contextual" models.[34] The impact of feminist theory, Latin-American liberation theology, and postmodern thought has forced this shift.[35] Pastoral theologians have also become more curious about the performative power of religious rituals to reveal, to harm, to help, or to

32. In reflecting on a statement of the Society for Intercultural Pastoral Care and Counselling, Emmanuel Lartey writes, "There is an express aim of reducing violence, imperialistic imposition and cultural indifference." Lartey, *Pastoral Theology in an Intercultural World,* 54. To read the full statement, see Society for Intercultural, "Mission Statement," 2.

33. Holifield, *History of Pastoral Care in America.*

34. See Ramsay, "Time of Ferment and Redefinition," 1–43; and Greider et al., "Three Decades of Women Writing for Our Lives," 21–50. Emmanuel Lartey defines pastoral theology as ". . . critical, interpretive, constructive, and expressive reflection on the caring acivities of God and human communities," Lartey, *Pastoral Theology in an Intercultural World,* 14.

35. The very meaning of the term "pastoral care" has expanded to include prophetic or social-justice oriented action as a compelling response to the needs of those who are marginalized or oppressed. Gustavo Gutiérrez explains his understanding of "praxis" as "a transforming activity marked and illuminated by Christian love." Gutiérrez, *A Theology of Liberation,* 131. Similarly, Hal Recinos describes Christian pastoral theology in the context of the American *barrio.* He writes, "Rereading the mission of the church from the perspective of marginal humanity will enable the church to discover that authentic Christian pastoral activity means participating in God's struggle to right the human condition by enabling trampled humanity to know historical salvation." Recinos, "Mission: Latino Pastoral Theology," 156.

heal. There is an increasing awareness of the potential of religious practices to shape, to expand, and to limit human imaginations.[36]

In light of these developments, pastoral theologians are continuing to try to find ways to care intelligently for whole persons and communities in complex socio-cultural contexts.[37] How can we bring a critical, holistic view of pastoral care to bear? One way to approach this question is by focusing pastoral theological reflection on actual religious practices. Elaine Graham writes,

> Christian practice is not just the acting out of predetermined moral norms, or application of doctrinal truths. Pastoral practices, as expressions of the Christian presence in the world, may therefore be seen as the foundation, and not the application of theological understanding.[38]

This view of practice challenges the notion of pastoral theology as "applied theology," a mere derivative of the classical theological disciplines. If theology more often springs from practice, then pastoral practices themselves are foundational to our understandings of God.[39] Our actions, habits, experiences, and ways of being in community reveal, inform, and shape our worldviews. It is what we do, and not just what we say, that finally reveals what we believe.

Here I use the word "believe" not to indicate mere intellectual assent. Rather, I am using Wilfred Cantwell Smith's understanding of "to believe" as, "to love" (from the German, *belieben*) or "to put the heart."[40] Belief in this sense involves will, emotion, commitment. What we do reveals what we value, to what (and to whom) we are committed. Our beliefs show up in our practices. As Graham points out, it is here that social relations are generated, and religious values are expressed, enacted, and/or brought into being.[41]

---

36. This greater awareness of the significance of practice grows out of the influential work of philosophical ethicist Alasdair MacIntyre; see *After Virtue*. Also see Browning, *Fundamental Practical Theology*. For an historiographic account of the development of the concept of practice in pastoral theology, see Graham, *Transforming Practice*, 83–141.

37. For example, L. Graham, *Care of Persons, Care of Worlds*.

38. Graham, *Transforming Practice*, 111.

39. Also see Happel and Walter, *Conversion and Discipleship*.

40. Smith, *Belief and History*, 41–45; cited in Parks, *Big Questions, Worthy Dreams*, 17–18.

41. Graham, *Transforming Practice*, 99.

In examining the social and historical impact of faith practices, critical questions arise. [42] In what ways have these practices been beneficial or helpful to the devout? What is the impact of the devotional practices on the devout's families, neighbors, and wider communities? In what ways do the devotions involve "empowering, nurturing, or liberating" functions?[43] Such questions help identify the practical wisdom embedded in practice. Likewise, it is necessary to ask how and when religious practices might be harmful or limiting. Whom do they exclude or objectify? In what ways are these practices liberating and in what ways are they oppressive? How do they cause pain and how do they alleviate suffering?

In order to reflect upon these questions deeply, multi-disciplinary lenses are needed. Emotionally and spiritually, immigration is a significant transition in the life cycle, involving intense adjustments along with complex emotions such as hope and fear.[44] What are the emotional needs, issues, and dynamics that particular devotional practices stir up, calm down, or enable persons to work through? In the psychological literature, the theory that I find most apt to explain these dynamics is known as object relations theory, a psychodynamic school that focuses on human needs for love and connection.[45] In particular, I rely on the work of Donald Woods Winnicott (1896–1971), a pediatrician and psychoanalyst in the British object relations school.[46] Winnicott's astute grasp of the important themes of union and separation in human experience is particularly helpful in trying to understand how religious ties and binds work in the context of immigration. Winnicott also offers a compelling view of the wider psychological importance of creativity, culture, and religion.

---

42. Graham notes that "critical studies of religion as a specific form of cultural practice might help to disclose its contribution in building subcultures of institutional and individual reality through which particular patterns of social relations are generated." *Transforming Practice*, 111.

43. Miller-McLemore, "Feminist Theory in Pastoral Theology," 151.

44. Carter and McGoldrick, *Family Life Cycle*, 388–90, 458–59.

45. For a good overview, see Greenberg and Mitchell, *Object Relations in Psychoanalytic Theory*.

46. See Winnicott's *Playing and Reality* and *Maturational Process and the Facilitating Environment*. My analysis also relies on the work of interpreters of religious experience who use object relations theory, such as Ana Maria Rizzuto, who analyzes God objects as parental introjects, and William Meissner, who offers a specific analysis of Catholic devotions as a form of symbiotic union with the mother. Rizzuto, *Birth of the Living God*; Meissner, *Psychoanalysis and Religious Experience*.

Taking history seriously is a form of critical caring. When we think about the image of Mary, Star of the Sea holding her fishing boat, it becomes obvious that economic and material factors have been woven into the religious bonds and loyalties of the immigrants. Such factors are implicit in all religious practices, of course. The disciplined study of the historical exigencies of group life helps us see the logic and function of faith practices more fully. Material realities such as finances, statues, buildings, fishing, and food all reveal and help constitute religious practices. In investigating the material cultural dimensions of the devotions, I rely on a three-stage method proposed by historian Colleen McDannell. This process begins with careful description (which is itself an interpretive activity), moves to various kinds of analyses, and then entails a more comprehensive level of interpretation.[47]

The social context of the devotions involves transnational bonds, awarenesses, and identities. Historian Thomas Tweed's theoretical construct of "translocative religion" helps elucidate the capacity of devotional practices to transport immigrants imaginatively back to their old lands even as these rituals assist people in the process of relocating in the new.[48] I draw on Tweed's thoughtful attention to the role of place in religious life.

A contextual theological analysis of the devotions involves keeping an "eye out" for the healing and caring dimensions of both private and communal rituals.[49] For example, a second-generation devout woman offered, "I'd rather do what I'm doing than go to a psychiatrist!"[50] This comment emphasizes the therapeutic or "cure" dimensions of the devotions and their perceived mental health benefits. This woman views her devotions as a spiritual alternative to secular therapy. She experiences the saints as sustaining and healing caregivers. The sentiments she expresses here are not atypical. In the course of my research in San Pedro, I often gained the impression that there is a kind of Catholic cognitive therapy frame implicit in the devotions, one that inspires strength and confidence. There is something about the ritual and repetitive nature of the devotions that appears to function in a way that is analogous to daily affirmations or what

47 McDannell, "Interpreting Things," 371–87.

48. Tweed, *Our Lady of the Exile.*

49. Lartey, *Pastoral Theology in an Intercultural World,* 47.

50. Interview #24.

cognitive therapists call "reframing," that may function as a hedge against depression and anxiety.

The same woman quoted above handed me a holy card when I left her home—her effort, clearly, to minister to me. "Take this home and read it. It will make you feel so good," she said, with confidence.[51] This vignette points to an aspect of the devotions that pastoral theologians would call "shepherding." This term, based on the biblical imagery of the twenty-third Psalm and the New Testament image of Jesus as the good shepherd, suggests religiously based pastoral care. In this setting, the shepherding that goes on sometimes involves clergy and sometimes does not. This care may take the form of an individual requesting supernatural aid or guidance from a saint. Sometimes the pastoral care is interpersonal—as in this woman's effort to care for me. Sometimes the care is communal and liturgical, as when a priest presides over a devotional feast, lending his human presence and ecclesiastical authority to the prayers of the people. This care is sometimes related to cure, and accounts of miraculous intervention abound. It sometimes has more to do with acceptance or endurance. The pastoral care element of the devotions is also evident in the practical ministries that the devotions encourage—such as providing public meals, which at Mary Star parish is called "Christian Care."

The theological perspective that I bring to this project is close to what theologian Sheila Davaney describes as "pragmatic historicism."[52] Davaney calls for contemporary theological analysis "as a form of cultural analysis, critique, and reconstruction, and as such it seeks conversation with those disciplines and methodologies that will better equip theologians to enter the world of lived beliefs and practices."[53] In the richness of interdisciplinary analysis, more comprehensive understandings can emerge. The tools of religious studies can inform and enlighten pastoral practice. I offer this critical phenomenology of pastoral practice as an example of how pastors and others can "enter the world of lived beliefs and practices" with attentiveness and care.

51. Ibid.
52. Davaney, *Pragmatic Historicism*.
53. Davaney, "Mapping Theologies," 40.

Organization

This book is organized into two parts. Part One is primarily focused on the case study. In chapters 2, 3, and 4, I offer analyses of three of the most striking features of the devotions: the visual aspects of devotions; the intertwined history of the local fishing industry; and the religious meaning of food, with corollaries to constructions of class, gender, and ethnic identity. In each of these chapters, I use data from the interviews to paint a picture of the devotions and to highlight the meanings that the people themselves suggest as they describe their faith practices. I then try to interpret what is going on in this setting, from a pastoral theological perspective.

In chapter 2, "On Seeing and Being Seen," I argue for the importance of the visual representations of Mary, Jesus, the angels, and the saints. Why should we begin this story of immigrant religious practices here, with a focus on images and objects? Protestants, in particular, may wince at this focus on the material and the mundane. Is not piety a more spiritual matter, apprehended through words rather than "graven images," and grounded in the study of scripture? Is not prayer better practiced in the darkness of tightly closed eyes? It might seem so. But perhaps the visual worlds in which we live and pray influence even this perception more than we realize.

David Morgan, who studied the primarily Protestant phenomenon of Americans who grew up with Warner Sallman's *Head of Christ* portraits in their homes, points out the profound role that religious art, artifacts, and architecture play in the social construction of reality. He writes,

> Images serve as a material means of conducting the rituals that define the public, domestic, and private spheres in which believers discern their identity and the characteristic horizons of reality that link them to one another and gather their experience into coherent worlds.[54]

The "coherent worlds" of the Italian Catholic devout in San Pedro have been formed and supported by numerous visual images of Mary, Jesus, and the Saints. These religious images are everywhere to be seen. They are found not only in the churches, but also in the homes, boats, and back yards of the devout. The significance of these visual surroundings and religious artifacts should not be underestimated, nor their pastoral

54. Morgan, *Visual Piety*, 18.

value overlooked. Historical theologian Margaret Miles has demonstrated convincingly the ways in which a piece of artwork can be viewed as an historical text, narrating the religious worlds of common people, including women and children, and others whose stories and voices are often missing from written accounts. By examining religious artwork, architecture, and even inexpensive objects, we can gain access to meanings inscribed in the material objects themselves. [55]

Chapter 3, "Fishing, Fear, and Faith" offers a more chronological historical analysis. The topics covered here include the rise and fall of the fishing industry, its financial benefits for some as well as its dangers and difficulties. People's experiences of losing loved ones at sea, and of fearing for this kind of loss, are explored. I also describe the financial support that Mary Star of the Sea has derived from the fishing industry, and two of the major collective rituals related to fishing: the Fisherman's Fiesta and the Blessing of the Fleet. The realities of the occupation of fishing, with its extreme risks and benefits, have functioned to intensify the devotions for some, and helped to promote the practice of devotions into the third immigrant generation. Fishing has had a profound impact on the prayers of the people, their way of life, their immigration to San Pedro, their love for this place and for their church.

In chapter 4, "Food, Famine, and Faith," I describe the relatively recent and lively Sicilian ritual of the St. Joseph's Table as it is practiced in San Pedro. I suggest a connection between poverty remembered and the cultural importance of food. The prevalence of pastoral care programs that offer public meals is also described. This chapter is tilted toward social analysis. I explore issues of class, gender, and ethnic maintenance. The importance of dining room tables, hospitality, communion, and community suggests a sacramental view of food that persists into the later generations.

In Part Two, "Practice, Transformation, and Religious Imagination" the discussion opens out into a broader view of immigration, identity, and religious imagination. In this section, I reflect on the ways that pastoral practices can lead to change, growth, and enlarged religious imagination. Chapter 5, "Holding On, Letting Go, and Being Held," is a "hinge" chapter to the second part of the book. Here I explain my theoretical perspective in greater detail, developing the links between practice, *habitus*, values, and

55. For good discussions of the value of material cultural evidence, see Miles, *Image as Insight*; McDannell, *Material Christianity*, 1–16; and Schmidt, "Easter Parade," 135–64.

transformation. I then suggest analogues and implications for ministry in broader Christian and religious contexts.

As contemporary theologians, pastors, and congregations seek to welcome and care for immigrants and other strangers in a shifting social landscape, we need ways to engage in care-*full* and attentive relationships. The pastoral theological reflection offered here models a way to lift up the voices of ordinary people, allowing them to tell their own stories, while piecing together emerging bits of theological wisdom and compelling care practices. While the particular insights of any community are situated and specific, theological reflection in one context can animate a broader discussion of transformative pastoral theology and practice.

In chapters 6 through 8, I discuss three specific "situated values" that arise out of the devotional practices: connection, multiplicity, and celebration. I try to plumb the wisdom of these values for diverse pastors and persons of faith, especially for those engaging in pastoral ministries with immigrant populations. In chapter 6, "Connection: Love as Union and Separation," I explore the value of a strong sense of connection —"Blessed Be the Ties that Bind"—in Protestant as well as Catholic settings. When is connection between and among the faithful life-giving and when is it smothering? We can see both possibilities in the San Pedro case study. In religious communities, human needs for union and separation are always at play. How do pastors tend the balance between offering supportive care and inspiring transformational growth? Pastoral practices that address human needs for both union and separation help empower the faithful in the quest to love God and neighbor.

In chapter 7, "Engaging Multiplicity," we see how a multiplicity of patron saints, once emblematic of ethnic tensions, over time has made way for a more peaceable but still distinct array of cultural societies and celebrations. The issues at play here are particularly timely for American religious communities that are encountering increasingly diverse populations and increasing kinds diversity—including theological diversity, ethnic and racial diversity, diversity related to sexual orientation, and diversity related to persons with dis/abilities. How can we come to terms with the issues involved in what Miroslav Volf terms "exclusion and embrace?"[56] How do we honor human distinctions, as Melanie May puts it, *and* give birth to life-giving connections for the glory of God?

56. Volf, *Exclusion and Embrace.*

Chapter 8, "Celebration and Incarnation," explores the value of celebration in religious life. In San Pedro, historical experiences of poverty
and hunger presage the community's current practices of lavish hospitality
and ministries to the hungry. The devotions reveal a sacramental view of
everyday life, an embodied wisdom that can enrich and enliven broad
models of pastoral theology and practice.

This book is not just about the particular practices of the devout in
San Pedro. It is also about "birthing life-giving connection to one another,"
in the words of Melanie May quoted in the epigraph of this chapter.[57] This
story of a small group of immigrants and their devotional practices opens
out into a broader pastoral theological discussion about the ways in which
religion works on us and through us, personally, socially, and culturally. By
attending closely to these particular faith practices—the devotions—we
can catch a glimpse of faith in action. The dynamic processes that come
into view through this case study find analogues in the ties and binds that
many other immigrants, Christian and otherwise, also experience.

I want to help "birth" some imaginative understanding through these
pages, so that the religious ties and binds of these ordinary immigrant
families can become more vivid and comprehensible. Because photographs have the power to portray the devotions in an immediate way, I
am linking this book to a website that includes several photographs. Of
course, depending on one's own religious and cultural roots, these photographs and this story may at first be confounding. To many Protestants,
these devotional practices will not seem very religious, or at least not very
Christian at all. The Italian and Sicilian Catholic devotions described here
often focus on Mary and the saints; the devout use holy images and rosary
beads in praying; the colorful festivals of faith will be wholly unfamiliar to
some readers. Rather than sparking recognition or connection, this story
of living devotions in an Italian Catholic immigrant context may provoke
cultural, aesthetic, and/or theological dissonance.

Nevertheless, as we learn from Antoine de Saint-Exupéry's *Little
Prince*, appearances may be deceiving.[58] I hope that these readers will try
to stay *with* the story, so that as it unfolds, some points of hope or insight
might become evident *through* the differences, as well. While differences
will remain, glimmers of contact and appreciation may also gradually

57. May, *Body Knows*, 25.
58. Saint-Exupéry, *Little Prince*.

come into view. My pastoral-theological aim is to help "birth" these points of connection, small sparks of engagement with people and practices that at first seem "other" or obscure. I hope that this story of devotion will become translucent, inviting readers' analogical reflections upon their own historical narratives, identities, and imaginations.

It is my own conviction that the transcendent power of the holy is always found embedded in cultural particularity. While the practical wisdom of any community is situated and specific, the theological insights arising from local settings suggest broader implications for transformative pastoral theology and practice. Attentive and engaged qualitative study can give rise to more appropriate, holistic forms of pastoral theology and care.

Part One

Devotions, Immigration, and Identity in Context

2

On Seeing and Being Seen

For now we see in a mirror, dimly, but then we will see face to face. Now I know only in part; then I will know fully, even as I have been fully known.

1 Cor 13:12

A N ornately framed portrait of a Madonna labeled "Rosa Mistica" hangs on a dining room wall in the home of an immigrant couple from Sicily (Figure 6). The caption in the lower right hand corner of the portrait reads, *"L'occhio sinistro della Madonna e vivo,"* which translates, "The left eye of the Madonna is alive." My hostess, whom I shall call "Maria," explains with great enthusiasm that there is a statue of Rosa Mistica, in a chapel back in Italy, that actually has one living eye that moves, following the viewer about: "Real, real," she says emphatically with her heavy accent.[1] When Maria looks at this portrait in her home, she not only sees a real supernatural Madonna in this picture of a statue, Maria also sees the living Holy Mother looking back at her.

Many of the folks who practice devotions in San Pedro are familiar with the experience of seeing and "being seen" by some holy image, whether it be the tortured face of Jesus peering down from a metal crucifix, a sculpted guardian angel hovering over an entryway, a prized portrait of a Madonna, or a holy card featuring a picture of one of the myriad saints. But it is the image of Mary that is the most constant. One hundred feet up in the air above Mary Star of the Sea Church, a ten-foot bronze statue of Mary stares out over the church and the neighborhood, facing

---

1. Interview #18. The statue that Maria is referring to is located in Montichiari in northern Italy. For more background on the devotion, see Sepeckbacher, "Apparitions of Our Lady," 6.

westward toward the water (Figure 7). I have been told that fishermen returning from the sea at night spot this statue in the moonlight first as they approach the San Pedro Bay.

The omnipresence of representations of the Madonna, with her firm and caring gaze, is also notable at ground level. The outside wall of the church on the Seventh Street side is adorned by a large mosaic portrait of Mary with the caption, *"Maria Stella Maris, Ora Pro Nobis,"* which means, "Mary Star of the Sea, Pray for Us" (Figure 8). The inside of the sanctuary is replete with images of Mary, including the towering central marble statue of Mary Star of the Sea holding the purse seiner (Figures 1 and 2), stained-glass window renditions of Our Lady of Lourdes and Our Lady of Fatima, a large mosaic of Our Lady of Guadalupe (Figure 9), a marble statue of Mary embracing the crucified Jesus, recalling Michaelangelo's *Pietà* (Figure 10), and a well-tended shrine to Our Mother of Perpetual Help (Figure 11).[2] In Mary Star's elementary school, adjacent to the sanctuary, classrooms host small shrines to Mary and the saints (Figure 12).

Similarly, in the homes I visited, images of Mary were everywhere. From large statues that dominated living rooms or bedrooms, to small holy cards held up by refrigerator magnets, some vision or version of the Madonna was present in almost every home.[3] In some cases, she could be seen in every room, and in backyard shrines as well. Portraits of Mary hanging in bedrooms often had been given as wedding gifts (Figure 13), and many statues of her have been passed down from parents or grandparents. One couple had a beautiful pencil drawing of Mary that the husband himself had made, hanging in their bedroom (Figure 14). Pictures of deceased loved ones were commonly arranged near images of Mary, the Sacred Heart of Jesus, or the saints on bedroom dressers or hallway tables (Figure 15 and Figure 16). Fresh or silk flowers, as well as candles or electric lamps, were often grouped together with the religious images in altar-like arrangements (Figure 17). One woman showed me three small medals engraved with likenesses of Mary and the saints that she wore regularly, affixed to her bra with a safety pin. The visual images of Mary and the saints that adorn the homes, churches, and, in some cases, the bodies of

2. In addition to the banks of electric candles glowing before this image and the ready supply of fresh flowers, there is a large book nearby in which the devout write their prayers of petition.

3. There were two homes that were exceptions. However, in one of these cases, the resident possessed rosary beads featuring small, sculpted images of Mary.

the devout serve as more than mere background to the Catholic religious devotions in this setting. Rather, these visual images are constitutive components of devotional practice.

Visual surroundings influence all of us, shaping our sense of what is normal and natural, what is sacred and what is mundane, what is good and what is evil. Whether or not we are conscious of it, landscapes, architecture, and art inevitably contribute to our experience and interpretation of the world.[4] In this particular local community, where religious images are both plentiful and prized, the power of visual environs to shape consciousness is perhaps more obvious than usual.[5] Here we can see how both the active, conscious practice of looking at religious statues, holy cards, and paintings, and the passive, less intentional practice of absorbing regular glimpses of Mary, Jesus, and the saints contribute to the viewer's ethos, identity, and worldview. These visual habits and experiences of both seeing and being seen engender certain shared psycho-spiritual capacities, expectations, and sensibilities.

What is it that the devout and their friends and loved ones are "seeing" in all of these portraits, statues, and medals? And what is it like to be so surrounded? These questions are at once phenomenological, psychological, and theological. Depending on the reader's point of view, these religious interactions with pictures and objects might be judged delusional, superstitious, unorthodox, or repressive. This visual piety at first seems to lend credence to Freud's hypothesis that religion is an illusion, much like an obsessional neurosis.[6] Even many co-religionists, post-conciliar American Catholics, might judge the reliance on images to be childish or embarrassing. Protestants, with a long history of both iconoclasm and theological disdain for Mariology, may find the centrality of Mary's likeness in "graven images" incomprehensible, if not idolatrous.[7] Many feminists will be similarly skeptical, though for different reasons. A con-

4. See Morgan, *Visual Piety*, 2–3.

5. While it is difficult, in a book, to convey a sense of the immediacy and power of the experience of viewing these religious representations, the photographs that are displayed on my website may help bridge this gap. Online: http://www.MaryMoschella.net/LivingDevotions. I hope, by the use of photographs, to "reveal the story" to the reader in a different way. Margaret Miles writes, "We must find the methods and the materials that reveal the story of contemporary and historical persons who have not been recognized as participants in historical and theological work . . ." Miles, *Image as Insight*, xii.

6. Freud, *The Future of an Illusion*, 54–57.

7. The issue of idolatry is addressed in chapter 7.

siderable body of feminist theological and psychological literature analyzes the symbol of the Virgin Mother and finds her to be an impossible and therefore damaging ideal for women.[8] Because all of these objections are often strong and immediate, some may be tempted to view the devout as primitive or "other"—persons who are far away theologically or culturally. How can we mitigate this felt distance and open the way for a more meaningful encounter between readers and the devout and their piety? I suggest that we begin this pastoral theological endeavor with patient observation and careful listening to these stories of ordinary people.

The three main themes that emerge through my study of visual piety in this setting are these: first, the devout frequently describe a pervasive sense of divine or supernatural presence when they are near these images; second, there is a connection between and among religious images, family ties, and natal lands; and third, the Madonna is the central figure in these images—Mary is the star of visual devotion here. In reflecting on my conversations in this community, it becomes clear that the people's visual practices help shape their historical memories of the past and also play an ongoing role in identity formation in the present. These visual practices embody an incarnational theology and highlight an important connection between sentience and subjectivity.[9]

Presence

By far the most frequent and striking bit of experience that my interviewees describe to me vis-à-vis their religious images is a sense of a divine or supernatural presence. While many do not share with Maria (described above) a conscious conviction that the statue or picture is alive, most indicate that the religious artwork in church and home instantly reminds them of the presence of God with them. Whether the focus of a devout's devotion is an image of Mary, a picture of the sacred heart of Jesus (Jesus

---

8. For a survey of critiques of the image of Mary, see Hamington, *Hail Mary?* For a critique of the cult of Mary in Italian popular Catholicism, see Carroll, *Madonnas that Maim.* For feminist psychological critiques, see Warner, *Alone of All Her Sex*; and Goldenberg, *Changing of the Gods.* For feminist theological critiques and analyses, see Daly, *Beyond God the Father*; and Atkinson et al., *Immaculate and Powerful.* For Catholic feminist and womanist attempts to rehabilitate the Marian image, see Ruether, *Sexism and God-Talk*, 150–53; Gebara and Bingemer, *Mary, Mother of God*; and Johnson, "Mary and the Female Face of God," 500–526; and Diana Hayes, "Black, Catholic, and Womanist," 113–15. For recent Protestant perspectives, see Gaventa and Rigby, *Blessed One.*

9. See Cooey, *Religious Imagination and the Body*, 62.

with blood flowing from his heart), or a patron saint, the devout exhibit a sense of reverence around these images, sometimes referring to the statues themselves with gendered pronouns—as if the statues are the supernatural beings, rather than mere images. Across the generational spectrum, interviewees repeatedly indicate that visual representations of Mary or the saints give them a feeling of calm and/or a sense of protection. These images serve as reminders, visual cues that indicate God's presence silently, regularly, reliably. One immigrant woman summed it up well when she said, gesturing toward the plethora of religious art in her home, "Wherever you turn, you see God." She added, "God is with me, on [at] my side."[10]

The visual power of these religious images became clearer to me during my frequent visits to the sanctuary of Mary Star of the Sea Church. Upon entering the building, I was often struck by the sheer number of representations. Designed by architect George J. Adams and built in 1958, the space is chock full of altars and shrines and stained glass windows. The ornate representations of Mary and the saints in this sanctuary seem to have survived the Catholic reform movements of the 1950s and 1960s that often simplified and masculinized Catholic Church art and architecture.[11] Here, Mary's image remains central, and her feminine presence is augmented by representations of a multitude of saints, many with long, flowing hair, occupying private altars along the church walls, giving the place an old-world European feel. In fact, the marble used to build these structures was imported for this purpose from Pietrasante, Italy, and most of the stained glass came from Dublin, Ireland.[12] The origins of these materials as well as the style and form of the representations serve as palpable reminders of the European homelands and ancestors of many current congregants. To this visitor, the combined impact of the fifteen life-sized statues, two mosaics, and thirty stained glass holy figures arrayed around the church is a sense of having company. Even if no one else is around, I find it hard to feel alone in this place.

Many people tell me that they like going to the church best when it is empty, when there is no Mass or organized devotion in progress. They speak of the peacefulness of it. They go to visit their favorite saints: Saint

10. Interview #15.

11. McDannell, *Material Christianity*, 167–86.

12. Monsignor George Scott, pastor of Mary Star from 1946–1975, who presided over the building of the sanctuary, is said to have gone to Italy himself to find the finest altar and religious works for "his church." Bobich and Palmer, *Mary Star Centennial*, 15.

Anthony, Our Mother of Perpetual Help, Saint Joseph, Saint Anne (the mother of Mary—Jesus's *nonna*), and Saint John-Joseph of the Cross. On any given day, these saints' altars are aglow with the red lights of electric candle banks, and just as likely adorned with fresh flowers. The oldest and most devout immigrants regularly dust these altars, wash the linens, purchase and place fresh flowers at the feet of the statues or mosaics, and buy tokens to light the electric candles. The devout treat these spaces as though they are sacred spaces, inhabited by the saints themselves. The devout speak of going to see their saint—meaning the image—whether at church or at home, as they do of going to visit with a friend or a family member. They talk to these figures candidly, "from the heart."[13]

Many people in my sample also commonly hang a crucifix or an angel in children's bedrooms, citing a feeling of protection. One well-educated, third-generation woman who holds a degree in science said, "I wouldn't feel right about putting my babies in a room without a crucifix."[14] Several men reported that crucifixes and saints also often hang on the inside walls of fishing vessels.[15] One man told the story of a captain grabbing the crucifix off the wall of the ship's cabin in a storm, going up on deck and holding the crucifix high in the air, only to find his boat mysteriously released from a swirling vacuum current.[16] I am told that holy cards with pictures of Mary or the Saints were also often taken to war with soldiers. One man describes a time when he was afraid of dying in World War II. He took a holy card out of his wallet and promised the saint he would name his first-born after her if she would get him home alive. His daughter now bears the saint's name.[17] These stories attest to a sense of supernatural protection that the religious images mediate for many of the devout.

But of course, not everyone in the community buys into this sense of supernatural protection. Though most of the people in my snowball sample who were willing to be interviewed were favorably disposed toward religious images, I did find one man willing to talk to me who strongly contested the idea of supernatural power in devotional objects and rejected the practices entirely. He is a 60-year-old immigrant who describes

13. Interview #7.

14. Interview #21.

15. One fisherman told me in passing that Portuguese fishing vessels typically have a chapel—an entire room—full of holy images.

16. Interviewee #15.

17. Interview #23. The name is withheld to protect the anonymity of the family.

himself as an atheist, though he still considers himself a Catholic "in the heart." He is a successful vocal artist with strong ties of friendship in the community, mostly due to his Italian musical performances at weddings and other religious feasts. His spacious and well-appointed living room in a neighboring suburb contained no religious images. (However, I did not meet his family, nor see other rooms in the home). This man expressed frank resentment toward the devotions that preoccupy many immigrants, including his mother. He believes that his mother, who is quite devout, is deeply deluded. Referring to her practice of devotions during Lent and Holy Week, when she weeps as she imaginatively identifies with the pain and suffering of Jesus, he said: "She never cried when my father died, but every Easter she cry [sic] like crazy."[18] The intensity with which the man speaks seems to indicate that he is angry about this, and perhaps hurt or jealous of the love that his mother reserves for supernatural beings, which, he implies, is at the expense of human ones. For him, the supernatural world of the saints is not merely false; it is also destructive and hurtful.

Nor is the spiritual or pastoral value of looking at art and artifacts unanimously agreed upon among the devout themselves. Some report finding the side altars a bit superfluous, a distraction from devotion to God alone. Some feel that paying homage to the statues is embarrassing or superstitious. When asked about the meaning of religious art or artifacts, several persons made comments decrying superstition, such as, "I'm not worshipping the statue,"[19] or "You don't really need the beads to pray when you're mature."[20] One man said, "It's just the idea of focusing on something. . . . I fix my eyes on the image of Mary. It helps you fix your thoughts."[21]

The devout find their profound respect for statues, paintings, and inexpensive holy cards hard to explain to outsiders. The devout know that their practices leave them open to ridicule. Some individuals are keenly aware of this and take pains to distinguish themselves from the stereotype of being childish or superstitious. They want me to know that they are not simplistic or foolish. One second-generation woman, after showing me several pictures of her favorite saints, explains,

18. Interview #14.
19. Interview #5.
20. Interview #19.
21. Interview #5.

> The saints are people that have lived, and you feel that they can
> help you by being an example. They help me live a better life. . . .
> They did extraordinary things. We pray to them and honor them.
> . . . Maybe it's only that we think it works and so it does. Whether
> it works or not it's your faith. It's nice to raise your child with
> security.[22]

These comments convey a certain degree of self-consciousness about devotional practices that are no longer mainstream, even for Catholics; they
also suggest the woman's recognition of the illusory or possibly illusory
quality of her practice. In spite of this, she asserts that these images work;
in particular, they helped her feel secure while raising her children. And
they help her live a better life.

What is going on here with these images? On one level, the woman
is praying to her saints for intercession, mostly prayers for the safety and
well-being of her family. She finds that this works, or at least it has seemed
to work well enough that she is going to keep on doing it. It makes her
feel secure. For some in this setting, particular saints are seen as patrons
or protectors; these patrons' images are venerated and their intercession is
sought. The saints are believed to have persuasive power with God. As one
man put it, "They are our lawyers." This view of the saints as intercessors
who will plead a case for the devout represents pre-conciliar theology—a
view no longer officially taught at Mary Star of the Sea—but one that is
still popular among the people. This is where the labels of superstition or
at least theological immaturity are most likely to be applied.

A more generous way of looking at this practice might be to see it
as akin to any prayers of intercession that people of diverse faiths as well
as the proverbial atheist in a foxhole may offer up. We can appreciate the
tendency to cry out to any "higher power" in times of distress. Prayer helps
people cope. In this community, the practice of prayer is aided by visual
and tangible images of figures thought to be living simultaneously here, in
the thick of life, and there, in heaven, pleading for us with God. Having
something tangible to hold on to, or an image to look at, "to help fix your
thoughts" while praying, can be viewed as a creative resource to aid one's
concentration. The Catholic saint who intercedes with God on behalf of
the devout is perhaps analogous to the members of a Protestant prayer
group who offer prayers of intercession on behalf of one another to God.

22. Interview #24.

Beyond prayers of intercession, some of the devout find inspiration and instruction for everyday living in the presence of their holy images. When Susan notes that, "The saints are people who have lived," she is pointing to their origins as historical human beings. She sees them as people who lived well; they are her ideals, exemplars, figures she tries to emulate. By praying to the saints and staying imaginatively connected to them through their pictures that she looks at when she prays, the sensation of their medals that she wears on her body, and their stories that she reads regularly, Susan believes she is able to live a better life. She consciously remembers these ideal figures, and draws inspiration, hope, or strength from their stories, which she uses in order to cultivate her own personal character. I think that what Susan has articulated here is a viable theology of the communion of saints. Susan's construction is not unlike the view of contemporary Catholic theologian Elizabeth Johnson, who stresses that the earliest Christians had some concept of connection between the living and the dead in Christ, and asserts that the practice of recalling the lives of faithful who have gone before us may indeed instill hope and courage in those among the living. [23]

This visual piety reveals itself as more complex than it seemed at first. For a few folks I talked with, the religious images are embarrassing, distracting, or evidence of delusion. For many, religious images convey solace or hope, especially in the face of fear or loss. The sense of divine presence is often experienced as soothing—though not always. Many other emotions, such as guilt, strength, and compassion, were also described to me. Some of the devout, like Susan, consciously use their images to mold their character and desires, or to undergird their commitments. Seeing and being seen by God so regularly and in such close proximity is a fraught experience, we could say: it is fraught with the feeling of family life.

23. Elizabeth Johnson writes, "The living press forward with the unfinished business of caring for the world. . . . Remembering the saints operates as a practical, critical, liberating force that energizes our resistance and protest, imagination and love." Johnson, *Truly Our Sister*, 320. The thread of meaning that runs through both Johnson's and Susan's interpretations is the idea that remembering the lives of the saints—in Susan's case, with the help of visual reminders—can inspire and support contemporary persons as they seek to love and care for the world.

Homelands, Family, and Saints

There is a "family feeling" about the way people handle and respond to the artistic representations of religious figures here. For example, when an Italian society at Mary Star holds a fundraising raffle, one of the major prizes being raffled will likely be a statue of a Madonna or a favorite saint. At the raffles I attended, social pressure notwithstanding, the winners of these prizes appeared to be genuinely pleased. The statues were carefully held up, admired, and handled with respect. This respect for religious images began to strike me as analogous to the respect that is commonly accorded to parents and grandparents in this community. Whatever the complex emotions the images evoke, there is a connection between these statues and the devout's feelings about their families and ancestral homes.

This association is evident in the Mary Star sanctuary, where many of the statues have been purchased or dedicated in memory of loved ones. In some cases, the statues themselves or the materials from which they were carved were imported from natal lands. I have been told, for example, that you can tell whether a statue of Saint Joseph was made in Italy by looking at the length of the saint's hair. Statues depicting him with long hair, like the one in the Mary Star sanctuary, are almost certainly of Italian origin. The presence of these patron saints of particular regions, such as Saint Joseph, patron of Sicily, and Saint John-Joseph of the Cross, patron of the Island of Ischia (Figure 18), further emphasize the ethnic origins of the devotions. When the devout "purchase" a perpetually lit candle for one of the saints' altars at church, the name of a deceased relative is actually printed on the candle, adding another visual and material reminder of connections between the saints and the deceased loved one. Both the natal land and the loved ones from the family of origin are memorialized in these altars and artifacts.

We can get some help in thinking about this phenomenon from historian Thomas Tweed, who theorizes about the significance of place in religious experience.[24] Tweed uses the term "translocative religion," which he describes as "the tendency among many first and second-generation migrants to symbolically move between the homeland and the new land."[25]

24. Tweed, *Our Lady of the Exile*, 91–98.

25. Tweed builds on the categories of Jonathan Z. Smith, who uses the term "locative" to mean local or native religion and "utopian" to refer to dislocated or Diasporic religion.

According to Tweed, religious artifacts have a particular significance for exiles and other migrants who are experiencing a sense of dislocation. Religious artifacts are both tangible and symbolic. They can function to transport people emotionally to the imagined homeland.[26] Immigrants' affection for their natal land, their "geopiety," in combination with their love for family members left behind or deceased, adds layers of feeling to devotional objects and practices.[27] Artifacts, because they occupy space, can also be a means through which displaced persons and groups form emotional attachments to a new place, such as an altar, a church, or a home. In doing this, migrants are engaging in the ongoing cultural work of "constructing a symbolic dwelling in which they might have their own space and find their own place."[28]

Certainly, for the devout immigrants in San Pedro who shared their stories with me, visual piety has served this purpose. By bringing so many striking tangible objects from the homeland into the public worship space of the sanctuary and into the private domain of the home, the devout have created visual reminders of their origins. In the context of prayer, then, as immigrants set their eyes upon these images, they are emotionally transported back and forth over the ocean, and over great distances in space and time. These visual and tangible reminders have served as spiritual anchors, through initial experiences of dislocation and in continual negotiations of economic, social, and personal upheavals in this new space. The hard work of making the dual transition to a new land and a new language, the two hallmarks of cultural identity, is aided by the presence of visual and tangible religious images. These images and artifacts bring a bit of the homelands into the new geographic place and help people carve out a sense of cohesion in the new cultural space.

My interviewees consistently displayed portraits or statues of their Italian patron saints next to or alongside of some of the more universal figures (such as the Sacred Heart) as well as portraits of parents, grandparents, or other family members. Many times I saw rosary beads draped over

---

Tweed modifies these categories and adds one, which he terms "translocative" religion. Translocative emphasizes a sense of "moving across" space and time, a going back and forth in religious cartography. Smith, *Map Is Not Territory*, 121–42; Tweed, *Our Lady of the Exile*, 93, 95.

26. Tweed, *Our Lady of the Exile*, 97.

27. Ibid., 87.

28. Ibid., 93.

a picture of a beloved mother (Figure 19). The presence of dresser scarves that resemble altar cloths, small lamps or perpetual candles burning in front of the images, as well as fresh or silk flowers enhances the religious quality of these groupings. These shrines often incorporate pictures of the most precious persons and symbols in the devout's life, and may be cluttered with personal items such as medications or hairbrushes (Figure 20). Sometimes a small American flag or a record of military service is part of the shrine, suggesting an attachment to or sacralization of the United States as the devout's new national identity.[29]

In some homes, these diverse items are found grouped together on a devout's bedroom dresser, in front of a mirror (Figure 21 and Figure 22). As a result, the person will regularly see these images together with his or her own image when looking into the mirror. The impact of this visual experience is significant, given that one is likely to glance in this mirror (that is also a shrine) at least twice a day, in the morning upon waking up, and at night before going to bed. David Morgan, in his discussion of religious images in bedrooms, speaks of the capacity of bedroom images to "measure and mark off a regular rhythm of daily life, and thereby to help insure a stable structure for the home and family. The bedroom is, after all, the place in the home where the diurnal cadence of dark and light is experienced."[30] The bedroom is a privileged space, and these symbols of saints, homelands, and ancestors are literally glimpsed together with the image of the self in the mirror with the regularity of the diurnal cadence.

How do the devout understand the group of people and saints that they see in the mirror each day? My impression is that many see themselves connected to these others, as members of an extended family. Ann Taves, in her book describing mid-nineteenth-century devotions in America, claims that the bourgeois family or household became a metaphor for the relationships between Catholics and the inhabitants of the supernatural world. This metaphor, encouraged by missionary preachers and popular devotional manuals, emphasized the nearness of the spiritual world, and fostered feelings of affection toward supernatural relatives.[31] Many San Pedro Catholics in my sample also think of the saints as something like

29. The tendency to sacralize the new land is also a feature of translocative religion, according to Tweed, as displaced peoples attempt to "map, construct, and inhabit worlds of meaning." Tweed, *Our Lady of the Exile*, 93.

30. Morgan, *Visual Piety*, 160.

31. Taves, *Household of Faith*, 47–88.

supernatural relatives. Certainly the faithful are still taught to regard Mary as their own Blessed Mother. They also tend to think of their deceased relatives as saints, or as being close to God, by virtue of the deceased's devout earthly lives and/or their current residence in heaven. Just as holy cards and family photographs abide together, side by side, a sense of fond connection to these dead relatives is kept vital through their association with favorite saints, and vice-versa.

"My mother's house looked like a shrine," one man notes. His devotion to Mary helps keep alive the memory of his now deceased mother.[32] The fact that the saints' portraits or statues that people display in their homes are themselves often gifts from family members, or inheritances passed down from parents, enhances the emotional link between loved ones and the statues as well as the saints they represent. A young woman I interviewed, a member of the third generation, has a shelf in her living room home entertainment center devoted to deceased relatives. Though she has no images of official Catholic saints displayed there, she emphasizes to me that these loved ones *"are"* their family saints.[33]

A second-generation woman tells me of her loss of two infant siblings, one death due to the Spanish flu and one to pneumonia. She reports that she began to think of the lost siblings as angels, living in heaven with God. When she had children of her own, she hung pictures of angels in their bedrooms. She told her children that they had two guardian angels, who would always be at their side.[34] In this case, the deceased infants actually became the referents of the angel portraits.

Some individuals have intentionally constructed shrines in their homes in memory of deceased loved ones. One woman, the self-described "fallen away Catholic," whose sister recently passed away, created an impromptu shrine on her kitchen counter (Figure 23). On this counter is a statue of Saint Teresa, the patron saint of Verona, the northern Italian family homeland. Along with Saint Teresa is a picture of the deceased sister, and a picture album that highlights the last year of her life as she struggled with cancer. Fresh flowers attend the memorial.

Another woman marked her mother's death by starting a tradition of building an elaborate altar for Saint Joseph in her living room for ten

32. Interview #5.
33. Interview #25.
34. Interview #24.

days each March, in celebration of the Saint's feast day and the traditional period of celebration that lasts from one to two weeks (see chapter 4). This annual creation takes over the mantle above the fireplace. Indeed, it dominates the whole room both with the bright colors of flowing fabric and the fragrance of flowers. The woman told me that she established this practice because she and her daughters felt that something "was missing" after her mother, a devout immigrant matriarch, passed away. For this family, the ornate shrine seems to invoke the presence of the deceased mother as much as that of Saint Joseph.

Historian David Morgan makes claims about the importance of religious images in the process of the construction of the self and its habitat. He writes, ". . . By becoming constant and virtually transparent features of daily experience, embedded in the quotidian rituals, narratives, and collective memories that people take for granted, religious images help form the half-forgotten texture of everyday life."[35] In these devotional practices, religious art and artifacts are indeed a "constant and virtually transparent" feature of immigrants' lives, signifying both particular and collective memories—memories of family and friends, as well as memories of family members, homes, and churches left behind in Italy or Sicily. These memories are constantly renewed through the presence of artwork that is in some way (either through style, content, or the origin of materials) both Italian as well as Catholic. Since this artwork surrounds people not only in church but also in the psychologically privileged space of the home, it becomes a part of the "half-forgotten quality of the fabric of everyday life."

I asked members of the younger immigrant generations how they felt about religious pictures in their homes or their grandparents' homes when they were growing up. They responded with comments such as, "I didn't think about it. It's just how it was." Or, "All my friends' houses looked just like ours. I didn't know anyone who didn't have them." A young second-generation woman said, "They were just always there, part of my life. I felt protected, secure, if anyone tried to break in."[36] A third-generation woman stated, "They were just a part of who we were and what

---

35. He continues, "As a part of the very fabric of consciousness, religious images participate fundamentally in the social construction of reality. . . . Again and again we have found that religious images assist in fashioning the impression of a coherent, enduring, and uniform world in which the self exists meaningfully." Morgan, *Visual Piety*, 207.

36. Interview #22.

we believed."[37] One third-generation woman said that they were "visual aids to remind us where we came from."[38] These comments suggest that the religious images were in fact so common that they appeared natural. They were unquestioned. A young two-thirds-generation woman said, "I just knew that we're Catholic and that's what Catholics do. When I started baby-sitting the neighbors' children, I first saw non-Catholic homes."[39] These comments suggest that the religious images in their homes efficiently contributed to the identity formation of children, wordlessly but regularly telling them who they were, both religiously and ethnically.

Here the power of the shared habitual experience of looking at religious art and artifacts comes more fully into view. The artwork itself, along with the meanings assigned to it by parents, grandparents, church teaching, and circles of Italian Catholic friends and neighbors, has helped to constitute and preserve memories of the past and link these memories to identity in the present. This practice indeed fosters the "impression of a coherent, enduring, and uniform world in which the self exists meaningfully." For families whose lives have been marked by the dramatic changes of immigration and the sense of contingency that this entails, the regular impression of a coherent and reliable world is especially salutary.

If images of Mary and the saints are experienced at least metaphorically as supernatural members of the family, then the profusion of portraits and statues of Mary in this setting raises the question of the meaning of her role as Holy Mother. The visual presence of Mary, if experienced as one's own supernatural Mother, is a phenomenon to be reckoned with. It is to this feature of visual devotion that we will now turn.

Mary (the) Star

The ubiquitous presence of images of Mary in the public realm—in the sky above San Pedro, in the inner sacred space of Mary Star of the Sea Church—as well as in domestic and personal spaces is striking. The persistent habit of keeping images of Mary nearby, even down through the immigrant generations of the people I interviewed, and even among those who say they no longer believe, is similarly remarkable. In all of the homes

37. Interview #27.

38. Interview #13.

39. Interview #20. By two-thirds-generation, I mean that one parent was an immigrant and one was born in the U.S.

I visited, with one exception, I saw at least one Madonna.[40] Even three women who described themselves respectively as "a fallen-away Catholic," "a non-practicing Catholic," and "converted to Christ alone," all had some statues or images of Mary in their homes; two carried rosary beads—Mary's honorific—in their purses. The presence of these items seemed important to these women. The self-described "fallen-away" Catholic who "married outside the church" has little altars and statues in several rooms of her home. She credits one of these pieces, a sculpted rendition of the Holy Family (Joseph, Mary, and Jesus), with helping her conceive her children.[41] Even in these cases where the women have mixed or hard feelings toward the Catholic Church, they appear to be comfortable with and fond of their images of Mary, the angels, and saints.

One of these women says she has always liked Mary Star's Pietà-like statue of Mary with Jesus (Figure 10). Though she no longer attends Mass, she remembers this statue fondly for its artistic value. "I'm a visual person," she claims. "I loved that statue. I appreciated the artistry in it."[42] The woman notes that she associates her appreciation of art and her interest in her own artistic expression with her experience of viewing that statue. The statue happened to be located directly in her line of vision from the pew in which she and her family always sat when she was growing up. This case brings to mind Margaret Miles's claim that "Images are powerful, and the most powerful images accomplish with skill and economy that which they do best: formation by attraction."[43] While the (third generation) woman in this case does not accept official church doctrine regarding Mary, and in fact pointedly rejects the virgin birth, she nevertheless claims that she was formed in some ways, or at least her artistic sensibilities were shaped, by her visual attraction to that statue. Interestingly, Sarah, another third-generation woman whose story I explore below, also singles out this particular statue. Sarah associates the piece with her own capacity for compassion, her ability to be moved by human suffering.

The facility with which these women notice the visual world, perceive Mary's beauty, or feel moved by a sense of her compassion, can be considered a kind of psycho-spiritual skill. This kind of skill or sensibility

---

40. In the one home that was the exception, my visit was confined to the living room, so I am not entirely sure that there were no religious items displayed in other rooms.

41. Interview #3.

42. Interview #21.

43. Miles, *Image and Insight*, 145.

informs religious and personal identity. According to religious philosopher Paula Cooey,

> Identity . . . is a dynamic, psychosomatic pattern of value mediated by social symbols. Religious life, centered on such symbols, serves as one primary locus for value-in-the-making as it creates persons in their solitude and in their community.[44]

What kind of persons does this devoted religious life, centered on images Mary, create in solitude and in community? Visually adept, compassionate persons? What other characteristics and values do these images of Mary convey to women, men, and children in this setting?

The answers to these questions are complicated, diverse, contingent. The number of and diversity of visual images of the Holy Mother that the devout, their children, and grandchildren view give us an inkling of this complexity. These particular figures include representations of Mary Star of the Sea, Our Lady of Fatima, the Madonna of the Bridge, Our Lady of Guadalupe, and Rosa Mistica, to name just few. These are images of multifarious forms of Mary, each with its own legends and each with varied versions of legends. Some devout know these legends and some do not. Given that the towering marble sculpture of Mary that dominates the main altar in Mary Star of the Sea Church is standing on a wave and holding a tuna boat, we might conclude that it is Mary's image as a protectress at sea that churchgoers view with the greatest regularity. Unless the eye should wander to the side-altar Pietà-like image, that is.

Whom and what each person sees in these images of Mary also changes over time, according to the beliefs, needs, and inclinations of the viewer. On a psychological level, the inner imaginative constructs of the Holy Mother of God are likely to be as varied as the inner imaginative constructs (or objects) of the viewers' real human mothers.[45] Theological beliefs about Mary are similarly various. Two persons interviewed made reference to Mary's virginity, while one explicitly rejected this teaching, finding it insulting to real mothers. Most said nothing about this doctrine. Many women spoke of Mary's love for her son and her heartbreak at his death. They expressed a sense of comfort in identifying with Mary as a mother who knew what grief was.

44. Cooey, *Religious Imagination and the Body*, 32.

45. For a fascinating psychoanalytic study of God images as and their relationship to internal representations of parents, see Rizzuto, *Birth of the Living God*.

The ambiguity expressed about these images and beliefs about Mary is compounded when we consider some of the feminist literature addressing this subject.[46] The traditional Catholic image of Mary as the ever-virgin mother of God's Son has long been rued as a harmful symbol of womanhood, one that keeps Mary isolated, "alone of all her sex" in the phrase of Marina Warner.[47] Because Mary is alone—one of kind, exalted for her unique status as a virgin mother, impossible for real women to emulate—she leaves real women falling short by comparison, and consigned to feelings of guilt, sinfulness, or inadequacy. Obedient, sexless, a mere vessel for the exalted male God, this Mary symbolically undercuts the agency and authority of living embodied women who look to her for guidance. This is a compelling critique, one that helps explain why having a towering image of a woman at the center of worship and devotion does not necessarily challenge the patriarchal structures of the church.

Yet this important critique does not account for other dramatically different popular interpretations of Mary. In some communities, especially in the context of suffering or marginality, a more subversive, unintended message has been perceived in Mary. Back in 1975, Rosemary Ruether described this phenomenon aptly. She wrote,

> There is the Mary of the Monks, who venerate her primarily as a virgin and shape her doctrines in an anti-sexual mold. But there is the Mary of the people who is still the earth mother and who is venerated for her power of the secret of natural fecundity. It is she who helps the woman through her birth pangs, who assures the farmer of his new crops, new rains, new lambs. She is the eternal image of the divine who understands ordinary people in their wretchedness.[48]

Many of the folks I spoke with tended to think of their Madonna in this way—as someone who understands hardship and childbirth; someone who loves them and their people.

Theological interpretations of Mary's impact on women continue to proliferate, with Protestant scholars now weighing in on the discussion.[49]

46. For an excellent review of this literature, see Johnson's "Fragments in the Rubble," in *Truly Our Sister*, 3–17.

47. Warner, *Alone of All Her Sex*.

48. Ruether, "Mistress of Heaven," 50.

49. Gaventa and Rigby, *Blessed One*.

Theologians from diverse cultural, racial, and/or geographical starting points tell conflicting stories, some judging Mary as a harmful, limiting, restrictive ideal for women. By contrast, Mexican-American theologian Jeanette Rodrigues claims that Mary manifests the "maternal face of God"[50] to "women whose humanity has been systematically denigrated."[51] Rodrigues asserts that Mary is a source of strength to Mexican women who are fighting to overcome their social marginalization. To this intensely mixed set of appraisals, Catholic theologian Elizabeth Johnson offers what she calls a "modest proposal:" that we begin viewing Mary as "a concrete woman in history who had her own life to figure out, a first century Jewish woman in a peasant village . . ."[52] I find this to be a creative and promising move in that it focuses attention on the messy, lived experience of the historical Mary. As such, it helps underscore the importance of the historical contexts of the communities in which Mary is venerated, as we try to assess her particular, local, symbolic and spiritual impact. In keeping with this approach, we will now turn to the particular experiences of four persons in this setting, to get a closer look at what is transpiring for them in their particular practices of devotion.

A Closer Look

Maria

"Maria" is a seventy-two year old immigrant from Sicily. When I arrive at her lovely home in an older section of San Pedro, she greets me warmly. Maria speaks to me alternately in English and Italian. She assures me that God will help us, bless us in this time together. Though she does not know me at all, she not only allows me this interview in her home, but she announces generously upon my arrival, "I dedicate this day to you."[53] Moved by her kindness, it does not take too long before I realize that I have found a true believer, a religious virtuoso. Maria's is an example of what William

---

50. Rodriguez, *Our Lady of Guadalupe*, xviii.

51. Johnson, *Truly Our Sister*, 14.

52. In making this move toward the historical Mary, Johnson seeks to bring our collective memory of Mary back down to earth, so that we might view her no longer as an ethereal symbol, alone of all her sex, but as a fully human woman firmly rooted in her own historical community, where she had close ties to other women. In her death, Mary may be viewed as a member of the communion of Saints. Johnson, *Truly Our Sister*, 104–13.

53. Interview #18.

James would call "first-hand religion."[54] She has an intensely personal relationship with God, and she is glad to share her original story with me.

Maria tells me that she has felt called by God ever since she was two years old. Her mother taught her the catechism, which she learned to recite by age three. She recalls that her mother would put her up on a table so that she could speak the catechism and sing religious hymns in front of friends. "I believe God call me when I was little. I believe." Later, as she approached adulthood, she again struggled with a sense of her religious calling. Should she marry or "go to sister"—become a nun? After much prayer, and with the urging of a persistent fiancé who waited two years for her parents' permission, she decided to marry. Early in the marriage, she had a distressing miscarriage when she was five months pregnant. Later, she gave birth to two male children. One of these pregnancies required nine months of bed rest.

When Maria and her husband came to this country in 1972, she left her parents and some of her siblings at home. She came to San Pedro so that her husband could fish. Because he went on long-haul fishing trips, lasting six to eight months, Maria was left here in San Pedro essentially raising her children alone for long periods of time. She recalls the difficulty of the early days, when she could not communicate in English. "When you don't know the lingua (language) everything is dark," she explains, quietly and tearfully. "And God is the light!" she whispers. Indeed, Maria's faith, and her association with Mary Star of the Sea Church, did light her path. Here she found other Italian-speaking people, became active in religious societies and ministries to the poor, and eventually became a Eucharistic Minister, assisting the priests by holding the cup for the service of Holy Communion. The church has given her a social network and a way for her to fulfill her spiritual sense of calling. Now, somewhat less active at age seventy-two, but still definitely involved in the parish, Maria begins her day in prayer, before she gets out of bed. She also reads the Bible in Italian every day, especially the gospels. When her women's society meets monthly to pray the rosary, she interprets the gospel to them. She claims that it is not she that speaks, but God who speaks through her. In essence, she preaches the gospel.

I am struck by Maria's faith practices, moved by story. An immigrant female Catholic preacher, steeped in bible-study, she seems to defy

54. James, *Varieties*, 337.

stereotypes. She follows the church's current teaching in that she prays most often, not to the saints, nor to their statues, but to God. She tells me that when she goes to church to pray, she goes directly to the Blessed Sacrament—specifically, to the monstrance that holds the sanctified host—the wafer that is believed to be the living Christ, "real, live." Looking at the host, she feels she is looking directly at God.

Maria is also the woman who has the Rosa Mistica portrait, described at the start of this chapter, hanging in her living room. Next to God revealed in Christ, the Madonna is Maria's closest spiritual contact. "She is our mother," Maria says simply. What happens exactly to Maria when she gazes into the face of the Madonna? Of course, she does not actually look into the face of Mary, but into a portrait of a sculpture of her face. Maria is, to some degree, aware of this distinction. But the border between Maria's visual perception of the physical portrait of the Madonna and Maria's spiritual and emotional experience of the presence of the Madonna in the room is permeable, blurred. In looking at the portrait in her living room (Figure 6), Maria imaginatively perceives the Madonna as present in the room ("real, real") and looking back, seeing Maria. What can we make of this?

THE TRANSITIONAL REALM

A general way of viewing what is happening psychologically for Maria, is through the lens of Donald Woods Winnicott's concept of the transitional realm, which he defined as, "an intermediate area of *experiencing*, to which inner reality and external life both contribute."[55] D. W. Winnicott (1896–1971), a pediatrician and a psychiatrist, first coined the term, "the transitional realm" in order to describe the emotional experience of newborn infants as they begin to take in the world around them.[56] The transitional realm is an emotional experience that originates in a baby's first dawning sense that he or she is not omnipotent—that is, fully in charge of

---

55. Winnicott, *Playing and Reality*, 2.

56. The use of object relations theory as a theoretical lens in the study of religion is controversial. Because this theory is based on infantile experience, it may seem as though I am reducing religious experiences to regressions to infancy. This is not my view. Rather, I find that object relations theory articulates some key themes that are echoed in human relationships throughout the lifespan. I think that religious relationships have psychological dimensions that cannot be denied. Yet religious faith is also more than a psychological experience. For a critique of object relations theory in the study of religion, see Wulff, *Psychology of Religion*, 318–68. For a collection of more recent essays related to this discussion, see Jonte-Pace and Parsons, *Religion and Psychology*.

his or her world. This awareness is terrifying for the infant, who is in reality vulnerable and absolutely dependent upon adult care.[57]

Though Winnicott based these ideas on the study of infants, he indicated that the need for illusion continues in childhood and throughout adult life. Playing is one way in which children and adults enter into illusory experience, taking a break from hard realities.[58] Play (such as vacationing) can be refreshing or renewing for adults caught up in the strain of daily living. According to Winnicott, the sense of formlessness and/or beauty available in or through these intermediate experiences can regenerate the human capacity to engage life creatively, and enable us to live out of a genuine sense of self, rather than merely conform to the realities of external existence.

Winnicott also claimed that religion and the arts belong to the transitional realm.[59] In this view, theology and religious practices always involve both bits of truth and bits of illusion, ideas that help us describe and cope with the vast unknown. Music and art also involve illusion—art more

57. More specifically, the transitional realm refers to the baby's experience of the world (focused at first on the breast, or the mother or other primary caregiver) as separate, distinct from the infant, and not completely malleable. According to Winnicott, the child's inner psyche gradually comes to terms with this frightening outside world through "illusory" experience of it. This experience is illusory in the sense that it is based on the child's perception of the world (or mother) and shaped by the child's emotional need to feel that he or she can depend on that world (mother). This illusion is, in most cases, partly real. That is, the child can usually depend on the mother or other primary caregiver to meet at least some of his or her basic needs. In the intermediate or transitional realm, the child uses imagination to help make the caregiver—and thus the world—seem better, more dependable, manageable, pliant, or supple.

58. According to Winnicott, "It is assumed here that the task of reality-acceptance is never completed, that no human being is free from the strain of relating inner and outer reality, and that relief from this strain is provided by an intermediate area of experience . . . which is not challenged (arts, religion, etc.). This intermediate area is in direct continuity with the play area of the small child who is 'lost' in play." *Playing and Reality*, 13. I take this passage to refer to the difficulty or strain which is inherent in adult living, including not only the strains of love and work, and the hardship of illness or want, but also the difficulty of coming to terms with the precarious nature of life and all of the dimensions of external reality that human beings cannot control.

59. Famously, Winnicott wrote, "I am therefore studying the substance of *illusion*, that which is allowed to the infant, and which in adult life is inherent in art and religion, and yet becomes the hallmark of madness when an adult puts too powerful a claim on the credulity of others, forcing them to acknowledge a sharing of illusion that is not their own. We can share a respect for *illusory experience*, and if we wish we may collect together and form a group on the basis of the similarity of our illusory experiences. This is a natural root of grouping among human beings." *Playing and Reality*, 3.

obviously so, perhaps. In the experience of beauty or vastness that people encounter in diverse ways, such as in worship, or in an art museum, or in a concert hall, we may experience the transitional realm.

According to Winnicott, people who feel the same way about particular theological beliefs, or schools of art or music, may naturally be found in groups together. This is part of his theory of culture. We can recognize differences in our cultural preferences while still appreciating the common need that we all have for some form of illusory experience. This theory of the transitional realm can help readers appreciate the role of illusion in visual devotions. Those readers whose religious experiences are extremely dissimilar to the ones I am describing (i.e., non-Catholics) may find it helpful to consider the devotions as psychologically analogous to other transitional phenomena, such as music or meditation.

In a general way, we can view Maria's experience of the presence of the Madonna in the portrait in her living room, as her experience of the transitional realm. The portrait of Mary, with her ambiguous left eye, may function for Maria as a cue or a gateway to the intermediate realm. The experience of the Madonna—the Holy Mother—as present and alive in the living room, looking at or watching over Maria, has probably helped Maria find relief from the strain of accepting the realities of dislocation and loneliness when she first immigrated, leaving her parents behind. Now, at seventy-two, she makes a practice of returning to her homeland for two months each year, in order to care for her mother (taking turns with her siblings in this care). Seeing and being seen by this powerful Madonna—whose eyes are said to weep real tears—may provide a sense of union that helps Maria redress the sadness, relief, or even the guilt that she may feel in these separations.

Similarly, Maria's capacity to see and feel the Madonna's presence during her husband's absence at sea may have aided her in her ability to construct a sense of her place in the world. Because the portrait of Rosa Mistica recalls a statue in a chapel in Italy, it may also be functioning as a bridge or a "transitional object,"[60] through which Maria can experience

---

60. Winnicott used this term to designate a child's first possession, an object that is not part of the child's body, but that is also not fully recognized as outside of the child's control. See "Transitional Objects," in *Playing and Reality*, 1–29. I am using the term in its more general and popular meaning, to signify an object that provides a sense of comfort and connection in the context of a separation.

her ties both to her homeland and to her current home—especially her domestic space—in this land.

MADONNA AS MIRROR

We can also look at Maria's visual piety in terms of a more specific phenomenon that Winnicott and other theorists describe, which is psychological mirroring. The important detail to consider here is Maria's claim that the portrait looks back at her. Maria not only sees the Madonna as mother in the portrait, she also experiences a strong sense of being seen by her. The psychological significance of this point is hard to overestimate. The importance of a loving maternal gaze to a child's wellbeing is frequently noted in psychological literature.[61] Winnicott put it succinctly when he wrote, "When I look I am seen, so I exist."[62] Seeing that recognition in the parent's gaze is essential for the child who is slowly building a sense of self. Even in adulthood, the need to be fully seen and recognized continues.[63] When we are recognized—through the warm gaze of a family member or friend, or through public attention or awards for our accomplishments— we gain a greater internal awareness of our own existence. We shore up a sense of ourselves.

Perhaps when Maria experiences herself as seen by the Madonna's watchful left eye, she is shoring up her sense of own existence. When we consider Maria's somewhat marginalized social status in this country, as an older immigrant woman who speaks little English, the experience of being seen in her new home takes on greater significance. During times of transition, when the sense of a coherent self is challenged by the continual need to change and adjust, the benefit of mirroring experiences is heightened.

Part of what a child needs to see "in the mirror" of his or her parents' eyes is a reflection of the self.[64] This longing for a sense of essential likeness

61. Ainsworth, "Infant-Mother Attachment,"16–19; Greenberg and Mitchell, *Object Relations in Psychoanalytic Theory*, 354–56.

62. Winnicott, *Playing and Reality*, 114.

63. Winnicott claimed that the continual striving to get oneself seen or recognized is a characteristic of normal human existence; it is only exaggerated in certain clinical cases. "What is illustrated by this case only exaggerates what is normal. The exaggeration is of the task of getting the mirror to notice and approve." *Playing and Reality*, 114. Heinz Kohut concurred: "We need mirroring acceptance, the merger with ideals, the sustaining presence of others like us, throughout our lives." Kohut, "Summarizing Reflections," 494–95.

64. According to Heinz Kohut, three conditions can enhance the mirroring experience that is needed for healthy development in the early stages of life. One of these three positive

is also referred to as "twinning." We can see this phenomenon in adult life, too, for example, in the pursuit of role models, friends or professional colleagues who seem like us in some important way. Consider also the value of support groups such as bereavement groups, veterans' groups, or Alcoholics Anonymous. We benefit from seeing and interacting with others who are in some ways similar to ourselves.

In Maria's case, we might think about the significance of the Italian origins of the figure of Rosa Mistica. When Maria looks into the portrait, she sees a culturally specific Italian holy mother, one with whom she may identify by feeling a "sense of essential likeness." Maria may also experience herself as mirrored or reflected in her circle of Italian-speaking women friends at Mary Star of the Sea Church. Maria's close-knit group shares similar immigration stories as well as common devotional practices.[65] Maria's religious devotion provides her with social support and cultural mirroring.

Maria's intense faith, and the spiritual aura that surrounds her, enable her to be seen in another significant way. Within her circle of Italian and Sicilian Catholic women, Maria's spiritual virtuosity is apparently recognized. She tells me that she reads the Bible in Italian every day and feels that God is communicating with her: "I learn the book, and I feel when I read. I *feel* it. Thank God I have a light. I feel communication with God." When Maria and her friends gather to pray, she often takes on the role of interpreter. "I explain it [the Bible] to them. God use [*sic*] me. I read the gospel and God use [*sic*] me. We [I] proclaim the words of God."[66] Maria indicates that her friends recognize her leadership and ask her to perform this interpretive role. She takes pains to tell me that this is not her own doing; it is God speaking through her.

Devotion to the Madonna constitutes only part of Maria's extensive religious practice. But it is a significant part of the whole of Maria's faith. The Rosa Mistica portrait invokes a female spiritual presence in an otherwise mostly male household. The portrait mirrors Maria's strong spiritual

---

conditions occurs when the primary care-givers or "self-objects," as Kohut calls them, "in their openness and similarity to the child, evoke a sense of essential likeness between the child and themselves." Mitchell and Black, *Freud and Beyond*, 159, paraphrasing Kohut and Wolf, "Disorders of the Self," 413–25.

65. Tweed notes that, ". . . translocative ritual behavior draws the displaced together," especially through "unifying mythic figures." Tweed, *Our Lady of the Exile*, 97.

66. Interview #18.

identity, signifying many things at once. Maria's sense of her own existence, her Sicilian and Italian identity,[67] her strength as a woman and a mother, and her coherent sense of her self as one called by God to religious leadership are all mirrored and undergirded when she looks at this portrait.

Josephine

Another woman, whom I shall call "Josephine," shares specific information about what she sees when she gazes into her Madonna's face. Josephine is also an immigrant, but would be more accurately described as a member of the one and a half generation, given that her parents brought her to this country when she was only two years old. She is now a high-school language teacher, age forty-three, the first one in her family to go to college. As the best English speaker and most educated person in the family, she is expected to help her extended family out with taxes and other legal paperwork. In this, she functions very much in the role of one from the second immigrant generation. Josephine is married to a man she met on one of her frequent return trips to her parents' homeland; the couple has two teenage children.

Josephine offers a classic description of her experience growing up as the child of immigrants in America. In middle school, she claims, "I was *very* American. That means: I didn't eat pasta; I didn't speak Sicilian; I ate peanut butter and jelly for lunch in front of the other kids. I didn't like that my parents didn't speak English. No one helped me with my homework. I would teach people how to read and write."[68] A language teacher now, Josephine has reclaimed her Sicilian heritage as an important part of her identity. She feels she is able to "take from both cultures." "My family and my faith is more the old world—my Italian culture. But because of my education, I'm a working mother." She sees advantages to this, and yet also acknowledges the burden of it. "Then you have that clash, that guilt. Because the guilt is so heavy, I usually drop everything and go down (to see her extended family when they call)." Josephine vividly describes both the joy of what she considers her dual cultural heritage and the labor and stress involved in maintaining this braided identity.

Josephine claims that her piety offers her some relief from this stress. Praying, in particular, she says, is "the one relief for me." Visual representa-

---

67. Maria refers to herself as Sicilian or Italian interchangeably.
68. Interview #16.

tions of Mary and the saints play an important part in this. In her beautiful suburban home just outside San Pedro, there are several impressive religious works of art, including a large ornately framed painting of the Madonna Del Ponte (Our Lady of the Bridge, patron Saint of Trapetto, Sicily) that dominates the formal living room (Figure 24). Notably, a white marble statue of Our Lady of Fatima resides in a bay window in Josephine's bedroom (Figure 25). Josephine regularly goes to this statue to pray. She says that if something is bothering her, she finds both repose and guidance from the Madonna. When Josephine is trying to work out a problem in her life, she goes to look at Mary's face. She says of this practice,

> This may sound crazy, but when I look at the Blessed Mother, if she's smiling, then I know everything's going to be okay. I feel that if I can go in my bedroom, and take a look at that Blessed Mother, if she's smiling, then we're okay. If she's not smiling, then I'm going, 'Whoa! . . . not a good sign.' Call it superstitious or whatever.[69]

When I queried Josephine specifically about how the statue smiled, she said, "I feel that she's smiling, because the statue's not going to change. But yet, my perception is, if I can look at that statue, and if I feel she's got that smile on her face, then I'm comforted by knowing everything's going to be okay."[70]

Josephine seems to know that her prayers to the Madonna take her into a different kind of perceptual realm. She implies that there is a certain ambiguity in her awareness when she says, "My perception is, that she's smiling . . . the statue's not going to change." Nevertheless, for Josephine, the statue mediates a relationship with the real Madonna, a supernatural mother for whom Josephine feels great affection, respect, and awe. Josephine's comments suggest that her devotion to the Blessed Mother functions to provide her with a kind of spiritual mirror that helps her gauge her comfort level with the vicissitudes of her daily life. Because the actual face of the statue of the Madonna is serene, Josephine's visual practice is apt to reinforce Josephine's own internal strength.[71] The comfort of

69. Interview #16.

70. Ibid.

71. According to object relations theory, this internal strength would have been established in early life, probably gleaned from her mother and other childhood caretakers. This prior experience may be what enables Josephine to perceive that the Madonna is smiling at her, much of the time. According to Winnicott, when a baby looks into the face of his or her mother, ordinarily, what the baby sees is himself or herself. *Playing and Reality*, 112.

perceiving the Madonna's smile is no small thing for Josephine. Her relationship with Mary, mediated through the statue, has assisted Josephine through several crises in her life, including two fairly extensive bouts with cancer. "I look to her for *strength*," Josephine says emphatically, and I believe her. Josephine speaks with the authority of one who has survived a fearful struggle with a life-threatening illness.

While Josephine's perceptual maneuvers may indeed "sound crazy," her ability to find strength and well-being through her devotions is certainly compelling. Perhaps we can appreciate Josephine's relationship with Mary as belonging to the transitional realm. This is the experiential realm in which the emotional and spiritual work of coping with a serious illness is done. As in the case of Maria, the concept of mirroring may help us understand the psychological dynamics of Josephine's practice. This theory claims that in childhood, we need to look at our caregiver and see in her three things: "essential likeness," approval, and an image of power and calmness.[72] Images of these caregivers or "self-objects" are then established internally, contributing to the child's developing sense of himself or herself.

Of course, the saints are not actual childhood caregivers, and statues alone could not provide the kinds of parental interactions that build a healthy sense of self in an infant or a child. At the same time, it is important to recognize that at least some of the devout in this setting are accustomed to experiencing Mary, the angels, and/or the saints as spiritual caretakers.[73] Visual representations of Mary and the saints, with their

That is, the baby picks up something in the mother's face that is related to what she sees, or how she feels about what she sees in the baby. If the mother—or other caregiver—reflects a harsh or angry mood to the baby, the baby will take this in. If the mother's face signals approval, warmth, or pleasure in the sight of her child, the child will take this in.

72. Heinz Kohut described three kinds of mirroring experiences that are needed in an environment that is conducive to the development of a healthy self. The child needs to be mirrored by caregivers who "respond to and confirm the child's innate sense of vigor, greatness, and perfection." These are caregivers who look with pleasure and approval on the child, encouraging his or her "expansive states of mind." Additionally, the child needs to be involved with powerful others "to whom the child can look up and with whom he can merge as an image of calmness, infallibility, and omnipotence." Kohut and Wolf, "Disorders of the Self and Their Treatment," cited in Mitchell and Black, 159.

73. Because the devout have grown up seeing and hearing about the saints, these figures are likely to be at least somewhat merged, experientially, with the devout's idealized images of their parents. Ann Taves, in her discussion of Roman Catholic devotions in mid-nineteenth century America, explores the significance of the popular use of parental metaphors in reference to Mary and the saints. Following Melford Spiro, Taves suggests

ethereal expressions, halos, symbolic garb, and ethnic identity markers, are well equipped to mirror a sense of vigor, greatness, and perfection, to adults who approach them seeking spiritual care.

Josephine reports finding strength, calmness, and vigor through looking into the face of Mary. She notes also a sense of essential likeness with Mary—the fact that she is female, and that she is a mother. While Our Lady of Fatima is traditionally considered a patroness of Spain, rather than Sicily or Italy, the statue does have long dark hair, and Josephine seems to identify with "her" as culturally similar. Josephine speaks of her statue as simply "*the*" Madonna, to whom she looks for strength. Josephine says of the Madonna, "She saw her son crucified. But she is not sorrowful or melancholy." Josephine's Madonna does seem to have a smiling face. This has mirrored back to Josephine a sense of happiness that undergirded her during her struggles with her health. Josephine elaborates, "I have a positive aspect on life. I've learned not to hold grudges. Happiness, health, and faith, it's almost like the Trinity. You have to have all three." Josephine's thoughtful theological construction has been wrought through her arduous and lengthy battle with illness and survival. She says of her cancer, "It made me a better person. My faith was able to get me through it. It's a positive thing that happened. It puts things back into perspective. You realize that affluence is not the most important thing."[74]

Josephine's story suggests that she saw in her images of Mary a joyful, approving, and encouraging holy mother. Josephine experiences her Madonna in ways that she has found both sustaining and curative during a difficult battle with cancer, and beyond. Now Josephine reflects on her theology, actions, and values, "checking in" with her image of the Madonna for guidance and wisdom, as she re-evaluates her former focus on affluence in light of the new meanings she forged through her illness.

From a theological perspective, Josephine's story is important. Josephine has been engaged in a battle to transform her own suffering (in this world). Paula Cooey notes that "the body lived becomes a crucible for both sustaining and changing human values."[75] In transforming her bodily

---

the possibility that the power of cultural images of supernatural beings, such as Mary and the saints, may rest in part on the blurring of the line between children's experiences of their natural and supernatural parents. This would help to explain the strength of the adult's faith in the supernatural world. Taves, *Household of Faith*, 83.

74. Interview #16.

75. Cooey, *Religious Imagination and the Body*, 43.

experience of cancer into "a good thing," Josephine relied on the image of Mary who "saw her son crucified but wasn't melancholy." Josephine's capacity to hold onto joy, inspired and affirmed by her perception of a smiling Madonna, proved to be a significant resource for her. She has now elevated the value of happiness and health along with faith to the status of a "trinity" of new values to live by. It seems to me that Josephine's visual prayer practices have assisted her, at a most basic level, in what Cooey would call "the symbolic construal of pain and pleasure." This important theological work appears to help her survive and enhance her human subjectivity, even as it transforms her values.

Sarah

Sarah, a member of the third generation, is thirty-five years old. She lives alone in an apartment not far from her parents' home in an older section of San Pedro. Several other members of her extended family live in the neighborhood. Sarah tells me that she does consider herself a Catholic, but not in the traditional sense. The child of an extremely religious mother and a father who is less devout, she rarely attends Mass. Her spirituality now involves meditation, massage, prayer to God, and faith in guardian angels. Sarah has several religious objects around her house, some of which she collected for me to photograph. They include four images of angels, a Native American dream-catcher, a scapular from her mother, and a portrait of Saint Michael (Figure 26).

Sarah grew up with lots of religious art and artifacts. In her home, the most prominent religious object was a statue of a patron saint in a backyard archway, which Sarah refers to as the garden saint. She also remembers the importance of rosary beads and the family Bible, from which each of the seven children in the family received a name. Sarah also recalls the Pietà-like marble structure of Mary and Jesus in the sanctuary of Mary Star of the Sea (Figure 10). She claims that it made an impression on her. "It had a strange effect. It looked larger than life. It moved me almost to tears, just looking at it."[76]

Sarah's form of piety seems, at first, quite different from that of Maria and Josephine. The first two women attend Mass and participate actively in the life of the congregation as well as in devotional societies. Sarah, by contrast, stopped attending Mass when she was a teenager, put off by what

76. Interview #29.

she perceived as the church's constant concern with fundraising. She also states that she was never really comfortable at Mary Star, except when she was there alone. While Sarah, for various reasons, does not participate in the traditional ways, she retains the habit of looking at religious objects and relies emotionally and spiritually on her sense of divine or divine-like beings watching over her. Interestingly, when she describes her prayer life, the tenderness she experienced as a child viewing the Pietà-like sculpture seems to still be with her. She says, "I have sometimes a tenderness. If there is a person going through a hard time, I'll take a few moments and I'll pray for them."[77]

Sarah notes that her guardian angels have become more important to her over the years. Interestingly, she states, "That's what carried me through a lot of things—belief that I was always watched by something other than God."[78] Sarah then very bravely elaborates on the things that the angels had carried her through. Slowly and steadily, she shares the story of her own embodied experience of pain and suffering, a lengthy period of domestic abuse at the hand of her ex-husband. Sarah met her husband locally, though he was neither Catholic nor Italian. He was a fundamentalist Christian, whom she met at a local church-based youth social. The violence began after their wedding and increased when the couple moved to another state, where Sarah was isolated from her large close family and her network of friends. "That's when it got worse. I tried to leave him more than once. I was in safe houses. I had my sisters mail me up my bond." Sarah became tearful as she spoke of the abuse and of her brush with death when she attempted suicide via an overdose so that she would not feel anything. She says, "I always believed in God. In the hard parts of my life, I don't think I would have made it if it wasn't for the man upstairs."[79] Indeed, Sarah tells me that her first prayer these days is one of gratitude for being alive. She then adds her thanks for family and friends.

Now, after being away from her ex-husband for many years, Sarah continues to work through her healing process. Therapy, meditation, massage, and prayer are among her resources. She now prays most often "straight to God." When asked what she looks at while praying, she mentions her wooden angel, carved by a friend of her sister, and the picture

77. Ibid.
78. Interview #29.
79. Ibid.

of Saint Michael, the archangel. "Everything I went through with my ex-husband . . . I don't think I could have done it if I didn't know that the angels were watching me and guiding me through, giving me strength. The guardian angels carried me . . . ."[80] Like the carved angel, the Native American dream-catcher is also a hand-made gift. Sarah keeps this gift hanging above her bed. The idea of it, she explains, is that it catches any bad dreams before you have them, and allows only good dreams to pass through onto the sleeper. This item holds special value for Sarah because her brother gave it to her.

Judith Herman, in her critical book on trauma and recovery, states that the two most important aspects of the recovery process for survivors of trauma are experiences of connection and empowerment.[81] Sarah's devotional habits of looking at the angels and saints, and experiencing their watchful presence in return, seem to me to contribute to her sense of being connected to God and other spiritual beings. In addition, the objects fortify her sense of social connection to the people who made them for her. Herman indicates that survivors of trauma can use pictures or objects to "enhance their sense of secure attachment through the use of evocative memory."[82] Perhaps this is one of the functions of these religious objects for Sarah. On the social level, Sarah's large and close-knit family as well as her friends and her therapist each provide some of the connection she needs as she works her way through this extended healing process.

Sarah's use of visual images may also facilitate a sense of empowerment. The placement of her diverse religious artifacts in her bedroom and above her bed suggests that they function as transitional objects, there for her when no one else is, helping her gain a sense of herself in a world that she is not completely able to control. Sarah demonstrates a creative use of religious artifacts in her strategy for recovering from post-traumatic stress. With these items, Sarah has been actively assembling a visually supportive environment.

It is interesting that Sarah, who now rarely attends church, freely mixes traditional Catholic pictures and symbols with diverse practices and objects. It may be that the habit of relying on visual representations of the holy, which Sarah observed and absorbed from her childhood and espe-

---

80. Ibid.
81. Herman, *Trauma and Recovery*, 133–54.
82. Herman, 150.

cially from her mother, is reflected in Sarah's entire repertoire of personal and spiritual resources for healing. Not only is her fondness for certain images preserved, but so is her very capacity to use tangible and visible objects in service of her healing and spiritual growth.

Sarah is reconstructing her identity, not by returning to Mary Star, but by drawing on social support, therapeutic resources, and visual piety, in which she finds herself affirmed, "carried" by angels, valued, and valuing. Like Josephine, Sarah uses her images to help her transform her own experience of physical suffering, turning a brush with death into a new appreciation for being alive. Visual piety mediates her sense of compassion for others even as she experiences herself as compassionately held in the presence of these artifacts.

Sarah's creative mixing of religious and spiritual traditions is significant, because such mixing has the capacity to dramatically change religious meanings and practices. She is improvising on a theme of devotion that she learned at home, adopting a creative use of visual skill and a range of symbols that goes well beyond the parameters of traditional Catholicism, even as it maintains ties to the Catholic images and figures that Sarah finds valuable and healing. This kind of selectivity and innovation is not uncommon among the folks I spoke with in the later immigrant generations, who tend to be younger and perhaps more clearly shaped by post modernity. The next story offers a different example of both thoughtful visual practice and conspicuous religious mixing. [83]

Matthew

Matthew is a young man from the fourth immigrant generation. At age twenty-four, he is extremely intense and thoughtful about his faith. This is immediately evident from looking around the living room of the apartment he rents in a windy section of San Pedro, down near the beach. On one side of the room is a bookshelf containing a considerable theological library. On the other side is an elaborate altar, built upon and around an antique table (Figure 27 and Figure 28). The altar features numerous sculpted Buddhas that Matthew has collected from Tibet, China, and Los Angeles. A statue of Saint Francis rests among the Buddhas, as do two

---

83. Catherine Albanese demonstrates that religion in America has always involved the mixing of various faith traditions and practices, including Native American influences. Albanese, "Exchanging Selves," 223.

candles, on either side of the table. A centrally located crucifix, with a cross made out of palm behind it, is mounted on the wall above the table. This crucifix once rested on the casket of Matthew's beloved uncle, who committed suicide some years ago. Above the crucifix hangs a prominent picture of Thomas Merton and the Dalai Lama, two of Matthew's most significant sources of inspiration. He says of them, "These are the two people who represent to me the core or pillars of the faiths that I gravitate to the strongest: Catholicism and Buddhism. Their teachings and their lives and their thoughts have shaped my understanding of who I am."[84] Notably absent from this shrine are any representations of Mary.

Matthew grew up attending Mary Star, where he was an altar boy for five years. He counted collection money in the church for many years as well. Matthew says that he loved being around the church, loved hanging out in the choir loft when his grandmother sang in the choir. It was when he took a world religions course in his Catholic high school, and read his first book by the Dalai Lama, that Matthew became interested in Buddhism and "was hooked" ever since. Matthew describes this as a scary time: "Finding things and doctrines that were not only different but contradictory to what I was taught...realizing that faith is not an easy thing, that it can't be swallowed blindly. It has to be sought after in order for it to really be faith."[85]

When asked whether he prays to any saints, Matthew says quickly, "I pray for the inspiration of what the saints represented. I pray for the drive and the charisma of Saint Francis. I pray for the totality of Ignatius . . . and I pray for the quiet of mind of Teresa of Avila, for the intense mystic spirituality of John of the Cross. . . . I don't pray to the Saints per se, but everything they represent is so real in and of itself, that I think it's almost the same thing." Matthew's religious practices do not seem to me to be "the same thing" as the more traditional practices of the devout. His faith is more searching, and he is more inclined toward theological and philosophical debate. He does not pray the rosary or make novenas. Furthermore, he has embraced the practices of Buddhism at least as much as his practices of Catholicism.

Matthew does not think of the Saints as his patrons, but moves beyond venerating the saints themselves to imitating the personal quali-

84. Interview #30.
85. Ibid.

ties that the saints' legends recall: inspiration, drive, charisma, totality of mind, and intense spirituality.[86] Somewhat like Susan, Matthew is using the stories of the saints as models or exemplars of the faith that he himself would like to emulate. He is consciously molding his own character, using the available historical memories and legends of the saints to aid him.

While Matthew is not a literalist, his faith is strong, and for this he credits his Catholic upbringing. He elaborates, "I owe my current religious practices to Catholicism. My prayer has taken on a different form, which is contemplative prayer and centering, emptying the mind of discursive thought. Saint John of the Cross and Teresa of Avila taught this meditation. To be schooled in different ways of prayer is highly valuable."[87] Matthew told me that he meditates almost every day—four to five times a week, though he would like to do more.

When interviewing Matthew, I remembered from my conversation with his grandmother that she, too, had been reading Thomas Merton. I asked Matthew if he had given his grandmother the book. To my surprise, Matthew said no, she had given him his first Thomas Merton book. He then went on to credit this (paternal) grandmother and his deceased grandfather with much of his inspiration. He said,

> The attitude of camaraderie has always been with my family. It's related to the Italianness of it. Kind of like the passion for life, and the ability to really enjoy life. You've met my grandmother, she's not a wallflower, she's a player in the game. She's been a big part of my life. . . . My grandfather, too, he was a huge role model to me. I wanted to be just like him. A person of incredible character, charisma, and strength, I'd like to think that I'm like him or at least in the process of becoming like him.[88]

In my brief meeting with Matthew, I gain the impression that he is well on his way to achieving these qualities; he impresses me as outgoing, ar-

---

86. Winnicott speaks of the subject's need to destroy primary objects, to attack them in order to move beyond them. *Playing and Reality*, 94. This is considered a sign of health and growth. Matthew's evolving views of the saints can be viewed in this light. Ann Ulanov suggests that the destruction of God-images is part and parcel of a faithful life. She writes, "Like a windshield wiper, imagination constantly functions to push away the preconceptions and subjective God-images we have so ceaselessly created, so that we can see afresh the God who is about to arrive." Ulanov, *Finding Space*, 123.

87. Interview #30.

88. Ibid.

ticulate, and joyful. He seems to approach many areas of his life with the same energy and passion he brings to his practice of religion. His way of speaking conveys strength and clarity, and yet exquisite sensitivity. For example, when I asked him if his prayers are answered, Matthew responded, "My prayers are answered every time a bird sings or a flower blooms. That's just what I thank God for, the beauty of creation, without any ulterior motive."[89] Matthew's demeanor is intense and genuine, moving.

Though Matthew's religious ideas and practices are more diverse than those of his grandmother or his father, the use of religious images and objects is a common practice across the four generations in his family. As in Sarah's case, Matthew's religious practice does not seem to have much to do with imagined or real Italian homelands. However, he does have a strong sense about his ethnic and religious identity: "Being an Italian Catholic—those terms are synonymous to me. . . . It's a big part of who I am. The root of me—inescapable, and I wouldn't want to escape it." Matthew's strong sense of Italian identity, which he describes as "FBI—full-blooded Italian," is melded to his sense of himself as Catholic. His choice of the word "inescapable" might suggest ambivalence. The weight of his parents', grandparents', and great-grandparents' stories provides him with a strong sense of rootedness, something that he loves and depends on and may also at times find confining. He describes some traditional Catholic doctrines as making him feel as if he were "in a box." Perhaps Matthew's Buddhist orientation, which he has innovatively incorporated into his home shrine, helps him move beyond the box. His regular association with Buddhist monks in Los Angeles also brings him into religious connection with non-Italians, moving him beyond the box socially and geographically—out of San Pedro. Matthew's visual piety, rooted in his childhood experiences at Mary Star, is one habit from his "inherited" repertoire of Italian Catholic devotional practices that he has not escaped, but which he is transforming into something new.

Though Matthew's forms of prayer and theological constructions have expanded, his level of participation in the Catholic church is no less frequent or profound. In fact, because his faith seems so vibrant, I ask Matthew if he has ever considered entering the seminary. He responds that, yes, he has, "as recently as three days ago," though he indicates that

---

89. Ibid.

he is not optimistic about the priesthood. "If I feel like I'm in a box now, how would I feel then?" he asks rhetorically.

Like others discussed in this chapter, Matthew's religious practices link him to the memory of deceased family members, particularly his grandfather whom he admired and an uncle. Matthew's beloved uncle and godfather, whom he was said to resemble physically, suffered from severe depression, and committed suicide at age twenty-three. Perhaps Matthew's religious and familial bonds of devotion were somehow intensified when the shared family memory expanded to encompass this tragedy.

When asked how he deals with adversity, Matthew said, "Pretty good. And a lot of that has to do with my faith." He recalled one point in his life, when his grandfather died, his parents got divorced, and he broke up with his girlfriend of two years, all in three weeks' time. He said, "I have a very sensitive heart, and that was the time in my life when that heart was aching. But everybody's got their own story. Everybody's been through stuff like that and far, far, worse than that."[90] Perhaps. Matthew did not mention that during the time these three significant events were unfolding, his father was also undergoing treatment for a life-threatening infection. Additionally, Matthew noted that his mother has suffered from a chronic condition for many years. Matthew's personal and family history and his "sensitive heart" may be held in a particularly important way through his meditation practice and through the religious objects that comprise his home shrine.

Many of these objects were gifts, such as the Saint Francis statue given to him by a priest in high school and the scroll with a scripture passage inscribed on it in calligraphy, given to him by a nun at a school retreat (Figure 29). As Matthew gazes at this altar, these items may recall the givers of these gifts, as well as the religious meanings assigned to them. Seeing these religious gifts from his tender high school years, just before the series of losses he described, may help Matthew redress the traumatic aspects of those times, by helping him re-experience the feeling of being seen, remembered, and/or held in community. Notably, the scripture verse on the scroll reads: "See, I will not forget you. I have carved you on the palm of my hand" (Isa 49:15). This is a striking passage, suggesting divine bonds of memory that are visual, and inscribed—literally—on God's body. Matthew's complex altar is also a mirror or reflection of himself, his

90. Interview #30.

life, and the intense faith that makes him who he is. It is a faith that, in his words, "is not an easy thing."[91]

Of course, religious images function in diverse ways at different moments in people's lives. There is no one fixed meaning or use for religious images or objects. There are instead what Leigh Schmidt might call "charged moments of encounter, exchange, practice, and relationship."[92] The near omnipresence of visual representations of Mary, Jesus, saints, and angels, along with their close connections to natal lands and family members, helps to account for much of the intensity and persistence of devotional practices. The image of Mary as a holy mother, an idealized woman of serene power (and perhaps as a vigilant observer), leaves diverse individuals with varying emotional experiences, ranging from comfort and strength to indifference to resentment. Nevertheless, the visual form of the devotions roots them in a bodily knowledge—a kind of knowledge that is hard to forget. The materiality of these images may indeed help foster the sense of God's immanence in mundane reality, along with the capacity to be alone.

The Capacity to Be Alone

The capacity to be alone—or to sit quietly in our rooms, as Pascal put it—has long been considered essential for self-knowledge.[93] The visual devotions that we have been exploring take place in public or private spaces, sometimes involve groups of people together but often involve the experience of being alone. In church or at home, the devout's sense of aloneness is mitigated by the perceived spiritual presence of God, Mary, angels, or saints. At home alone in front of a bedside shrine, a devout may feel accompanied even as she is, literally, sitting quietly in her room.

In 1958, Donald Winnicott wrote an important essay on "The Capacity to Be Alone," in which he described the way in which infants develop this capacity.[94] When an infant is left to him or her self in the presence of the mother, the child may become absorbed in play, manipu-

91. Ibid.

92. Schmidt, "Practices of Exchange," 72.

93. Margaret Miles, *Practicing Christianity*, 2.

94. He wrote, "The basis of the capacity to be alone is the experience of being alone in the presence of someone. . . . Gradually, the ego-supportive environment is introjected and built onto the individual's personality, so that there comes about a capacity actually to be alone." Winnicott, *Maturational Processes*, 36.

lating manageable bits of the external world, while feeling secure in the knowledge that the caregiver is close at hand, there if needed. Winnicott noted that this experience is critical to normal social and emotional growth; it must occur frequently in order for the child to gradually attain the mature capacity to feel secure in one's own company. The important dynamic needed here is that the child's caregiver be present, but not constantly interacting, so that the child can "float" in and out of the awareness of the caregiver's presence.[95]

Adults also need some way to re-establish the sense of a dependable external environment. "Houses" of worship can provide the space for this experience of being alone in the presence of someone. Consider how many Americans attended worship services on September 14 through 16, 2001, after 9/11 shook our trust in a national sense of safety. Many diverse religious practices function in such a way as to provide the psychological experience of being alone in the presence of someone. We gather together perhaps in order to find the courage to sit quietly with ourselves. In Buddhist temples, where people meditate side-by-side, they may experience the feeling of being alone in the presence of each other. In mainline Christian worship services, to take another example, during periods of silent prayer or during a boring sermon, worshippers sometimes find themselves "lost in thought." This free-floating experience, supported emotionally by the presence of other worshippers and sometimes by the presence of a symbolic caregiver such as a member of the clergy, provides a bit of this vital experience of being alone in the presence of someone.

But then, we must ask, does visual piety mainly offer security, familiarity, and comfort? Or do these religious practices actually help foster solitude and thus enhance the capacity to know oneself? The answer to this will vary from person to person, just as one person may attain greater maturity and wisdom from the practice of meditation, while another may merely feel distracted or stuck. All four of the individuals described here give examples of how they have used their visual practices to transcend

95. According to Winnicott, the non-intrusive presence of the mother or mother figure allows a child to begin safely to experience herself as a separate being. This happens because a sense of the mother is introjected, brought into the child's psychic structure, becoming part of his or her personality. When this happens enough times, the actual mother can leave the room, without the child feeling bereft or overwhelmed by fear. This is because the child is still experiencing something of the maternal presence. The child gradually begins to feel safe and calm when left alone and develops trust in the dependability of the external world. This is also called the ego-supportive environment.

difficult or painful personal circumstances; they also express concerns for other people who suffer. At least three of these persons are actively engaged in care-based ministries. We cannot claim that visual representations of religious figures necessarily lead people to live "an examined life." But we can see that in many of the stories described in this chapter, the devout employ their religious images in creative quests to transcend suffering, to hone personal character, and to come to terms with life in the world.

Icons and Incarnation

Christians have debated the theological validity of religious images at least since the Iconoclastic Controversy of the eighth and ninth centuries. Theodore the Studite, a monk and an abbot (later canonized), vigorously refuted the iconoclasts of his age, defending the veneration of images of Christ. For Theodore, the key issue at stake in these debates was the doctrine of the incarnation of Christ. If Christ truly was, "born in the likeness of men and being found in human form" then, Theodore reasoned, Christ could be "circumscribed," portrayed in his bodily form.[96] For Theodore, these portrayals were not graven images that limited God, because they portrayed Christ's human image. He argued,

> But Christ incarnate is revealed within these limitations. For he who was uncontainable was contained in the Virgin's womb; He who is measureless became three cubits tall; He who has no quality was formed in a certain quality; He who has no position stood, sat, and lay down . . . [97]

For Theodore, it was tantamount to heresy to deny the particularity of Christ's earthly life. Picturing Christ's human image was a way of embracing the doctrine of the incarnation.

Through the centuries, Christians have continued to wonder about images, however. The issue came alive especially during the Reformation, when Protestants called for simplifying visual worship environments in favor of an emphasis on the aural sensation of hearing the word of God read and expounded through preaching.[98] Knowing God, for some, is still thought to be mostly a matter of words—hearing, listening, and thinking,

---

96. Phil 2:21–22; *On the Holy Icons*, 98.

97. Theodore the Studite, *On the Holy Icons*, 82.

98. Kapikian, *Art in Service of the Sacred*, 9.

rather than a sentient experience. Of course, the senses also play a role in these experiences. Also, music is a central element in many Christian worship services. Furthermore, Protestants also get attached to their visual environments, and associate their sanctuaries with the sacred. Anyone who has ever tried to alter a worship space will quickly realize this; people can form attachments to bare walls that are every bit as intense as others' attachments to religious images. William James' reflections on the role of aesthetic sensibilities in religious experience come to mind.[99] The almost visceral theological objections to Catholic uses of religious images that some Protestants experience are probably related to aesthetic sensibilities as much as they are to theological issues.

The visual devotion of the folks I interviewed in San Pedro persists for all kinds of reasons, including tradition, *habitus*, and aesthetic sensibilities. Theologically, though, the practice is related to the doctrine of the incarnation, the word made flesh. It is interesting to note that for Catholics, the crucifix, rather than the bare cross, is used to recall the image of Jesus. This is an example of the particular, human image that Theodore was concerned with. Visual piety involves the act of looking with limited human eyes at religious pictures or statues made by feeble human hands. It is an embodied form of devotion that requires a sentient action. This practice also reinforces sentience in a particular way in that the artwork often depicts actual bodies and faces. We could say that the practice emphasizes the flesh of both the devout and the object of devotion. Theologically, this emphasis is critical. Awareness of the incarnate "God with us" here, close at hand, in the messy reality of earthly life, helps remind us of our humanity, and our ties and obligations to one another.[100]

The devotions at Mary Star of the Sea are visually and viscerally related to one of the community's most significant shared historical experiences: the local fishing industry. Fishing was the underlying "pull" factor for many diverse immigrants to San Pedro. In the next chapter, we will turn to the subject of fishing, to see how this history is entwined with the ongoing practice of living devotions.

99. James, *Varieties of Religious Experience*, 459–61.
100. Cooey, *Religious Imagination and the Body*, 16–18.

3

Fishing, Fear, and Faith

A windstorm arose on the sea, so great that the boat was being swamped by the waves; but he was asleep. And they went and woke him up, saying, "Lord, save us! We are perishing!" And he said to them, "Why are you afraid, you of little faith?"

Matt 8:24–26a

Anyone who has been through a severe storm at sea has, to one degree or another, almost died, and that fact will continue to alter them long after the wind has stopped blowing and the waves have died down. Like a war or a great fire, the effects of a storm go rippling outward through webs of people for years, even generations.

—Sebastian Junger, *The Perfect Storm*

SEBASTIAN Junger's words summarize the impact of a major Atlantic storm on the people of Gloucester, Massachusetts, a New England fishing village. Junger's vivid reporting of the story of one lost fishing vessel, the *Andrea Gail*, suggests the layers of grief and lasting change that such a tragedy can impose upon "webs of people for years, even generations." San Pedro, like Gloucester, has seen its share of tragic fishing accidents at sea. In the last hundred years, the commercial fishing of tuna as well as white sea bass, mackerel, squid, and sardines employed thousands of diverse immigrants and proved lucrative for business and cannery owners. But fishing here has been a difficult and dangerous enterprise, too, and numerous lives have been lost in these waters. Many folks in San Pedro were reluctant to tell me this part of the story. They were happy to tell me about the beauty of living near the sea, its wonder and inspiration. Many informants also gladly told me what they could remember about the rise and fall of the fishing industry in this place, the wealth and abundance that fishing and canning once brought to the region, and the inter-connections between Mary Star of the Sea parish and the fishing industry. But the stories of the storms, accidents, and hardships related to fishing seemed almost too difficult to tell. These tragedies at sea have altered the people, their families, friends, and faith.

The economic uncertainty of fishing as an occupation added another layer of intensity to the family stories I heard. The great wealth and happiness of good times when the nets were full and the prices high contrast with the stark poverty and desperation of hard times when fish stocks and/or prices dwindled. This occupation, with its financial and emotional highs and lows, has exerted considerable emotional strain, not only on fishermen themselves, but also on their families. The intermittent and unpredictable nature of these variations added a sense of urgency and desperation to the fishing enterprise that drew diverse immigrants throughout the twentieth century. Since the late 1980s, the marked decline and arguable end of the fishing industry in San Pedro have added stress, fear, and loss—both financial and cultural—to the lives of families who have depended on occupations related to fishing.[1] Local devotions reflect, celebrate, enact, and memorialize this history.

This story of Italian and Sicilian Catholics in San Pedro and their historical memories of fishing and faith illustrates the important role of economics in both immigration and religious practice.[2] The classic functions of pastoral theology and care—healing, sustaining, guiding, and reconciling[3]—do not adequately address issues of power, money, or marginality in churches and in communities. This case study suggests a compelling need for pastoral theologies and practices that engage the whole intricate web of spiritual, emotional, social, economic, and political life.[4]

1. Sahagun, "Commercial Fishing," B1, B11; Fulmer, "End of the Line," C1, C6.

2. This chapter tells the story of Italian and Sicilian fishermen, their families, and their descendants. I am not suggesting, nor do I wish to imply, that Italians were the sole or major influence in the fishing industry in San Pedro or in the development of Mary Star of the Sea. Of the many diverse groups of immigrant fishermen, the Croatians had the largest number of boats.

3. For discussions of the classic functions of pastoral care, see Hiltner, *Preface to Pastoral Theology*; and Clebsch and Jaekle, *Pastoral Care in Historical Perspective*.

4. Miller-McLemore, "The Living Human Web," 14. For pastoral-theological work at the intersection of economics and theology, see for example, Couture, *Blessed are the Poor?* and Poling, *Render Unto God*.

It has been the genius of the pastors of Mary Star of the Sea parish over the years to allow and encourage the donation of artifacts, the establishment of numerous ethnic organizations such as sodalities, confraternities, and choirs, as well as a proliferation of feasts and rituals that address the exigencies of the fishing life. These practices have encouraged loyalty to the church by establishing strong bonds between Mary Star, immigrants with their distinct national origins and patron saints, and the fishing occupation. The devotional societies have functioned as pastoral resources to help immigrant fishermen and their families address the spiritual, emotional, and practical crises related to the dislocation of immigration as well as the difficulties of fishing. This pastoral strategy has also helped bring diverse immigrants and their descendants together within one parish, gradually mitigating intense ethnic tensions between groups. This ministry to and with diverse immigrant groups has been no small task for the congregation and its leaders. Almost from the church's founding in 1896, multiple immigrant groups populated the pews, speaking different languages, praying to different saints, all while vigorously competing with each other for their livelihoods on the precarious waters of the Pacific Ocean.

Fishing and Mary Star of the Sea

Perhaps the best place to begin this part of the story is in the sanctuary of the Mary Star of the Sea Church. Both the abundance of the Pacific Ocean and the loss of life therein are memorialized in its art and artifacts. The large centrally placed marble statue of Mary standing in a wave while holding a tuna clipper is an impressive testament to the historical connections between fishing and faith in this community. Her right arm is extended upward, in a gesture that suggests halting the dangers of the sea. Mary holds the purse seiner in her left arm as she might hold the Christ child, symbolically protecting it and sacralizing it at the same time (Figure 2). No worshipper could miss this imposing image, with its gold-trimmed marble pillars that frame the central altar from which daily Mass is offered.

According to some of my informants, tuna money paid for this sculpture. I am told that there was initially some resistance on the part of Mary Star's clergy to the idea of having such a large and prominent statue of Mary, rather than a crucifix, in the center of the chancel. Supposedly, the will of the cannery owner won out, when he threatened to withhold significant contributions.[5] This story reminds us of the power of financial contributors to influence the form and style and symbolism of sacred space.[6] A connection between the particular layout of a sanctuary and the will of donors is not surprising; it is a mundane feature of the history of religion in America. Still, this statue and its placement demonstrate, in an unusually overt way, both the power of a donor to shape sacred space and the prominence of fishing in the history and identity of the parish.

At Mary Star of the Sea, the two largest stained glass windows on either side of the sanctuary also tell the story of the link between fishing and faith. The window on the right, depicting Jesus stilling the Galilean storm (Figure 4) bespeaks the danger of life at sea, as well as the people's hope that God's power will save them or their loved ones from peril; the window on the left side, illustrating the gospel story of the abundant catch (Figure 3), captures the people's hope for a good livelihood. This hope has motivated many immigrant fishermen, cannery workers, net-menders, boat builders and owners, seafood merchants, restaurateurs, and fish processing plant owners alike.

While some have derived great wealth from these industries, many workers have just managed to make a living, enduring strenuous physical labor and times of severe economic hardship. Their livelihoods have hung in the balance over the years as they have dealt with continually changing weather conditions, fish stocks, habitats, prices, and national and international fishing regulations. The size and placement of these windows reflect the reality of the community's economic reliance on the sea, and suggest divine sanction of their way of life, by associating it with Jesus. These stained glass windows, created and installed in the church during boom times, also signify the optimism of the church and the fishing industry at mid-century.

Prosperity and the Pastorate of George M. Scott

The height of prosperity that the fishing and canning industries in San Pedro enjoyed coincided with the tenure of the church's longest-serving pastor, the Very Reverend Monsignor George M. Scott, 1946–1975. When Scott arrived at Mary Star, World War II had boosted San Pedro's popula-

5. I have not been able to document the details of this story.

6. For reflections on the commodification of sacred space, see Chidester and Linenthal, *American Sacred Space*, 12.

tion to approximately sixty thousand. At that point, San Pedro was the largest commercial fishing port in the United States. In 1948, San Pedro's year-end catch was valued at $30,000,000. Nearby Terminal Island was the home of several profitable canneries, including Star-Kist, Van de Camp's, Pan Pacific Fisheries, and South Pacific Canning Company. According to Joe Canetti, owner of Canetti's Seafood Grotto since 1949, the smell of fish cooking at the canneries was as familiar as it was welcomed. People called it "the aroma of money" because the smell was a sure indication that the fishing boats had returned full. Canetti explained that when the boats were really laden down, the fish at the bottom of the haul would be crushed—"mashed and mushed."[7] This part of the catch could not be sold for consumption, so instead it was cooked up and sold as fertilizer. The cooking process gave off the welcomed aroma. During this time, wholesale and retail fish markets and boat works also thrived. Along with the busy oil and lumber port, and the sizable military installation at Fort MacArthur, the seafood industries constituted one of the three pillars of San Pedro's growing economy.[8]

Members of Mary Star of the Sea parish were among the beneficiaries of the strong fishing economy. A 1949 article in *The Tidings*, a local Catholic weekly, stressed the connection between Mary Star of the Sea, the "Harbor Parish," and the fishing industry. The article noted parishioners' involvement in the various industries related to fishing, citing prominent names such as Aniella Scalo, fisherman, Giosue Di Masa, a wholesale fish dealer, and John Jerkovich, "twice head of the Holy Name Society, who markets seafood throughout the Los Angeles area." Thousands of church members were employed in the Terminal Island canneries.[9]

The early, strong connection between Mary Star and the fishing industry can also be seen in the clergy's long record of involvement with fishermen. Father Luigi Pecorella, an Italian priest appointed as an assistant pastor in 1918, served as a federal mediator in San Diego in a dispute

---

7. Informational interview # 02.

8. Informational interview # 01. A list of 1950 businesses compiled by Charles Queenan includes: "Shipping lines, commercial trucking companies, transcontinental railroads, petroleum and lumber companies, ship and boatbuilding and repair firms, canneries, stevedore companies, ship chandlery and marine supply firms, marine surveyors, pleasure craft berthing, customs brokers and others." Zangs, "Terminal Island History," 25.

9. Vita, et al., "Sixty Years," 51.

between striking Italian fishermen and sardine packers.[10] Later, many pastors became chaplains to fishermen and other seamen through the "Apostleship of the Sea," an organization that Father James McLaughlin (pastor from 1934–46) helped found. McLaughlin is also reported to have entered the fray of the "notorious longshoremen's strike of 1938,"[11] providing housing and food and securing a priest to preach a mission among the longshoremen.

When Monsignor George Scott came to the harbor area in 1946, the Mary Star parish was still housed in the 450-seat wood-frame structure built in 1905. But the church was already outgrowing its space. In a commemorative booklet that the church put together for California's Centennial in 1949, there is a photograph of the outside of this sanctuary with numerous people standing nearby. The caption reads, "Any Sunday: People Wait in Line to Enter Church for One of Ten Masses." Taking advantage of both the crowds of people and their post-war prosperity, Scott soon began a million-dollar building campaign that funded a new convent and established the church's first high school. The project expanded to include the building of the church's current sanctuary at 870 West Eighth Street.

Scott had arrived at an opportune moment. His predecessor, Father James McLaughlin, had already nurtured church growth during the population expansion of the war years. He had also cleared up an inherited debt of $100,000.[12] When Scott arrived, he built upon this legacy. By this time, several parishioners who were immigrants from Croatia and Italy had achieved financial success through the fishing industry. Notable were Joseph Bogdanovich and his son Martin, whose company, Star-Kist, had become the largest fish-canning company in the world.[13] When people tell me that fishing built the church, part of what they are indicating is that donations from such successful individuals funded the building projects. At the same time, many smaller, but crucial, donations from devout fishing families complemented this munificence. The immigrants' faith in the

10. Ibid., 53.

11. Ibid., 26. The year of the strike to which the author was referring was probably 1934 rather than 1938. For a description of the major longshoremen's strike of 1934 that stretched from Bellingham, Wash. to San Diego, see Markholt, *Maritime Solidarity*, 76–103.

12. Bobich and Palmer, *Mary Star Centennial*, 13–14.

13. Bartlett, "Islands of San Pedro Bay," 34.

Madonna, brought with them from homeland fishing villages, now found local specificity and concrete expression in their growing allegiance to San Pedro's own Mary Star of the Sea. Their financial contributions to the church helped build a sanctuary and a church staff that could house and handle the diversity of cultures that the immigrants represented.

Ethnicity and Americanization at Mary Star

In a 1975 interview, Monsignor George Scott claimed that when he was sent to Mary Star, San Pedro was "the most unwanted parish in four counties. The 'foreign element' was not understood. No one wanted to tackle the ethnic mixture."[14] But Scott, whose father was a well-known judge in Los Angeles, and whose mother had taught him to speak Spanish and French as well as English, relished the challenge. During the course of his tenure at Mary Star, seven priests, several of whom were also multilingual, assisted him. They reportedly heard confessions in Croatian, Italian, Spanish, French, German, Portuguese, and English. Articles about the church often boasted that the church membership represented fifty-one of the fifty-two nationalities listed by the US Census Bureau.[15] Scott's vision was to create more unity, to calm the ethnic tensions, in the diverse parish. Early on, he stated his goal of making Mary Star of the Sea an American parish in both language and system.[16]

Scott had his work cut out for him, in part because his predecessors had taken a different tack. In the early decades of the century, San Pedro was a Mecca for fishermen from all over the world. The waters off the coast were rich with abalone and sea bass, as well as numerous smaller fish. These fish stocks, along with the temperate climate and relatively unrestricted access to fishing, attracted large numbers of immigrants from Japan, Scandinavia, Italy, Portugal, and Croatia. Mary Star's earlier pastors responded to the influx of diverse immigrants by encouraging the establishment of separate social and religious organizations within the parish. This allowed various groups to gather together, speak their own languages, and devote themselves to patron saints from their native lands. These organizations were frequently divided along the lines of gender as well as nationality. Some these early sodalities still in existence include: the

14. "Pastor Calls San Pedro 'God's Country—Special,'" *San Pedro News Pilot*, A1.

15. Vita, et al., "Sixty Years," 51.

16. Ibid., 27.

Altar Society, founded in 1889, to care for linens, vestments, and clean the sanctuary; Saint Anne's Society, founded in 1929, "for Italian Ladies" (but soon expanded to include those of Italian descent); and the Velike Gospel Society, for Slovenian women, established in 1932. These groups have served many of the functions that ethnic parishes accomplished in other parts of the country.[17] They have provided physical and cultural sacred spaces where immigrants and their descendants have been able to mingle together, recall and celebrate their national origins, and find relief from the stress of dislocation. These organizations have also addressed the material needs of immigrant fishermen and their families through charitable activities and the pooling of resources for mutual aid.

Scott's predecessor, Father James McLaughlin, had continued to encourage this pattern of ethnic organizations. During his tenure, from 1934–46, the number of parish organizations increased to twenty-seven. McLaughlin also arranged for missions to be preached each year in English, Italian, Slovenian, and Spanish, "for the various national elements of the parish then still quite divided."[18] Much of the ethnic division in the church was related to competition among the fishermen from various countries. The desperate competition between Italian and Slav fishermen is particularly well known. One informant tells me that there were times when fishermen from these groups would wake up early, ready to leave the shore in their boats, only to discover large holes in their nets, caused by acid that their competitors had applied to the nets during the night.[19] Older members of the church also recall the days when ethnic groups worshipped separately, at their own Masses, in their own pews, refusing to speak to each other. For pastors trying to retain these diverse and desperately competitive immigrants in one parish, there may have been little choice but to allow for separate Masses and devotions.

Monsignor Scott, the church's first American-born pastor, searched for ways to unify the parish. His approach was in keeping with the popular post-war rhetoric of the melting pot. He is quoted as saying that it occurred to him that there was one word that all the groups in the church understood—Fiesta.[20] Even as the town was busy organizing its first Fishermen's

17. Dolan, *American Catholic Experience*, 158–220.

18. Vita et al., "Sixty Years," 25.

19. Informational interview #04.

20. "Angel's Gate Salutes . . . ," Angel's Gate Council, No. 1740, Knights of Columbus, circa 1975.

Fiesta, Scott called for the church to establish an annual fund-raiser: Mary Star's own Annual Parish Barbecue and Fiesta. This church-wide celebration, in which each of the separate organizations established booths, sold ethnic foods, and organized games and contests, had the effect of bringing the various groups into closer proximity while still showcasing their ethnic distinctions as they worked side-by-side for the common goal of expanding church facilities and programs.

Scott's repertoire of strategies for establishing ethnic unity also included a more startling tactic. In the church's *Sixty Years Commemorative Booklet*, I discovered an undated photograph of a minstrel show. The text notes that Father Scott encouraged "the founding of a Parish Minstrel Group to produce and stage an authentic minstrel show each year." The booklet claims that both the parish Fiesta and the minstrel shows "were intended to weld the various national groups and their descendants together for the general benefit of the parish."[21]

When I drew attention to this photo in an early draft of this writing, one of my interviewees later remembered the event in which she herself performed as teenager. She wrote to tell me that the minstrel show was held at Mary Star only once, and this was in 1948. As teenagers, she and her sisters and best friends were in the show, which she remembers as amusing. She notes that the minstrel show was discontinued the next year because of "some community controversy."[22]

I found this event, and this characterization of it, rather shocking. Historically, minstrelsy was a disturbing phenomenon in America, involving the theatrical practice of non-blacks putting on blackface paint in order to entertain by making fun of African-Americans.[23] David Roediger and other historians of race and ethnicity in America, see the phenomenon of minstrelsy as a strategy that employed distorted images of African-Americans to function as the "other," over against whom diverse European immigrants could join together and identify themselves as primarily (white) Americans.[24]

21. Vita, et al., "Sixty Years," 27–28.

22. Interviewee #4, written communication, 2 October 2003.

23. For an historical summary of the phenomena of blackface and minstrelsy in America, see Roediger, *Wages of Whiteness*.

24. See Orsi, "Religious Boundaries," 313–47; and Barrett and Roediger, "Inbetween Peoples," 3–45.

In San Pedro during World War II, the sharpness of ethnic and racial distinctions became especially clear. During this war, an entire community of Japanese fishermen and their families—three thousand residents of nearby Terminal Island—were evacuated and sent to internment camps, such as Manzanar, in California's Owens Valley. Because the Japanese fishermen's homes were razed to make room for military operations, very few of these citizens ever returned to Terminal Island.[25] This enormous loss of a well-established community was one of the casualties of the war. The Japanese residents were not new immigrants. They were long established in this area, had been avid fishers and cannery workers on Terminal Island for years, preceding many European immigrants. Yet they were wiped out of their home when the war propaganda cast them as foreigners and enemies.

Even as George Scott attempted to unify ethnic groups at Mary Star in the years following the war, this painful example of what it meant to be considered less than fully American must have loomed over people in the Port of Los Angeles. The patriotism of many immigrants had been questioned during the war. By asserting the goals of unity and assimilation, Scott was also firming up the American status of both the Catholic Church and the particular members of Mary Star of the Sea parish.

The church-sponsored minstrel show, with the stated intention of bringing ethnic Catholics together, seems to participate in the strategy of immigrants "becoming white" in order to become fully American.[26] Because skin color does not "melt," it often became the difference over against which many immigrants and their descendants could gain stature

---

25. Zangs, "Terminal Island," 23. Among the earliest groups of fishermen was a colony of Japanese, who lived since 1903 in an enclave on what is now called Terminal Island. While the Japanese immigrants had little to do with Mary Star of the Sea, many credit them with teaching other immigrant fishermen how to fish in commercial quantities. Some claim that the Japanese had the best fishing techniques, which they soon taught to the Portuguese, Italian, and Slav immigrants. The Japanese are credited with the introduction of braille-net fishing and the use of hand-net fishing for albacore. Bartlett, "Islands of San Pedro," 36. Because of this reputation for fishing skills, early canning and packing companies such as South Coast Canning Company built apartment houses for the Japanese fishermen on the island. By the 1930s, the area on Terminal Island known as East San Pedro had become a thriving Japanese community. Zangs, "Terminal Island," 17. Also see Perkins, "Terminal Island Japanese;" and Kawasaki, "Japanese Community of East San Pedro."

26. For a broad description of the history of whiteness in America, see Jacobson, *Whiteness of a Different Color*. For a fascinating theological interpretation of the process of becoming white, see Thandeka, *Learning to Be White*.

as full U.S. citizens. In 1949, when Mary Star of the Sea celebrated its sixtieth anniversary, the church's historians wrote, "In scarcely two generations the melting pot of Catholicism and Americanism has done its beneficent work."[27] Looking back, we can question the beneficence of this work, not least because the inter-ethnic unity gradually being honed at Mary Star parish at this point in history left many racial divisions in place.

Even aside from the important question of who was left out or harmed by this "beneficent" work of the melting pot, the sixtieth anniversary claim was probably an optimistic assessment of the church's progress on ethnic harmony within its own ranks. Nonetheless, these were prosperous and upbeat times. The success of the growing church brought pride and a qualified sense of unity to the parish. Both the melting pot ethos and the mood of prosperity found expression in what was to become an extremely popular San Pedro tradition, the Fishermen's Fiesta.

The Fishermen's Fiesta

The Fishermen's Fiesta is the San Pedro institution that most clearly demonstrates the overlap between the heyday of the fishing industry and the glory days of Mary Star of the Sea parish. Established in 1946, the traditional celebration combined a secular civic event with a Catholic religious ritual. Many of the older persons I interviewed remembered the Fiesta fondly; some showed me pictures and spoke proudly of winning awards for their boats' decor. They expressed nostalgia for the days when the wharf was a safe place to go. As I listened to my interviewees affectionately describing these events, I had a sense that their devotion to God, their love of country (America), their fondness for their Italian heritage, and their love for Mary Star of the Sea church were blurring together in glorious nostalgic harmony.

The Port of Los Angeles Fishermen's Fiesta was initiated in 1946, as a victory celebration marking the end of the war. Numerous unions and local business associations joined to gather to stage the celebration. These included the Fishermen's Cooperative Association, the San Pedro Chamber of Commerce, the Federated Boat Owners Association, the Seine and Line Fishermen's Union, and the International Fishermen and Allied Workers

27. Vita et al., "Sixty Years," 33.

of America, Local 33. The colorful dockside festivities were repeated in 1947, and then halted for a year for the construction of new docks.[28]

Before the celebration resumed in September of 1949, Monsignor George Scott received an invitation from the Fishermen's Fiesta Committee asking him to arrange for the Archbishop of Los Angeles to come to the event and give his blessing to the entire fleet.[29] This invitation was striking in that it offered a visible and prominent role to the Catholic church's local leader, signifying perhaps that here, in San Pedro, the Catholic church had finally attained the fully American status that George Scott valued so highly. Thereafter, the Fisherman's Fiesta featured an annual Blessing of the Fleet. Photographs and news articles covering the Fiestas of this era show long street processions of Catholic clergy, altar boys, and the faithful carrying lighted liturgical candles down to the wharf, while crowds of people line the streets. Down at the wharf, movie stars, mayors, and Catholic Cardinals rubbed elbows as they piled on and off the boats. The Fiesta remained a civic celebration, sponsored by the San Pedro Chamber of Commerce from 1949–1957, with additional financial support from Los Angeles County and the LA Harbor department beginning in 1954. At the same time, this wildly popular event, which in 1951 rivaled the Rose Bowl parade in attendance, continued to feature the Catholic Church, giving it a special place through the Blessing of the Fleets. This is an indication of the success of the largely immigrant parish, winning a place in the "sacred space" of the patriotic public ritual, and thereby asserting its presence and influence in San Pedro.[30]

The influence of the church's largest two immigrant constituents—Slavs and Italians—was on display in these activities. Mary Star parishioners were active on the Fiesta Committees, and participated in the tradition with pride. The Fiesta grew to become a three-day event, featuring, among other things, a beauty contest for an annual Fiesta Queen. The prize for the winner was an authentic Hollywood audition for an acting part in a movie. There were also contests for decorating the boats with colorful flowers and flags, arranged to represent pictures with religious or popular themes. There were net-sewing contests, to see who could tie knots and mend nets the fastest. Many of my interviewees remembered

28. "History of the Fishermen's Fiesta," 9.

29. Vita et al., "Sixty Years," 29.

30. Chidester and Linenthal write, "In its material production and practical reproduction, sacred space anchors a worldview in the world." *American Sacred Space*, 12.

their family boats being decorated and entered, and some winning prizes. Monsignor Scott saw the fundraising potential, and encouraged the various organizations within the church to set up booths at the wharf. Ethnic food was plentiful at these booths, which featured a variety of seafood. Interviewees who were teenagers during the Fiesta days offer vague recollections of eating lasagna on the boats. *Cioppino*—an Italian bouillabaisse or fish soup—was also served up in abundance. One woman recalls setting up a booth to sell "Holy Mackerel"—fried mackerel—to visitors. The Fiestas celebrated the prosperity of the fishing industry in ways that were simultaneously Catholic, ethnic, and American, with a good bit of Hollywood-style celebrity and fanfare thrown in.

Thomas Tweed has written about the ways in which exiles and other dislocated groups engage in religious practices that help them establish a space and find a place in their new land.[31] The fishermen's fiesta is a prime example of a public ritual that expressed the immigrants' cultural identity while establishing a claim upon this particular place. Through activities laden with both American patriotism and Catholic symbols—such as the procession to the wharf—the immigrants did the difficult cultural work of relocating in America, laying claim to their new land, their livelihood, and their devotions. The Fisherman's Fiesta allowed them to practice their "translocative" faith, imaginatively recalling their homelands even as they firmly asserted their presence in the Southern California landscape.

While the Fisherman's Fiesta illustrates the boom times for San Pedro fishermen as well as Mary Star parish, there is a subtext of hardship and loss for many of the persons I interviewed about their early experiences of fishing. We can get a better sense of this if we focus on the workers—the fishermen who were crewmembers rather than boat owners; and the women and men who worked in the canneries. Crewmembers and cannery workers made modest though somewhat predictable wages during the heyday of fishing. They lived in inexpensive houses below Pacific Avenue,[32] within walking distance to the wharf and the ferries that transported cannery workers to Terminal Island. Some of them lived in homes right on the coast, on property that would later become quite valuable. But even during good times, fishing and canning were difficult and dangerous occupations.

31. Tweed, *Our Lady of the Exile*, 136.

32. Pacific Avenue is a main thoroughfare in San Pedro that runs perpendicular to the shoreline, five blocks inland.

The Fishing Life: Realities for Workers

While the smell of tuna cooking was an indication of prosperity, the smell of raw fish that cannery workers regularly absorbed and endured is reported to be especially foul. One informant cringed with the memory of this odor and told me, "You could smell it on buses, at banks, everywhere."[33] The advent of unions, from 1930–1950, also suggests that the working conditions and wages of cannery workers were less than ideal. A stanza from a poem written by a female fish packer who worked in a San Diego branch of the Van de Camp Company gives us an idea of what this occupation was like:

> It is cold in a cannery and wet,
> Salt wind blows through,
> And the feet freeze fast to the
> slimed and rotted floor,
> And the fingers grow stiff on the knife,
> numb, jointless, and sore,
> Cutting the heads and guts from the little sardines as they pour
> Out of the chutes that is always
> belching sardines, always more, always more.[34]

These harsh odors and cold and hazardous working conditions may be part of the reason that some Italian men preferred that their wives not work in the canneries. These jobs, however, were often filled by immigrant women, beginning with Japanese women before the war,[35] and eventually including Mexican, Croatian, and Italian women as well.

For reasons that are unclear, one of the elderly immigrants who shared her story with me neglected to tell me that she had worked in a cannery. Her daughter later informed me of this, noting that for close to ten years, her mother would get up and walk to Beacon Street, where she and the other women workers waited for the 4:00 a.m. ferry to Terminal Island. While it was considered dangerous for women to gather there in the dark, the ferry was the only available means of transportation at the time.[36] The cannery worker's daughter recalls the ubiquitous smell of fish: mackerel,

---

33. Informational interview #01.

34. Edith Summers Kelly, "The Head Cutters," 126, Used by permission.

35. The Japanese women were called "tuna nurses" because they wore crisp white hats to work.

36. The current Vincent Thomas Bridge had not yet been built.

anchovies, and "red devils"—a kind of scorpion used in soup.[37] Several other persons I interviewed told me of mothers or aunts who worked at the canneries intermittently from the 1930s through the 1950s. They did this routinely to supplement family income when their fishermen husbands were injured, or when their boats were being repaired, or when they were enduring a period of dwindling prices or elusive fish stocks. Some women found social support and connection in these jobs, as well as needed income.[38]

Canetti's Seafood Grotto

I learned a great deal about both canning and fishing through the kindness of "Papa Joe" Canetti, a local restaurateur. At Canetti's Seafood Grotto, a waterfront establishment that has served as a gathering ground for fishermen, gill-netters, longshoremen, international crews, fish-buyers, and yacht owners since 1949, stories of both hardship and glory can still be heard. One can also find evidence of these fish tales on the walls of the restaurant, which feature old photos of tuna seiners, overloaded sardine catches, and popular Fishermen's Fiestas. From the early 1950s, when over 300 vessels routinely went off to sea, to the present when fewer than twenty boats go out, Canetti's has been a haven for fishermen. In an interview for a 1998 article in *National Fisherman* magazine, Canetti recalls a time when a group of fishermen in their purse seiners unexpectedly found a school of giant bluefish tuna near Santa Rosa Island, a windfall of significant proportion. "There were guys comin' in here after making million-dollar sets, sets where crewmen earned fifteen thousand dollars apiece. When that happened, this place turned into a giant party. I've never served a happier bunch of fishermen."[39] Occasions like this were a rarity, but they illustrate the extreme height of abundance that fishermen could hope for on an expedition. Hopes for such good fortune were high, especially in the early days, before, as one fisherman put it, "things went bad."[40]

It is hard to date precisely the downturn of the fishing industry in San Pedro. The man who spoke of things going bad fished only from 1946 until 1952, before he switched to another occupation. The waning popu-

37. Interview #16.
38. Interview #24.
39. Kronman, "Breakfast at Canetti's," 26.
40. Interview #8.

larity of Fisherman's Fiestas, notable since 1967, is sometimes also pointed to as an indication of the end of the boom.[41] When I asked the locals what caused the downturn, I was usually told that the industry simply "fished out the bay." From as early as the 1950s, I am told, tuna could no longer be found close to the shore. Local fishermen were gradually forced to go out further into the ocean to fish, which meant staying away from home longer, usually a week or more. Similarly, sardines, which once attracted scores of Norwegian fishermen from the state of Washington every June, had disappeared.

Changing national and international laws over the years have brought restrictions on local fishing as well as unprecedented competition. Canetti cites as an example the restrictions on local sea bass, which now can be fished for only two or three months per year. In the meantime, tuna have been moving south and out into deeper waters, where the United States does not have complete jurisdiction, and where small boats must compete with large-scale international fishing vessels. Locals have also had to obtain additional licenses to fish in these waters, or risk being caught and fined, or worse. Newspaper clippings from the 1970s and early 1980s report on the "tuna wars" that erupted after the governments of Mexico, Ecuador, and Peru started seizing and fining unlicensed American fishing vessels found within two hundred miles of their coasts.[42] Fishermen from San Pedro who opted to take their chances and forgo purchasing the expensive licenses (such as $26,000 in Ecuador alone), would be arrested, fined heavily, and sometimes detained—thereby losing valuable fishing time. The United States government got involved in these disputes, but didn't succeed in stopping the seizures. Eventually the government set up a fund to help American fishermen who sustained heavy losses due to these seizures. But the fund started running out of money in 1980, leaving many fishermen and the industry to absorb their own losses. By this time, the downturn in American tuna fishing was indisputable. It is not surprising that in the last thirty years, the majority of the small fishing boats have been retired. These boats occupy a small strip of the harbor that one local referred to as "starvation row"[43] (see Figure 30).

41. Ibid.

42. "Ecuador Captures Eight Boats," A1; Lagies, "Two Sides of Seizures;" and Davies, "U.S. Runs out of Money," A1, B1.

43. Informational Interview #01.

The canneries gradually disappeared as well, with only two remaining in 2000, when I initiated this research.[44] Since then, both Heinz Pet Food Products and Chicken of the Sea International have closed their San Pedro plants. While the County of Los Angeles once had more than 18 canneries, providing an estimated 17,000 jobs, no operating canneries are left on Terminal Island today. Lower operating costs in low-wage areas, such as Samoa and Puerto Rico, have lured these businesses away.[45]

Pescatore Desparate

In 1988 the Corporation for Public Broadcasting filmed a segment of a nationwide documentary film series, entitled "Listening at the Luncheonette," at Canetti's Seafood Grotto. The segment was called "*Pescatore Desparate*," or "Despairing Fishermen." In the documentary, the narrator allows the "regulars" at Canetti's to speak casually to each other, with little interruption. The patrons in the restaurant openly describe the painful collapse of fishing in San Pedro. One of the principals volunteers, "You know what to call this film? Call it 'Despairing Fishermen,' 'cause there's no happiness here."[46]

In the documentary, one man laments the closing of the canneries, which he blames for the drop in prices. He speaks angrily to a market owner, also a regular: "Why aren't we getting a price? When the canneries were here, we never had any problems. We always had a price. But now we're working for you guys." "Go cry in church!" replies the market owner, in a sarcastic reference to the devotion of fishermen. The first man apparently ignores this sarcasm, and goes on with his lament. "I worked for thirty years in that cannery . . . a thousand women cleaning fish at a

44. In 1991 Mary Zangs wrote, "There were 17 canneries in the 1930's thru 1950's. That number dwindled down to seven canneries in 1972. In 1975, only Pan Pacific, Star-Kist, and Van Camp remained. Van Camp Seafood Company, which canned tuna under the brand names of Chicken of the Sea and White Star, had come under ownership of Ralston Purina. It moved to San Diego in 1976 and Pan Pacific took over its Terminal Island plant. By 1983, tuna canneries moved most production from Southern California to American Samoa and Puerto Rico. Star-Kist, now owned by H. J. Heinz, closed its Terminal Island tuna cannery in October 1984, though it still has a mackerel pet-food operation here. In 1987, the local Fisherman's Cooperative Association, which runs a fleet out of Fisherman's Slip, took over the Star-Kist plant #1, calling their endeavor United Food Processors, Inc." Zangs, "Terminal Island History," 29.

45. Sahagun, "Commercial Fishing," B1, B11; Fulmer, "End of the Line," C1, C6.

46. "*Pescatore Desparate*," in "Listening at the Luncheonette."

time. Look at all the economy going down the tubes. A thousand women all dressed up like nurses going into those canneries, singing at Christmas. . . . It's broken now."[47] A sense of depression dominates the film. Men worry that their grandchildren will have no work. They complain about laws that protect endangered species at the expense of fishermen: "Now when you bring in the fish, there's only two left, because there's eighty billion seals out there, and they bite the net. The seal goes along the net and takes the bellies off. You come in, and you've made a hundred dollars for a whole month's work." The talk turns to prices, and one man blames political corruption in Washington. Another argues that the United States prices were so much higher than the rest of the world that "we got to come down if they're coming up." Still another claims that some good things have come out of the loss of work. "We've got to learn to get back to community. One of the nice things about working less is you have more time. If you can make the transition back to just having enough, that is."[48] This attempt at meaning making is not picked up by others.

In spite of this dispirited conversation, there are some very joyful moments in the recorded hour. One comes when an international fisherman plays his guitar and improvises a song about fishing. Another comes when a woman speaks of her love for San Pedro, the sight of the ocean, and her feeling of belonging in this place. More smiles emerge when one of the well-known locals, with the help of his wife, describes one of his best nights of fishing. His wife begins the story: "It was on a Friday night after supper. John (her husband) calls at 6:00 o'clock. His usual helper couldn't come. I offer to go in his place. Once we're out there on the water, he was grumbling. He says, 'We're late. We're not going to get our spot," then, 'Okay, let's put the net in the water.'"

The man picks up the story from here:

> It was a beautiful evening. The ocean looked like glass . . . wonderful warm water. About ten o'clock we start pullin' and here come the sea bass! We got to relax. There was no breeze. It was wonderful, warm weather. The fish were glimmering in the moonlight; . . . one, two, three, four of 'em. Just in big bunches. You could just see them off in the water shimmering because of the moonlight.

47. "All dressed up like nurses" is a reference to the cannery women's white hats.
48. "*Pescatore Desparate*," in "Listening at the Luncheonette."

That night we had over one hundred sea bass. It was one of my best nights ever.[49]

As the couple tells this story, they are glowing. I gain the impression that even an occasional night of fishing marked by this kind of exquisite beauty and good fortune could keep them going for some time. Perhaps it is the hope for this kind of beauty and bounty that has motivated many fishermen to endure the numerous hardships that their occupation entails.

Separation from Families

Along with the strain of economic loss, fishermen in San Pedro have had to endure frequent separations from their families. As fishing in the San Pedro Bay itself declined, the length of fishing expeditions increased, compounding the dangers men faced at sea as well as their isolation from their families. These separations from family and friends have been marked by both hopes and fears. One woman I interviewed, whose brothers-in-law were fishermen, remembers the worry in her sisters' faces when their husbands were gone. She points out that not all fishermen owned boats, and not all were prosperous. Sometimes the men would go out for a week and come back with nothing.[50] The uncertainty of income, as well as the uncertainty about the safety of the men, had an impact on them.

During these separations, many mothers functioned as single parents, running their households and raising their children alone. One woman told me that her husband was away when she had her baby.[51] These frequent separations led to closer reliance among extended family members as well as neighbors and friends. As one woman put it, "Hillary [Clinton] talks about 'the village.' Well, we had a village a long time ago. We needed a village! We took care of each other's children. If a child was hurt, my mother would carry him inside or bring him to the doctor if need be. We helped each other in those days."[52] Sometimes relatives moved in to live together during these extended periods.

When mothers were also working outside the home, live-in grandparents played a larger role in raising children. Two third-generation sisters explained that their grandmother, in essence, raised them. They credit her

49. Ibid.
50. Interview #16.
51. Interview #17.
52. Interview #24.

with teaching them to speak Italian, as well as passing on her devotions to the saints. "She kept us in line," one granddaughter claimed. She described her grandmother as a very strong woman, who taught them how to be strong, how to pray, and to trust that everything would eventually be okay.[53] When I asked one of these daughters whether she worried as a child, when her father was away, she replied, "My grandmother wouldn't let us get worried. She cheered us up. Distracted us. She told us about the saints." I pressed the question, "But did you worry about your dad?" She answered, "My grandmother wouldn't let you know how worried you were."[54] This answer suggests both how worried families really were about losing their loved ones at sea, and how efficiently they used their faith and devotional practices to counteract those fears. This grandmother was determined to banish any thought of fear in her grandchildren before it could set in. Nevertheless, the children were at times fearful, even if their grandmother quickly (and anxiously?) distracted them with stories of the saints. We can even wonder whether these inadmissible fears became embodied or emotionally stored in the repetition of devotional practices.

Other children of fishermen were profoundly affected by separations from their fathers. One third-generation woman I interviewed told me of her father being gone most of the time, and how much of a disciplinarian her mother became. She is now especially determined to make sure her husband is present in her sons' lives. She also told me of her husband's memories of his father being gone for long periods. Because his father sometimes went to Alaska to fish for salmon, he was gone for up to seven months at a time. The child used to cry inconsolably for his father. His mother, an extremely devout immigrant who spoke little English, must have also endured considerable stress.[55]

Carmela, a thirty-four year-old member of the second generation, remembers praying for her father's safety from the time that she was very young. Before he left on a fishing trip, her father would send Carmela or one of her siblings to the church to get holy water, so they could sprinkle it on the net. She remembers that he always had a cross and a statue of a saint on board to protect him. She also describes her role as teenager in the Mass at Mary Star preceding the Fishermen's Fiesta: at the offertory

53. Interview #19.
54. Interview #13.
55. Interview #25.

Carmela would bring a boat and a piece of net up to the altar. Then she would do the scripture reading. These seem to be pleasant memories for Carmela, who had a role to play in her father's leave-taking rituals. Perhaps sprinkling holy water on the net was fun for her and her siblings. Carmela also spoke of the concern that she felt even as a child praying that God would bring her father home safely. She sometimes found herself thinking of what it would be like if he never came home. She said, "When he would walk through that door, there was a sigh of relief."[56]

Even into her adulthood, Carmela's prayers and concern for her father have continued. She tells the story of her father's boat going down recently, less than a year ago. He was part owner of the vessel, which was fishing just off the coast of Monterey. It was a seventy-five foot commercial fishing boat, with a crew of nine on board. When the boat became overloaded and sank, the Coast Guard came to the rescue of the crew. Carmela sounds upset as she recalls the incident. "They hit the water. He's a large man. It took them a long time to get him up."[57] Carmela's concern for her father is palpable. I get the impression that she has gone through the cycle of prayer and worry many times, and it has never been easy.[58] This story also illustrates another dimension of the hardship of fishing: the increasing strain and risk that men face as they age in this occupation.

These stories demonstrate how fishermen's families have endured and coped with periods of separation from husbands, brothers, and fathers. Mothers and grandmothers left home raising children often relied on the practice of devotions, repeating the prayers of the rosary while holding the beads, or dipping their hands into cups of holy water. The devotions, in part because of their use of visual and tangible items, could include children in ritual activities that were impressive, intriguing, fun. The camaraderie of extended families drawing together was a source of comfort and/or joy for some of these children, though others seem to remember mainly their own weeping or a mother's escalated disciplinary practices. Whether children in this situation were "allowed" to be afraid or not, it seems apparent that they absorbed the anxiety of the situation, even as it was addressed or deflected, and sometimes ameliorated, through the practice of devotions.

56. Interview #22.

57. Ibid.

58. Because Carmela has lost her mother to illness, her concern for her father's safety is all the more poignant.

Loss of Life at Sea

After I had already completed several early interviews, I began to wonder about the number of fishermen lost at sea. I began to ask people routinely whether there were any stories of boating or fishing accidents in their family history. Often, I was initially told, "No, not in our family," or, "No, not that I am aware of." This disclaimer was sometimes followed by a story of a friend's family's loss. Then a closer story of loss might be told, such as the story of an uncle's uncle whose boat went down at sea. Finally, and often with much difficulty, stories of personal experiences of emergencies, accidents, and losses of loved ones would emerge. Just as likely, one family member might fill me in on a story that another family member had omitted.

I do not think that the people I interviewed were being duplicitous with me in omitting or "forgetting" these stories. In many cases, as persons spoke to me, it seemed that there was no initial recollection of the deaths at all. When I asked the question, several people responded by describing the effectiveness of the Coast Guard, and suggesting that deaths at sea are a thing of the past. However, as our conversations proceeded, stories of recent as well as older catastrophes would emerge. I began to suspect that these stories were initially "forgotten" not because they were rare or distant memories, but because they were fairly commonplace and recent enough to be extremely frightening.

In one of my informational interviews, I consulted "Paul," a seventy-year-old businessman of the second immigrant generation, for his description of the local fishing scene. I listened eagerly as he offered many stories from his close connection to the fishing industry. He supplied me with stories and colorful details that others had omitted. When I asked him about accidents and the fear of fishing accidents, he praised the Coast Guard and dismissed the current danger of dying at sea. He then made reference to an employee of his, and told me that her husband's boat was destroyed in a storm six months earlier, noting that the Coast Guard had saved the crew. He assured me that this was no big deal; a new boat was already under construction. This description seemed to minimize the both the danger that the man and his crew had been in and the broader impact of such an event.

Paul then began speaking in hushed tones, as he related a story about his own experience in the water, an event that had taken place many years earlier. Paul told of going out on a skiff with a high school friend, when they were eighteen and nineteen years old. They were not far from shore when the sea became choppy, and one oar dropped. "I said, 'Hey, you want me to go get that oar?' and my friend said, 'No, Paul, I'll go.' Then he swam out to get it, and he never came back." Paul was shaking visibly as he spoke. I asked him what happened then. He said he just stayed in the boat, screaming "like a madman." Eventually someone picked him up. The other boy's parents never spoke to him again. "I should have died. Not their son, I should have died," he repeated several times. Paul went on. "I'd be in a lock-up today if it wasn't for the priest. He took me places and helped me get back." Close to tears, Paul added, "It's always with me. It's right there."[59]

It is my impression that a number of tragic deaths at sea are "right there" beneath the surface of everyday life for many in San Pedro. Almost every one I interviewed celebrates the beauty of the ocean and its inspirational quality. The fishermen's "live-for-today" bravado, celebrating the joys of the open air and the solitude of life at sea, is real. But this pleasure in the present is also linked to an uncertainty about the future, and to the painful knowledge that fishermen are engaged in one of the most dangerous occupations in the world.[60] While many fishermen and their families may try not to think about the risks, some awareness of the danger is unavoidable. One of the devout immigrants, whose fisherman husband was twice rescued from the Pacific Ocean, puts it this way: "I love the ocean. It's something very powerful. Because when it gets mad, it's very powerful. Nobody could stop it. Only God."[61]

In the course of the thirty-one core interviews I conducted, no fewer than twenty different fishing accidents were reported to me. (More than one person in a family reported some accidents to me, but I was careful not to count the same accident more than once.) This number is substantial, especially when we take into consideration people's reluctance to talk about these incidents and that I did not directly ask every person I interviewed about accidents. These were serious incidents, where the vessels involved either overturned or sank. Frequently an overloaded hull was cited as the cause of sinking; sometimes storms or explosions on the boats were noted.

59. Informational interview #05.

60. Sebastian Junger reports that "More people are killed in fishing boats, per capita, than in any other job in the United States." Junger, *Perfect Storm*, 88.

61. Interview #15.

These accidents involved either the men I interviewed themselves, or the fathers, uncles, crewmembers, husbands, or more distant relatives of the persons I interviewed.

These twenty accidents resulted in eleven fatalities. In one additional case, a whole crew was said to have gone down. Given my small sample, these numbers are high. The effects of these losses on family and friends and churches are hard to calculate. Even in cases where the fishermen were rescued, the impact of the near-fatal experiences should not be under-estimated. As Sebastian Junger's words suggest, the experience of almost dying remains with someone long after the storm subsides. My interviews indicate that these experiences remain as well with the wives, siblings, children, and friends who have feared their loved ones lost.

Research at the San Pedro Bay Historical Society further confirmed my hunch that serious fishing accidents continue to occur with some regularity in the waters off the bay. In a newspaper-clipping file, I found reports of twenty-seven sunken boats in local waters between 1951 and 1991. In the majority of these cases, the captain and crew of the vessels had been saved by rescue efforts. However in some cases, there were fatalities, and in others, survivors told harrowing tales of their boats overturning in storms, catching fire, or exploding. Putting aside the devastating financial losses that these accidents involved, especially to uninsured boat owners, these incidents as reported seem extremely frightening. In one case in 1987, three crewmembers died, while six were saved in heavy seas after spending seventeen hours clinging to debris in the cold of night.[62] I suspect that experiences such as these have stayed with the people involved and their families. These events have also surely made an impression on long-time residents of the area, who have learned of these stories and absorbed their emotional impact with some regularity.

Paul's experience of excruciating emotional pain and terror at the death of his young friend has clearly stayed with him for over fifty years. He recalls it as though it were yesterday. Similarly, the sudden losses of friends and family members in accidents at sea, and the fear of such losses, inhabit the consciousness and prayer lives of many of those I interviewed. In addition to the trauma of any sudden loss, Paul exhibits a sense of survival guilt, evidenced by his claim that he should have been the one who died.

62. Pack, "3 Die, 6 Saved," A1.

Survival guilt is one of the common sentiments that interviewees expressed when describing these accidents. One family very haltingly shared a story involving these emotions. Only by interviewing several family members was I was able to piece the story together. Some years ago, two devout immigrants, a woman and her brother, owned a boat together. It was a small fishing vessel, named after their patron saint. One day, the woman's brother (and part-owner) was out fishing with a small crew. They caught too much squid, and the boat went over. The brother was saved, but one crewmember, a 30-year-old immigrant, was lost. As one of the owner's daughters put it, "That family lost a husband, a son." A new boat was eventually purchased, and a new saint's name was given to it. But there is a palpable sadness, a sense of responsibility or guilt that comes through in cast-down eyes when members of the older generation tell the story.

The traumatic stress of these incidents, as well as survival guilt, compounds the grief and mourning processes. It is not surprising that Catholics would turn to their faith for pastoral support in the face of such losses. In Paul's case, though he has never considered himself very religious, he credits his priest with helping him adjust to life again in the aftermath of the traumatic event of his friend's drowning. Apparently the priest spent time with Paul, helping him endure some of the intense fear that set in after the trauma. By offering him connection and a supportive presence, the priest probably helped Paul avoid a prolonged period of constriction after the trauma.[63] Given the amount of guilt Paul was feeling, and the reality that the other boy's family was blaming Paul for their loss, the priest's presence at Paul's side may have also helped him feel worthy enough to make his way back into society. Paul did not become devout, but he remains grateful.

While a sudden loss of life at sea does not automatically correlate with increased religious devotion, there does seem to be a tendency toward intensified prayer among those who were devout to begin with. The family described above was already devout before the incident involving the loss of a crewmember. While the couple did not tell me specifically how they had come to terms with this incident, they indicated that they continued to feel some responsibility for it. Interestingly, I did not get the impression that the couple blamed God or faulted the saint for the loss of their crewman. The woman indicated that she sometimes wonders what she

---

63. For an excellent book on trauma and healing, see Herman, *Trauma and Recovery*.

may have done to provoke the saints or cause "bad things" to happen. The woman in particular has remained intensely devoted to her saints and to Mary Star of the Sea, a church that seems particularly fitting for her. In the presence of the Madonna that cradles the tuna boat as if it were the Christ child, many have grieved their losses at sea. Here the devout can commit their loved ones to the care of God or the Madonna or the saints. Here they may also find a way to experience themselves as held in loving arms as they live with their hopes and fears and losses.

Some individuals report that a brush with death at sea has caused them to re-think the meaning and purpose of their lives. This was the case for Lisa, a forty-four-year-old member of the two-thirds generation (second generation by one parent, third by the other). Lisa is the only woman who shared a story of her own frightening experience at sea. Lisa and her husband both come from fishing families, and though they have chosen other occupations for most of the year, they go salmon fishing in Alaska in the summer. She reports that she and her husband were out in their boat in the chilly Alaskan waters one summer, when a nearby boat started taking on water. She and her husband lent a pump to the people on the other boat, radioed for help, and stayed near the other boat until the Coast Guard arrived. Lisa then tells of another experience, when the boat she was in took on water. She becomes more intense as she speaks. "It was a scary thought that I could die." I asked her how that experience has affected her. "What it does to you is it makes you realize that life is so precious. Life is a gift."[64] She then goes on to describe a brother-in-law who had a serious illness. "We look at my brother-in-law as if he's a gift." Lisa emphasizes how beautiful her children have become to her. She notices this especially when they are in the role of altar boys during the Italian Mass on Sunday nights, when they look like little angels to her. Lisa uses her traumatic experience to remind herself of what she values—her family tops the list—and to keep in check any impulses to complain about daily trials.

Another story is less sanguine. "Philomena," the very first woman I interviewed in San Pedro, was a ninety-one-year-old immigrant from Trapetto, Sicily. She came from a family of fishermen: her father, grandfather, husband, and sons were all fishermen. She immigrated to this country in 1946, with her two sons, in order to join her husband, who had already come to San Pedro. Philomena graciously welcomed me into her

64. Interview #25.

living room for an interview on short notice. She is a woman who prays almost continuously. After she told me the story of her extensive daily devotions, I asked her if she had children. Philomena immediately began to weep, and pointed to a large black and white photograph of a fishing vessel displayed on her living-room wall. It turns out that her first son was killed in a fishing accident, as was her husband. One of Philomena's friends pointed out to me that Philomena has continued to keep an old Italian custom of wearing black as an expression of her mourning, even now, more than forty years after her husband's death. She prays for her husband and son daily, as she prays for all the dead. In fact, she prays the rosary and sings devotional songs in Italian almost continuously throughout the day. Philomena's grief is obviously complicated. Her devotions do not seem to bring resolution, as much as they help her stay imaginatively connected to her son and husband. Her sadness is perhaps made more bearable through prayer and song.

As I suggested above, even in cases where there has been no fatality, the experience of storms or other fishing accidents can be extremely frightening. While I was not able to get many of these accounts from the fishermen themselves, their wives frequently told me the stories. Sometimes the husbands were present in the room, and interrupted occasionally to add a word or make a correction. "Joy" is a devout immigrant who told me the story of her husband Mike's two accidents at sea, in which he almost drowned. In one case, Mike was part of a crew fishing in waters a good deal south of San Pedro, when the boat encountered a hurricane. The boat went down, and Joy's husband Mike was in the water for thirty-six hours. She reports that she was praying for them the whole time. Mike was rescued when a Japanese freighter came along, picked up the crew, and brought them to Panama.

A similar event some years later involved Mike fishing on a job for his uncle. This time the boat sank near Mexico. The crew stayed with the life raft, until a Chinese and Japanese ship rescued them. Joy recounts these stories as miracles, similar to other miracles in her life, such as the time she injured herself and needed surgery to live, and the time five years ago when she was able to overcome cancer. "I never give up," she claims. "I always have hope." She adds, "I help anybody who comes to my door." Joy's English is good, so she continually helps her friends with translation when they go to doctors, or to the welfare office, or shopping. She has helped other immigrants with forms and with studying for citizenship.

"God rewards me," she claims. "All the saints and angels . . . anytime I need them, I call upon them and I know they help me." She understands the saints to be her intercessors. "The saints give me a lot of miracles. Saint Anthony—I prayed to give my husband back. He prayed to Jesus and the Virgin Mary. God sent this big ship." Joy also credits her husband's faith with his safe return: "His faith bring [*sic*] him back fishing."[65]

Joy demonstrates the way in which many immigrant fishermen's wives have worked the risks of fishing into their faith systems. "My faith is really, really strong," says Joy. "Sometimes I can feel and see Jesus. I am very, very, Catholica." Joy practices her faith, relying on her prayers at home and at church, her Italian Bible reading, her numerous works of religious art in every room of her house, her large social network of church friends, and her participation in religious societies at Mary Star to help her get through the frightening times. Helping the people who come to her in need is part of her devotional practice. It is part of the bargain she has made with God, to do whatever is asked of her, in return for miraculous help when she needs it. I have no doubt that her kindness to me in granting me an interview was part of Joy's practice of faith. Perhaps on some level it is her fear of catastrophe that motivates her acts of kindness and the zeal with which she performs them. I suspect that these practices help her gain some sense of personal control. Joy seems to embody her faith, to have taken it into her personality, so that it is automatic. She says, "Faith comes from your heart. From your brain and your heart. The way you're thinking towards God in your heart."[66] There is intentionality here, a purposeful direction of her own thoughts ("your brain and your heart"), toward the saints and toward God. And there is the earnest joy she expresses in reflecting on the modest life that she has lived this way. Joy is grateful and apparently at peace with the life that she has hewn out of fishing, fear, and faith.

San Pietro Society and the Blessing of the Fleet

Joy, along with several others whose stories I have described thus far, is a member of the San Pietro Society. This organization, along with its annual feast-day celebration, the Blessing of the Fleet, memorializes the inter-relationships between fishing and faith and the Italian Catholic presence at Mary Star of the Sea. The San Pietro Society, founded in 1996, is an off-

65. Interview #15.
66. Ibid.

shoot of the local Italian American Club. Those who started it wanted to "bring the devotion of San Pietro to the Italian community and a patron to fishermen."[67] San Pietro, or Saint Peter, is thought of as the patron saint of both fishermen and all of San Pedro. He is usually pictured holding a key, representing the keys of the kingdom that Jesus gave to his disciple Peter, a fisherman himself. A large mosaic on the exterior of the Eighth Street side of the Mary Star sanctuary depicts this scene (Figure 31).

The extreme joys and sorrows of the fishing life, as well as the fluctuating fortunes of the history of the industry, are expressed and memorialized in the Society's annual event, the Blessing of the Fleet. This ritual is held in late June, on the Saint's feast day. Though I was not able to attend one of these events, I watched a videotape of the first one that the Society sponsored, in 1996. One of the women I interviewed, a founding member of the Society, showed me the videotape in her home. The video captures the start of the feast day at morning Mass at Mary Star of the Sea. For this Mass, a large statue of Saint Peter, usually housed at the Italian American Club, is brought to the church in an open car. It is carried in ceremoniously, with members of the local chapter of the Knights of Columbus standing on either side of the aisle, their swords drawn. The pastor blesses the statue, and proceeds to walk down the aisle, blessing the congregation and sprinkling holy water. The gospel reading includes Jesus' words to his disciples, "I will make you fishers of men." In the course of the Mass, prayers for those who have passed away at sea are offered. The recessional hymn, "America," recalls the patriotic origins of the old Fishermen's Fiestas.

After the Mass, the people process down 6th Street toward the Marina. A truck decorated with crepe paper pulling a trailer carrying the statue of Saint Peter follows them. At the Marina, a noisy crowd of brightly dressed people awaits the arrival of the pastor. The founders of the devotion are wearing white gowns and brown sashes, and some of them have Hawaiian-style garlands of flowers around their necks. The children are dressed in Italian costumes, most of which were hand-sewn for the joyful occasion. When Monsignor Gallagher arrives, the statue of St. Peter is placed on a boat in the water. Standing on the wharf, the pastor prays that God will "bless these boats, and those who use them, for work and for pleasure. As the Lord calmed the Sea of Galilee, we commend these boats to his care. . . . May God protect them, and their equipment, and be with them. May

67. Program, San Pietro Society, 29 April 2000.

Christ who calms the storm fill their nets, and bring us all to the harbor of peace and love." As I watch this videotape with Maria, I see that she is gently weeping. The Monsignor's prayer touches her and seems to capture her prayers and the prayers of so many of her friends.

The theology of this ritual is enacted as well as spoken. The priest's words claim God's presence, protection, and provision, and invoke the values of peace and love. The ritual as a whole does these things too, through activities that express the community's particular history and identity. The practice of walking down to the wharf recalls religious processions in Italian homelands as well as in the Fisherman's Fiestas of old San Pedro. This may be a way of ritually re-establishing the community's sense of identity, which is now constituted over and against the backdrop of dislocation, both in relation to national homelands and in relation to the decline of local fishing. If Italians made their mark (found their place) in San Pedro through their involvement with fishing, the decline of this occupation represents a loss that is both cultural as well as economic. In this yearly ritual event, the people go down to the shore, place Saint Peter in the water, and the priest puts the anchor into the sea, the sea which has given the people life (and caused some deaths). In doing these things, the people ritually relive their dual history of immigration and fishing, celebrating it, blessing it, mourning its losses, and grieving the virtual end of this way of life. Supported by the pastor's presence, his caring words and sensitive use of scripture, the people hold onto their memories before letting them go, casting them upon the sea as if scattering a loved one's ashes.

A lively party follows the priest's blessing on the Marina. Singer Tony De Bruno and his band entertain, singing mostly Italian songs. There is much food, animated conversation, and dancing, lasting well into the afternoon. It is a small-scale event, when compared to the original Fisherman's Fiestas, as it inevitably is. Everyone knows that fishing in San Pedro isn't what it used to be. Nevertheless, this is a celebration of the fishing life in San Pedro, the way it was and the way it is. In this feast-day celebration, the precarious nature of fishing in San Pedro is lifted up and addressed through scripture, ritual, and prayer. The priest's words recall both the beauty and bounty of the sea and those whose lives were lost in these waters. And finally, as the priest tosses an anchor into the sea, the intensity of it all is released, transformed into dancing and celebration. In this way, the pastor and people re-enact their past, interpret it as sacred story, and assert their continuing presence in this place.

Summary

The fishing industry has left an indelible mark on the practice of Catholic devotions at Mary Star of the Sea. The wealth that this industry once created enriched many members and enabled the church itself to prosper and expand over the years. But the vicissitudes of the fishing life have also included significant hardship and loss for many of the devout. Fishermen and cannery workers have led difficult and dangerous lives here. Through devotional prayers and rituals, the people have sustained themselves, held on to memories of loved ones lost, and found the spiritual strength to endure uncertainty and fear. The large-scale rituals described here can be viewed as a performative, communal form of pastoral care, that lend a sense of spiritual value and coherence in the lives of the devout.

At Mary Star of the Sea, off in a far right corner of the sanctuary, is a statue of Saint Restituta. Saint Resituta is the female patron Saint of Ischia, the birthplace of several immigrants. This statue was donated to commemorate a boat with the same name, a boat that went down in a fishing accident in the early 1940s. One man tells me he is the nephew of the nephew of the man who drowned when the boat sank. This popular image draws many of Mary Star's devout over to pray, suggesting that the shrine memorializes not only the man who died and his boat, but also many other fishermen, both in Ischia and in San Pedro, who have been lost to a similar fate. Though these stories are not easily told, they are still present—"right there"—for the devout and for the community. They are noted at particular times on the calendar—such as Saint Peter's day, and in particular places in the sanctuary—such as Saint Restituta's altar. These ties to the dead add weightiness and meaning to the devotions. While many post-Vatican II Catholics have let go of devotions to the saints, following the church's renewed emphasis on the theological primacy of Christ and downplaying the intercessory role of Mary or the Saints, devotion to Saint Restituta endures, both in Ischia and in San Pedro.

From a pastoral point of view, we might also begin to see the importance of mourning and remembering in religious ritual and practice. John Patton has written eloquently on the links between remembering and caring.[68] When we are remembered, or when our stories are remembered accurately and retold, we feel cared for, confirmed in our beings. Religious rituals take on life when they succeed in evoking important shared memo-

---

68. Patton, *Pastoral Care in Context*, 32–36.

ries. We feel moved by religious rituals that help "bring back" our family histories or community stories through visceral experiences as well as through verbal recitation. Place plays a significant role in this memorializing process.[69] We speak of the value of being "grounded" or "putting down roots." Caring for and connecting to a community involves attending to its history, respecting its sacred spaces, and remembering its story.

This narrative also suggests ways in which religious identities forged in the transition of immigration and in the struggle to survive are marked by particular capacities and skills as well as limitations. Traumatic experiences leave rippled and lasting effects. People need spaces, rituals, and practices in which their histories can be shared as they unfold over time. Shared historical memories, when expressed, can be mourned, celebrated, or resolved in creative ways. Both the good memories and the less sanguine parts of our stories ought to be recalled, so that healing and hope may increase.

Thus far, we have only introduced the history of ethnic unity and diversity in this place. We will be coming back to this story and to its theological ramifications, particularly in chapter 7. We will now turn to another important dimension of the devotions: food. Food is the substance and goal of fishing. People fished, and some continue to fish, in order to eat, to survive. These devotions, which celebrate survival, often do so through the preparation, consumption, and sharing of food. The presence of food is not accidental or incidental to the devotions, but like fishing, part and parcel of the peoples' embodied piety.

69. Quoting Edward Casey, Patton writes, "Places are congealed scenes for remembered contents; as such they serve to situate what we remember." Ibid., 34.

4

Food, Famine, and Faith

> O taste and see that the Lord is good.
> Ps 34:8

THE date is March 19th, 2000. The celebration of Saint Joseph's Table, an annual tradition at Mary Star of the Sea Parish, is well under way. It began earlier with processions in the street before and after the 11:00 a.m. Mass. Approximately one thousand people filled the sanctuary for the Mass; fewer than that—perhaps five hundred—have gathered in the auditorium for the dinner and festivities that follow. A large U-shaped table is set up near the stage, at the feet of the statue of the saint. The table is elaborately decorated and completely covered with food. The host struggles to be heard over the noise. Shouts of *"Viva, San Giuseppi, Viva!"* inflected with a heavy Sicilian dialect, stir through the crowd, conveying intense emotion.

Many things are happening at once in this room: bedecked members of the Knights of Columbus are posing for photographs around the light-studded statue of Saint Joseph; five elderly women wearing blue sashes identifying them as the founders of the devotion are seated off to the right side of the main table, praying the rosary; other members of the Saint Joseph's Table Society are busy selling plates of homemade Italian cookies and raffle tickets, as well as glasses of beer, wine, and soda; meanwhile a sizable crowd of people, including my son and me, scramble for seats. At the center of it all is a large and ornately decorated table that is covered with food and dedicated to Saint Joseph (Figure 33 and Figure 34).

The food at this table is fresh, ripe, and choice. It displays the bounty of Southern California agriculture in springtime. Citrus fruits—lemons, grapefruits, and oranges—are particularly plentiful. They are arrayed in large, overflowing baskets. Numerous vegetables including eggplant, cucumbers, huge artichokes, peppers, and cauliflower, are also carefully arranged on the table. They are interspersed with multiple loaves of fresh bread, which have been made in a diversity of shapes and sizes. Four symbolic loaves of sesame bread are prominently positioned near the feet of the Saint: one formed in the shape of a halo and one in a cross, signifying Jesus; one a staff, for Saint Joseph; and one a palm frond, signifying Mary (Figure 35). Too, there are overflowing bowls of raw mushrooms, carrots, tomatoes, lettuce, broccoli, radishes, cabbage, and cantaloupe. Nestled in among all of this are dishes of marzipan—a kind of candy made from almond paste—that has been intricately sculpted and painted into small replicas of carrots, figs, and strawberries. There are also numerous small cakes, baked and decorated to resemble stained glass windows, crosses, lambs, Easter eggs, shells, fish, and one shamrock (a bow to Saint Patrick, whose feast has just passed).[1] There are apples, grapes, plums, bananas, stalks of celery, nectarines, watermelons, and tall jars of uncooked pasta. Bowls of fennel, corn, beans, chestnuts, pineapple, pears, kiwi fruit, strawberries, and mangos alternate with plates of cookies, muffins, candy-covered almonds, braided sweet breads, and marshmallow chicks. A small dish of cooked fish—including sardines, anchovies, and crab—has been placed on each side of the U. Finally, and perhaps most imaginatively, there are three small plates of chocolate pieces, made in molds to resemble wrenches and hammers—Saint Joseph's carpenter's tools (Figure 36).

I am struck by the sheer abundance of the food on this table, its variety and zest, the boldness of its presentation. I think of the money spent on procuring the food, and the time invested in its careful arrangement. Obviously, many of the individual items hold particular symbolic meanings. But the overarching message that the table proclaims is that food itself is sacred. This grand display of this bountiful substance broadcasts its importance for life. The ritual reveals the community's religious conviction that its life is a gift, as ripe and beautiful and perishable as every item on the table. The crowd's refrain of *"Viva, San Giuseppi, Viva!"* asserts with rare candor a basic human yearning to eat well and stay alive.

The food at this table also expresses the ethnic identity of the people who prepared it—the Sicilians and Italians and their descendants. The table proclaims this community's will to sustain its life and presence here

1. The shamrock might also be interpreted as a bow to the Monsignor, who is an Irish immigrant.

in Los Angeles. Many of the foods displayed here recall the foods grown and consumed in Sicily, where this tradition began. In particular, the abundance of citrus, almonds, beans, bread, and fish reflect the Sicilian diet that many of the immigrants here remember. This helps explain the immigrants' fondness for southern California, where so many kinds of fresh produce, particularly citrus fruit, grow. One immigrant stressed that she had never eaten meat when she lived in Sicily, as the people were all fishermen or farmers, and too poor to buy meat. Along with preserving ethnic identity, the devotion memorializes and redresses familial experiences of hunger and the struggle to survive. It is no wonder that the bonds of gustatory memory, preserved in the body through tastes and textures and aromas, evoke both comfort and anxiety for the devout.

While conducting my research in San Pedro, I found that abundant food, painstakingly prepared, was everywhere I went. The prominence and bounty of Saint Joseph's Table was echoed in other large-scale rituals revolving around food, in pastoral care ministries that provide meals for the hungry, and in the ubiquitous presence of large and well-worn dining room or kitchen tables in the homes I visited. Like the braided loaves of sesame bread found on Saint Joseph's Table, the phenomena of food, famine, and faith are braided together in the lives of the devout. The members of the later immigrant generations do not all remember being hungry, nor do they all embrace the same sense of ethnic identity; but the heightened significance of food, like a strong aroma, lingers on.

Saint Joseph's Table

According to tradition, Saint Joseph, the "stepfather of Jesus," once saved the people of Sicily from a terrible drought. In response to the prayers of the starving people, Saint Joseph miraculously sent rain that made the crops grow overnight. In gratitude and in the hope of staving off future famines, the people in several villages set up annual devotions to Saint Joseph, marking the mid-Lenten feast day of the Saint, March 19th. Traditionally, three of the poorest members of the village, a man, a woman, and a child (possibly an orphan) would be selected to play the roles of Joseph, Mary, and the boy Jesus. They would then enact a sacred drama, walking through the village and knocking at the doors of three homes, begging for food. This "holy family" would be refused at the first two homes they approached (recalling, of course, the plight of Mary and Joseph seeking shelter in Bethlehem). At the third door, marked by a palm frond or an olive branch, *I santi*, "the saints," as they are called, would be welcomed and treated as honored guests. This home would be the pre-arranged location for the Saint Joseph's table, which would have been lavishly prepared in advance. The three guests would eat first, sampling all of the finest foods, which would have been blessed by a priest and dedicated to Saint Joseph. After the honored guests were fed, the whole village would be offered a "poor man's meal," consisting of fava beans, pasta, sometimes sardines, and always bread and fruit. Afterwards, the honored guests would be given the remainder of the blessed foods to take home with them.[2]

The Saint Joseph's Table at Mary Star of the Sea Parish maintains several elements of this tradition, with the addition of a few interesting touches. Begun in 1973 by six women, themselves Sicilian immigrants, Saint Joseph's Society maintains a deep devotion to Saint Joseph year-round. But the feast day in March is clearly its largest and most time-consuming event. Legal permits for the procession must be obtained. The letter-writing process begins months in advance, in order to get the hefty fees for these permits waived. Extensive planning and purchasing also go on for months in advance of the feast. Hundreds of cookies are baked and frozen. Donations of flowers, bread, beverages, and food for the public dinner are tediously solicited from local merchants, as are items for the raffle that follows the dinner. A few key leaders of the devotion go around town to various businesses, seeking these donations. This practice of asking, or begging, is an important feature of the tradition. It is thought to cultivate humility, which is a virtue believed to be particularly pleasing to the humble carpenter saint. But more than humility is needed to orchestrate this event. It is an organizing feat of serious proportions, requiring time, effort, money, and leadership.

I got to see some of the behind-the-scenes work that takes place on the day before the feast, when about fifty core volunteers start gathering in the church auditorium to work on preparations. Food is the central focus of this day as well. Large scale cookie baking goes on in the morning. The women are in charge of the baking, but several men assist. The work is heavy and the kitchen gets hot. But the mood is upbeat: many old friends greet each other, and proudly display the cookies they have brought to contribute.

2. Del Guidice, "St. Joseph's Tables," 18–19.

The day of preparation is marked by its own customary foods. When I arrived to observe, it was close to lunch hour, and the volunteers were just lining up for an elaborate lunch buffet. I was immediately encouraged to eat. A cold squid salad, Italian cold cuts, and exquisite homemade rolls were plentifully spread. The rolls had been baked that morning by one of the founders of the devotion. These particular rolls were not served at the dinner the next day; they were made expressly for the day of preparation. They were remarkably fresh, light, and flavorful. I complimented the woman who made them, wondering if she had passed this recipe along to anyone yet. She only smiled and encouraged me to eat more.

After lunch, a group of the devout gathered together, sitting on folding chairs, to pray the rosary and sing hymns to Saint Joseph in a Sicilian dialect. This prayer time seemed to flow naturally into the afternoon activities. It provided a period of physical rest, as well as spiritual activity for the oldest members of the Society. Different women took turns leading the decades of the rosary,[3] and passing out small printed copies of the hymns. The prayers were familiar, and the women seemed to relax into a rhythm as they recited them. They were not just fulfilling a duty, but also earnestly engaged in prayer and song. The hymns brought tears to some eyes.

Meanwhile, some of the organizers kept working, albeit more quietly, in the kitchen nearby. Throughout the afternoon, hundreds of plates of cookies were wrapped for sale (Figure 37). I watched as the amount and variety of food at the Table grew to wild proportions. It seemed that everyone had a job there, or just knew what to do. The praying, baking, socializing, singing, decorating, and eating seemed to flow together, as if in a pattern. Eating as well as prayer punctuated the day.

Later that evening, as the preparations continued into the dinner hour, a number of men arrived with Sicilian pizzas and salad for dinner. Again I was encouraged to eat. The longer I stayed, the more interesting the food and the rituals of preparation became. After dinner, I watched a group of women work in the church kitchen to prepare a chick-pea flour paste, which was quickly rolled out into a thin layer, cut into squares, and fried. I was of course encouraged to sample this *panelli*. The women worked deftly; meanwhile they were also laughing, posing for me to take their pictures, and apparently enjoying themselves immensely. They spoke

3. Decades of the rosary are five sets of ten beads each. The "Hail Mary" prayer is recited at each of these beads. The decades are separated by larger single beads, at which the "Our Father"—the Lord's Prayer—is recited.

in Italian part of the time, and in English the rest. Around 9:00 p.m., as I was getting ready to leave, they heated up the griddle for yet another dish—*Cassadelli*. This is a sweet made from frying a batter made of flour, eggs, wine, Crisco, and a little sugar, shaped into a shell. The shell is then filled with a mixture of ricotta cheese, sugar, chocolate chips, and cinnamon. I was not allowed to leave that night without taking home a warm and heavy plate of these aromatic creations—"to taste."

None of these particular foods were in evidence the next day, at the feast itself. Rather, these foods were reserved for the day of preparation and the inner circle of volunteers. The practice of preparing and sharing these additional foods is striking, especially on a day when the group had already been working steadily for over twelve hours to prepare the following day's food and festivities. What stood out for me in what I observed that day was the camaraderie of the women, their pleasure in being there together, in speaking Italian, and in preparing and eating these special foods. The foods seemed to reinforce their bonds to each other, to their Italian heritage, and to their faith. The women made a point of telling me that the chickpea flour was imported from Italy; so were other ingredients that they had purchased at specialty markets in Los Angeles. The preparations were joyful, but also precise: it seemed important to get it right; the elders of the group were often consulted on matters of taste or consistency. This was, I think, a demonstration of respect for the older women, many of whom were too tired to keep working late into the night, but who were nonetheless sitting nearby, enjoying themselves and their stature as the elders, the keepers of the tradition, and as expert consultants on the taste and quality of the food. That a good number of the group would pause in the midst of these preparations for an hour and a half of praying and singing seemed perfectly natural. In the devotional world that I entered that day, the spiritual and material aspects of devotion were clearly braided together.

Humility, Grandeur, and Class Roots

This annual event requires hard work, and some of the individuals who do most of it tend to wear themselves down. Their family members expressed concern over this to me. Nevertheless, as Anna, the main organizer, describes her role, she is smiling. She seems to exude a sense of satisfaction, finding fulfillment in pulling the event off successfully each year. The word "pride" comes to mind, but it is an odd kind of pride: a pride in one's humility, in the behind-the-scenes quality of her work. Anna avoids public recognition, and reserves the honorific roles—the front lines of the procession—for the founders, the elders who no longer actively manage the festivities.

This odd matching of humility and grandeur marks almost every aspect of the Saint Joseph's Table tradition at Mary Star. Each year, a young family from the church is selected to play the parts of Mary, Jesus, and Joseph. This is considered a great honor, often reserved for the founders' children and grandchildren.[4] But of course, the actors recall Sicily's poorest persons. The little group leads the procession before the Mass, knocking on two doors in the church building complex, before finding a welcome from the pastor at the door to the Rectory. The pastor and several other priests then join the procession, which circles the church buildings between 7th and 8th Streets, wheeling along the large statue of Saint Joseph, decked out with red and white flowers (Figure 38). Numerous church societies fly their banners in the procession, including the Knights of Columbus, the Italian Catholic Federation, and Saint Anne's Society. A group of children dressed in traditional Italian costumes also walk along. An Italian marching band from Los Angeles brings up the rear, offering a variety of Italian and American anthems (Figure 39).

Amidst all the fanfare and ethnic pride, the event retains a focus on devotion to Saint Joseph and his miraculous intervention to feed the poor. The table is a commemorative ceremony with many precise details that are repeated year after year, even if some new features, such as the band, are added. According to social theorist Paul Connerton, a calendrically observed ritual has a kind of "echo effect from the perceived order of a cosmic sequence."[5] The "echo effect" renders the past—or a certain memory of it—emotionally potent in the present. The words of Anna, the chief organizer of the Saint Joseph's Table feast (who is also the daughter and niece of two of the founders), bore this out. In describing the feast day to me in advance, she said, "You will get goose-bumps."[6]

---

4. This change is an example of the way in which the tradition is altered in its new location. While the poorest person in a Sicilian village might have been easy to locate and honored to play a role in the sacred drama, this is probably not the case in San Pedro. Here, the immigrants and their descendants play these parts themselves, and thereby slightly shift the emphasis of the symbolism toward immigration and ethnic identity.

5. Connerton, *How Societies Remember*, 66.

6. Interview #7.

There is indeed a moment in the ritual when emotions run high. It follows after the Mass and the second procession. The statue of Saint Joseph has been carted back into the auditorium, and placed at the head of the Table. The people press in to get a look at the food on the Table. Some pin money onto a sash attached to the statue (Figure 40). The founders, tired from walking, take their chairs near the table and begin praying. One of them, in her eighties, has walked the procession barefoot. It is at this point that someone tries with the aid of a microphone to address the crowd, and the shouts of *"Viva San Giuseppi!"* begin, creating an audible "echo effect." The intensity of this moment, the feeling of "goose bumps," has something to do with the belief that the Saint is still alive and present here, in the community of immigrants, with its venerable ancestors. Implicit in the cries of *"viva,"* "live!" is a fearful story of hunger and desperate struggle to survive: if it were not for the goodness of God, won by our devotion and the intercession of Saint Joseph, we might not be here; furthermore, without the continuing benevolent aid of the Saint in the present, even in this land full of plenty, we might perish. So "Live, Saint Joseph, live!" Through this invocation, the people say to themselves as well as to others, "We are here!" Here, that is, in a country in which we may still sometimes feel unsteady or out-of-place.[7]

The emotional power of this event also lies in its bold reminder that people need food to live. Though the presentation of the food is stylized and the rituals around it are performative, there is still something disarmingly simple and direct about so much fresh produce. It is humble, in the original sense of the word: earthy. Again, we can note the juxtaposition of humility and grandeur. The cornucopia of food suggests lush abundance and plenty. Yet its raw form lays bare for the devout the reality of human dependence on the earth. Food comes from the earth; it is something that human beings cannot make. Bread, the most basic food here, is made of wheat; its production wholly depends on nature's power, God's power, to give rain or to take it away.

This presentation of food is humble in another way. Pierre Bourdieu describes the food space as one field in which class differences are embod-

---

7. In a reflection on European immigrants' experience, Chidester and Linenthal write, "The old world was, in part, recreated in the midst of the new world. . . . Disorientation, dislocation, and alienation were imbedded in the immigrants' consciousness, try though they might to use their former identities as a buffer to soften the impact of their new condition." Chidester and Linenthal, "Introduction," 26.

ied and displayed.[8] The food on Saint Joseph's Table, in its raw form, fairly announces its material reality, its substance. This primacy of substance might be read as a marker of the working class. By contrast, according to Bourdieu, the middle and upper classes are more concerned with food's form than its function.[9] While Saint Joseph's Table is itself a ritualized social ceremony, with its own ethical and aesthetic tone, the ritual as a whole emphasizes substance and function more than form. The noise, the crowd itself, and the non-hierarchical seating for the public, the plain and undisguised form of the food—these are all reminders that this popular religious practice is rooted in poverty and starvation. The importance of eating—"the basely material vulgarity" of it—is held up here. It is not only on display, it is rendered holy.

Several additional practices at the celebration reinforce this impression. As the ritual unfolds, each guest views the main table and then pays a visit to the five surviving founders, who are sitting off to the side of the table. Along with warm embraces, guests receive a small brown paper bag containing the essential symbols of the devotion: a holy card, featuring a picture of the saint, a lemon, and a small loaf of bread. This practice, which recalls the Sicilian tradition of packing up leftovers for the poor to take with them, rekindles the memory of famine. It reminds the people of how basic eating really is, and how close at hand poverty once was, and for some still is.

The meal that is served to the public on Saint Joseph's day also reflects the peoples' consciousness of class distinctions. It is called a "poor man's meal." It consists of bread, *pasta e fagiole* (pasta with beans in soup), salad, and *calamari* (fried squid). While these foods are somewhat refined and stylized (and currently available in certain bourgeois restaurants), they are

8. Bourdieu, *Distinction*, 169–225.

9. "It is also a whole relationship to animal nature, to primary needs and the populace who indulge them without restraint; it is a way of denying the meaning and primary function of consumption, which are essentially common, by making the meal a social ceremony, an affirmation of ethical tone and aesthetic refinement . . . . The manner of presenting and consuming the food, the organization of the meal and setting of the places . . . the seating plan, strictly but discreetly hierarchical, the censorship of all bodily manifestations of the act or pleasure of eating (such as noise or haste), the very refinement of the things consumed, with quality more important than quantity—this whole commitment to stylization tends to shift the emphasis from substance and function to form and manner, and so to deny the crudely material reality of the act of eating and of the things consumed, or, which amounts to the same thing, the basely material vulgarity of those who indulge in the immediate satisfactions of food and drink." Bourdieu, *Distinction*, 196.

modest in that they are inexpensive and they emphasize basic nutrition. In the context of a now mostly middle-class setting, this is clearly meant to be a simple meal, emphasizing substance, intent on reminding people of their basic humanity, their humble roots, and their need for food. Many of the older Italian and Sicilian immigrants in the room will probably also remember times when their daily fare was much more sparse, and some of these very foods were their staples. In smelling, tasting, and sharing these foods, the memory of that experience of poverty is rekindled.

Generally speaking, the people in this room no longer live in fear of hunger or starvation. Many of the immigrant families have done well financially. Many members of Saint Joseph's society now live in beautiful middle-class homes, some of which are located on the upscale Palos Verdes Peninsula. Though these devotees of Saint Joseph are no longer poor, they almost all have working class roots. There are also class differences among the members of devotional societies at Mary Star, even among the Italian ones. Among these societies, Saint Joseph's Table Society is self-consciously proud to be the most modest.

Saint Joseph's Table Society's approach to putting on church dinners demonstrates this modesty. For example, the dinner tables at this feast are attractively decorated, but on a simple scale. A few fresh flowers grace each table, and paper plates, tablecloths, and disposable utensils are in use. Donations to the society are accepted and encouraged from those who eat the dinner, but no particular amount is expected or required. It is stressed that no one will be turned away. The society raises approximately two thousand dollars through the Saint Joseph's Table festivities each year. With this, they fund four local high school scholarships (two for students attending Mary Star High School, and two for San Pedro High). Those in the society who organize the dinner pride themselves on their practice of promptly turning over the remaining receipts to the church.

Again, one senses a kind of pride in the humility of this. They are proud that they don't waste money on fancy table decorations, as they perceive that other societies do. They are proud that they don't hoard their money in separate bank accounts, as they claim other societies do. They are proud that their money is used to help the church and the needy. The fact that they fund high school rather than college scholarships can also be read as an indicator of class. In particular, the fact that they help public school students who don't have to pay tuition, as well as Catholic school students who do, suggests an awareness of the ongoing poverty of some families in town.

When the pastor recently asked this society to raise money for the purchase of a new chalice for the parish, the members gladly complied. The cost of the chalice was high, approximately ten thousand dollars—the cost of commissioning a work of sacred art. The symbol that was chosen, which was to be sculpted into the chalice, was a staff of wheat. The symbol of wheat is of course a key ingredient in bread, a central element in the Sacrament of Holy Communion. But wheat is also of particular importance to this group, which harbors the memory of famine and the importance of basic foods such as bread for survival.

One of the organizers of the fund-raising for the chalice said that she felt it was an honor that the Monsignor has asked their society to raise this money. She suggested that the Monsignor knew that Saint Joseph's Table Society would work hard to raise the money—and not just ask one wealthy parishioner to write a check. This hard work, this earnest sacrifice involved for the solicitation of many contributions from those who have less, presumably adds religious value to the task. There is a kind of pride in offering the "widow's mite."

The reverence for poverty, struggle, and thrift is perhaps an example of what Bourdieu has called turning a necessity into a virtue.[10] It may also be a means of remembering and redressing the devout's experiences of hunger, and trying to insure, through faithful sharing of resources, that they will never be hungry again. Additionally, there is some intra-congregational cultural capital at stake here in maintaining modest and poverty-conscious ways in this setting. The favor and approval of the busy pastor, Monsignor Gallagher, is one example of this. When the Monsignor commends Anna for her piety, her closeness to Saint Joseph, she is very pleased indeed.

The food on Saint Joseph's table will not be eaten on the day of the Feast; on this day it is here for the Saint. Saint Joseph is thought to enjoy all of this fanfare, and even to go out of his way to insure good weather for the procession.[11] The next day, the food will be distributed to the poor—through "Christian Care," an ongoing ministry of the church that

10. Bourdieu, *Distinction*, 189.

11. I am told that once, a few years ago, rain was predicted on the feast day, and it did in fact rain during the feast day Mass. The woman organizing the event prayed to Saint Joseph to improve the weather, and the sun burst forth from the clouds just in time for the procession. "He wants his procession," she said. Interview # 7.

feeds lunch to fifty to sixty persons per day. This practice, too, is in keeping with the roots of the devotion in Sicily, where the tables often directly fed the poor as a form of communal or public charity.[12] Saint Joseph's Table underscores the people's sense of their religious duty to provide food for the poor, a duty that is widely evidenced among the devout in San Pedro. It is to these food ministries that I shall now turn.

Food for the Hungry

During an interview in her home, Anna, the organizer of the Table, mentions in passing that she has worked for Christian Care for four years. For at least one of those years, she was the sole person making sandwiches for the lunch program; it took several hours each day. "The Monsignor ask me, so I do it," she says simply. "We do a lot of stuff for him, he do [sic] a lot of stuff for us."[13]

Anna's food-serving ministry was not unusual among the devout. Though I did not specifically ask, at least seven of my thirty-one interviewees mentioned that they were involved in feeding ministries, as a critical expression of their faith. Had I inquired routinely, I suspect the number would have been higher. I was moved not only by the considerable commitments of time and resources that people routinely devote to these ministries, but also by the thoughtful theological reflection and spiritual devotion that these ministries represent and express for the devout.

One man, whom I shall call Rocco, has been working for Christian Care for eleven years, since his retirement from a successful seafood business in San Pedro. He is a member of the second generation, and feels that he has been blessed throughout his life. It seems to follow quite naturally, to him, that he should do what he can to help those who have not been so fortunate. His wife Susan helps at Christian Care too, but she points to Rocco, and says, "He does the most."

Rocco's daily routine involves leaving the house between 6:30 and 7:00 a.m. and driving around town in his pick-up truck, gathering leftover or slightly dated foodstuffs from restaurants and grocery stores. He then brings the food down to the church and unloads it. He stays to help out in

12. Del Guidice, "St. Joseph's Tables," 18.

13. Interview #7. Anna offers an example of the pastor's reciprocity, noting that he has sometimes allowed her to put flowers at the church altar to Saint Joseph on his feast day, even though the feast usually falls during Lent, when flowers are not permitted in the sanctuary.

whatever way he can, and finishes volunteering around noon each day. He clearly loves the work and can't understand why it is so hard to get more committed volunteers. He says, "They help out for a few months, and then stop, because they don't get anything out of it." He claims that it can be difficult work, dealing with, "druggies, winos, and people who never tell the truth." But he feels it is his calling. "I believe with all my heart that the Lord wants me to do His work, not Mass fifteen times a day."[14] Here Rocco is perhaps taking a swipe at the more liturgically inclined devout.

He and his wife also show me the busy traveling schedule that they enjoy in their retirement. "These people (the guests at Christian Care) don't get any of this," they point out. Here, Rocco is telling us something about his awareness of his own good fortune, and his appreciation for the hardship that his less wealthy neighbors endure. His comment about "Mass fifteen times a day" indicates his sarcasm or at least impatience with the devotional habits of the devout who do spend hours and hours in church. That kind of practice doesn't appeal to him. Rocco would rather express his faith through ministries that address the concrete needs of people. His independent spirit comes through in the way he speaks so plainly about his calling.

Before he retired, Rocco was the well-known owner and operator of a successful door-to-door seafood business. He sold fish all over San Pedro and in several inland communities as well. He started out with nothing but an old truck and bed full of ice, and built a wildly successful business. He could have expanded it, had he been willing to hire others. But he chose to work independently, with no one to answer to but his customers. He feels very fortunate indeed to have made such a good living doing something he truly enjoyed. Rocco and Susan are also proud that they were able to put their three academically motivated children through college. "I've had a wonderful life," says Rocco. "Great kids. A great marriage." At this his wife looks at me meaningfully and insists, "Nothing is perfect, dear, nothing is perfect." The couple laughs easily. For them it seems clear that their good fortune is the gift of God. They know that life is tenuous. Perhaps they don't want to tempt fate—or the divine—by hoarding their good fortune. They claim that they are meant to do God's work, and this involves providing food for those who need it.

14. Interview #23.

The couple tells me many miraculous stories from their day to-day lives. They speak with emotion and conviction. Rocco notes that when he was a boy of fourteen, he was supposed to go fishing one day with his father and several other men. The night before, he couldn't sleep. He kept seeing a dark shadow in his bedroom and it scared him. The next morning, he was too tired to go fishing, so he stayed home. That day, the boat blew up. Two men died, two had third degree burns. Rocco's father was wounded and had to go to the hospital. "That shadow saved my life," Rocco claims. As a result of this, he suggests, he has a responsibility to try to save others. Whether pangs of survival guilt are operative here or not, Rocco demonstrates the way in which this accident has stayed with him, intensifying his appreciation of life and informing his religious practice.

But it is not just a sense of indebtedness that fuels the couple's efforts. It is also their spiritual sense that God is operating through them. Rocco admits that he was not really very religious as a young man, but feels that he has become more spiritual in recent years. Susan encourages him to tell another story. "Tell her about when you were thrown out of your chair!" she exclaims. He tells it less dramatically than she does, but the basic gist of the story is the same. Late one night, after the couple had gotten ready for bed, Rocco had settled into his favorite chair. He then had a strong bodily sensation, a feeling that he needed to get up. "Something was telling me to go to 19th and Pacific (streets). I told my wife, 'I've got to go pick up bread and food and give it to the homeless.'" "I thought he was crazy. I said 'I'm all ready for bed. I'm not going with you,'" said Susan. Rocco quickly dressed and got his truck, picked up the food and found that there were indeed homeless people waiting for his delivery at 19th and Pacific. This is what he means when he says he feels "more spiritual" now. He feels he is in tune with God in his work to deliver food to those who are hungry.

Pastoral ministries that provide food to the public are part and parcel of the faith at both Mary Star of the Sea and at Holy Trinity, the second largest Catholic church in San Pedro. These ministries require considerable volunteer labor from church members. This form of practical pastoral care appears to be linked to the devotions, to the memory of poverty and the struggle to survive that the devotions reinforce, and to the embodied form of spiritual practice that they encourage. The teaching and preaching of the Catholic churches here also articulate a link between faith and concrete service to the needy. Monsignor Gallagher, the pastor of Mary

Star for fourteen years, has particularly stressed the need for the practical care-giving ministries of the laity. When I asked him about the emphasis on ministries to the poor during his tenure, he quoted the gospel of Matthew with ease. "We've become more conscious of the needy person, the homeless person, the hungry, the imprisoned. After all, Our Lord tells us that what you do unto to least of these, you do unto me."[15]

Similarly, Matthew, whose complex home altar I described in chapter 2, also contends that faith must lead to action. This action revolves around food, as did our interview. Over bowls of *tortellini* he served in a highly spiced tomato sauce, Matthew told me of his intense and searching faith, a faith that finds practical expression in a ministry of food distribution at Holy Trinity parish. He told me about this work with some apology, as if to guard himself against bragging. "The only reason I say this is really for the sake of your interview, because I don't like to pat myself on the back. But I'm in charge of a really large service organization at Trinity that I started, founded, and run." I encouraged him to tell me more about it. He explained,

> I just decided to call it the Outreach Program. And we minister food every week to families in the area that are poor, and you know, having a hard time fending for themselves right now. We deliver. We have a team of people that come in and pack, and another team of people that come in and drive the food, we have people that pick up the food at the food bank, and we've got probably about 150–200 people in the parish involved in it. So that's my, that's my membership in my church, because to me that's much more important than sitting there and talking about it, that's getting out and doing it. That's a large part of the way that I live and the way that I pray. Because prayer is found in your devotion and in your active devotion in your work. I think it's James that says that faith in itself without works is dead.[16]

Matthew explicitly refers to his practical efforts *as* his devotion. While his youth, his education, and his combined study and practice of Buddhism as well as Catholicism[17] distinguish his experience from seventy-eight-year-old Rocco's, the two men's lives concur in their religious commitments to

15. Informational interview, 31 May 2000.

16. Interview #30.

17. See chapter 2.

provide for the hungry. Each man believes that he possesses the talents and resources needed for this kind of ministry. Each seems to be possessed of an intense spiritual conviction that he is meant to do this work. Or, as Matthew says, with youthful candor: "If I've been given the gift to be able to do a charitable thing and I don't do it, then I spit in the face of the giver." The obligation to provide food for the hungry is a "natural" and obvious Christian duty in this setting.

A third story illustrates a more literal form of pastoral feeding ministry at yet another Catholic church in San Pedro. It involves a very dignified second-generation immigrant, age eighty-five, the only person who volunteered to be interviewed. "Linda" saw my notice in the Mary Star bulletin, though she attends Mass at Little Sisters of the Poor, a parish related to a home for the elderly in the northern section of town. Linda has led a long and interesting life. She was a public health nurse, a veteran of World War II. She is also credited with starting the "Life Line" program in San Pedro, which placed electronic units in the homes of elderly persons, allowing them to call for emergency help with the push of a button.

When asked what devotions mean to her, Linda says that for fourteen years, she visited the lonely and fed the handicapped at the nursing home each Sunday. Because of a health crisis of her own a year ago, she had to stop practicing this ministry for a while. She says, "I want to go back and feed in the feeding room. Somebody has to feed them." She explains that these are the patients who are handicapped in ways that prohibit them from feeding themselves. While the nursing home staff feeds these patients on weekdays, the home is short-handed on weekends. Linda adds, "I want to do something worthwhile. Not just be in the Women's Guild. I want to do something more than just get dressed up and go to a rich man's banquet."[18]

Linda grew up in poverty, but indicates that she is fairly well off now. She is somewhat critical of Mary Star of the Sea parish, which she finds ostentatious. "Mary Star is a much richer parish. Here we have close to two hundred people. Some really from poor families, or have *no* family. Some people have no visitor that ever comes." Linda supports the church financially, but emphasizes the importance of her pastoral ministry of

18. Interview #26.

feeding. "I give a donation every year—*ten percent*. My Sunday *duty* is to feed in the feeding room."[19]

Like Rocco, Linda believes that she has been blessed throughout her life. She speaks movingly: "I marvel every day at how much the Lord has given to me. Much more than I deserve. I own this home and my life is good. Every illness I've ever had the Lord has helped me through. I've said my prayers. 'Thank you for the things you've done for me, dear God.'"[20]

Also like Rocco, Linda experienced a brush with death as a teenager. At nineteen, she had pneumonia. In 1934, without penicillin, it was not unusual to die from this disease. Her mother cared for her diligently, praying the rosary continuously. Her mother lifted Linda up and shifted her back and forth between two beds, so that she could change the sheets frequently, washing the linens by hand each day. The doctor stopped in to see Linda each morning. Over time, the illness abated and Linda survived.

Linda tells this story vividly. She says it affected her whole life, and gave her a feeling of closeness and gratitude to her mother. Linda points to a picture of her mother at her bedside table, over which a rosary is draped (Figure 19). I cannot help but wonder whether the experience of this illness also influenced Linda's career choice of nursing and her lifelong charitable efforts to help the sick, including her current desire to help feed the disabled persons in the nursing home. Did her own experience of helplessness and close brush with death "stay with her" in the way that fishing accidents, losses, and experiences of poverty have stayed with others in this community? Perhaps in caring for patients, and alleviating their helplessness and hunger, Linda is creatively redressing her own frightening experiences. These efforts may also help her feel connected to her deceased mother.

Rocco, Matthew, and Linda all engage in various food-based ministries. It may be that the experience or story of poverty or illness has helped inspire these ministries. It may be that the traumatic brushes with death in their families' histories have intensified their attitudes toward life and faith, and helped motivate pastoral ministries geared toward survival. It seems clear that these individuals from the second and fourth immigrant generations experience an obligation to provide food to those who need it as a spiritual and moral duty.

19. Ibid.
20. Ibid.

Maria, whose story we explored in chapter 2, also participates in a ministry of feeding, referring to it matter-of-factly as if it is a basic spiritual duty. In the course of our interview, she drew a connection between her participation in the sacrament of Holy Communion and her work in preparing food for individuals and families who need it. Maria is an immigrant who struggles to speak English. In explaining how her work at the church helped her "enter" this country, i.e., become actively involved in the life of Mary Star of the Sea Church, she said, "Now it's okay. I am minister Eucharistica (a Eucharistic minister who serves communion). Every morning I give the cup at the 8:00 Mass . . . before I make sandwich[es] for the poor people." Her words suggest a natural flow between giving the cup and making sandwiches, spiritual and material eating, drinking, and sharing.

The current pastor of Mary Star, Father Gallagher, drew the connection between communion and food-provision ministries more explicitly. He said, in reference to Christian Care, "It's at 5:00 a.m., out here on the sidewalk every morning that the real breaking of the bread takes place." This sacramental view of food provision finds an echo in community attitudes toward family meals and the common practice of hospitality.

Hospitality, Italian Style

One of the things that made my interviews so pleasant and so warm was the overwhelming hospitality of the people I interviewed. If there is one striking commonplace about the homes I visited, it was the presence of a large, serviceable dining room or kitchen table. It was at these tables that most of my interviews were conducted. On these tables, plates of delicious and fresh homemade Italian cookies constantly appeared. Along with the cookies, tiny (*demitasse*) cups of *espresso*—dark Italian coffee—seemed always at the ready. If an interview ran into the lunch or dinner hour, I would often be invited to stay and eat. Bowls of homemade soup were frequently ladled up. Often I would leave with a plate of beautiful, fancy cookies to take home. After a while, I got the hang of it, and took a part in the ritual of hospitality myself. I would sometimes arrive at my interviews with a small gift of food, such as loaf of bread, or a coffee cake from Ramona's bakery down on Gaffey Street. The pleasure of these small exchanges was immense.

In one case, when I requested an evening time for an interview, I was invited to dinner. I immediately said, "I don't want to put you to any trouble." My informant replied wryly, "We eat every night." When I agreed to come, my hostess, whom I shall call "Rosa," invited another immigrant couple to join us, so that I could interview them as well.

Around a huge dining room table, we ate and drank together. It was a leisurely meal of several courses, offered with homemade wine. Rosa's husband, Martyn, an immigrant from Croatia, did the cooking. After appetizers and pasta, he served the entree of grilled white sea bass. Martyn is a retired fisherman, and a fabulous cook. He had prepared his own marinade and grilled the bass to perfection. He served it with green beans, a tomato salad, and fresh warm bread. Throughout the evening, the courses kept appearing, the wine flowing, and my tape recorder (with permission) was rolling.

Around this table, some wonderful moments were shared. These were four dear friends, gathered to tell me their stories. They were all immigrants who had come over as children. They were from different places: Rome, Sicily and Croatia. But they were of similar ages (fifty-five through sixty-one), they had experienced similarly frightening adventures in immigrating, and they shared similar faith and devotional practices. They took turns answering my questions, often launching into stories that illustrated a point. Some of the deeper stories, the more painful ones, emerged with tears. These poignant moments were quickly followed by funny or joyful comments.

I kept getting the feeling that something significant was happening there at the table. I was glad to be a part of it. The food was plentiful and delicious, and it was matched by a depth and quality of conversation that surprised me. While my questions certainly had a role in prompting such reflections, I had the sense that these were stories that needed to be told, and stories that could only be told around a table. There was a vibrancy, an intimacy, that seemed connected to the food itself, as well as to the considerable pleasure of consuming it together with this group of friends. It was after 10:00 p.m. before I tried to pull myself away from the table and the conversation in order to start my long drive home. But when I turned off the tape recorder, the conversation got better, so I stayed a while longer.

We can look at what was happening here at many levels. Bourdieu might see it as an example of the distinct "food space" of the working class. He wrote,

The art of eating and drinking remains one of the few areas in which the working class explicitly challenges the legitimate art of living. In the face of the new ethic of sobriety for the sake of slimness, which is most recognized at the highest levels of the social hierarchy, peasants and especially industrial workers maintain an ethic of convivial indulgence. A bon vivant is not just someone who enjoys eating and drinking; he is someone capable of entering into the generous and familiar—that is, both simple and free— relationship that is encouraged and symbolized by eating and drinking together, in a conviviality which sweeps away restraints and reticence.[21]

Certainly these friends and I were entering into the "generous and familiar," simple and free relationship that eating and drinking together encourages. (I hasten to point out that very little wine, less than a carafe, was consumed). This conviviality certainly seemed to sweep away "restraints and reticence," and allow the speakers to tell their stories openly. One man described the pain and shock and tears that immigration entailed for him as a boy of fourteen. He offered a detailed and gripping description of cramped housing, offensive odors (from the canneries and oil refineries), and the fear of going to school when he spoke not a word of English. This man is now a successful electrical contractor, an upbeat and affable fellow, whose immigration story is probably not widely known or frequently told. But in the context of a dinner with friends, he offered it with tender emotion.

Some weeks later, I interviewed "Antonia," one of the daughters of Rosa and Martyn, the couple that had hosted the dinner. Antonia is thirty-four, and a teacher at Mary Star's elementary school. She strikes me as joyful, like her parents. She speaks with pride of her husband, an immigrant whom she met in Sicily, who learned to speak English and in other ways made his own immigrant transition to this country very well. Antonia tells me that they have a four-year old son. In speaking of her son, she fights back tears. They have just learned that he has been diagnosed with a serious developmental condition. "Believe me, if I didn't have faith, I'd be in trouble. He's doing well, and I have to thank God for that."[22] She went on to tell me that she has made a practice of putting holy water on her son's body.

21. Bourdieu, *Distinction*, 179.
22. Interview #13.

Of the saints, she says, "They hold us up. Through all these statues and novenas. They give us a little boost. They remind you you're on the right path. You think back: you've had such a great family tie. It keeps me strong."[23] Clearly, Antonia is relying on her devotions emotionally and spiritually, as she adjusts to this news about her son. She is also relying on her strong bonds of connection with her family for practical help in raising him. Her father, Martyn, takes care of the boy most days when Antonia is teaching.

When asked if there was anything else she wanted to say about the meaning of faith or spirituality in her life, she said, "Love begins and ends it all. That eating together really does it . . . eating, communicating, kissing, loving!"[24] Her eyes welled up with tears. Having eaten at her parents' table, I could appreciate Antonia's words. I could see how generous and genuine her family really was. I could see, too, how love, faith, and food were, in this family, habitually intermingled.

While this dynamic was perhaps more pronounced and compelling in this family, it was not unlike the dynamics I witnessed in other homes, at other tables. The habit of sitting down and eating together, while conversing and relaxing, was extremely common. These shared meals and coffee breaks frequently expand to include guests and extended family members. The depth of communication and caring that characterizes these occasions certainly varies. But an emphasis on the importance of sharing food together is taken for granted. Sharing food is a basic form of care. Food is a means through which the devout and their descendants sustain themselves, each other, and those who are hungry—persons whom they may not know but for whose plight they have some appreciation. This practice is itself religious, in that it expresses an ethical obligation to sustain life and to maintain social networks of support and connection.

Food, Ethnic Identity, and Gender

A discussion of the religious importance of food in this setting inevitably leads to questions about gender roles. Who is preparing all of this food that is so generously offered? Who is baking the cookies and making the coffee? Martyn, a retired fisherman, prepared the delicious meal for the dinner party. In this particular household, this is quite common; his wife

23. Ibid.
24. Ibid.

Rosa still works full time, and Martyn likes to cook. In fact, one of the "saving graces" of the fishing occupation, from the point of view of some women, is that the men who spent so much time away at sea were forced to learn to cook, and many of them became quite good at it—at least at preparing fish. Men in this setting also prepare pizza, and sometimes do "heavy" cooking tasks such as frying squid or grilling other entrees for large-scale devotional events or fund-raising dinners. Still, by and large, I have the impression that it is the women who do much of the daily food preparation, and most of the baking.

The preparation of food is also inevitably mixed up with constructions of ethnicity in this setting. We can get a glimpse of these intertwining issues by looking at the stories of three women, ages forty-four to fifty-one, who are all good friends, and who are all connected to this community of devout whether through family, marriage, and/or their own devotional practices. Lisa, a member of the "two-thirds" generation (second generation by one parent, third by the other), exemplifies unusual zeal about matters of food preparation in relation to her constructions of motherhood. Lisa, forty-four, says of herself:

> I am an *intense* mother. . . . *I* make my children's breakfast, *I* make
> their lunches, and *I* make their dinner. I make dinner five nights
> a week. I feel they need the nutrition, I cook fresh fish, fresh veg-
> etables, so they get vitamins. We have dinner together every night.
> And it's hard because of my husband's business. He rarely gets
> home before seven or seven-thirty. My kids say, 'Mom, I'm hun-
> gry.' I say, 'Have a snack.' It's important that we wait for him.[25]

Some of Lisa's intensity about waiting for her husband to come home for supper may be related to the painful experiences that both she and her husband endured as children, when their fathers who were fishermen were often away at sea. But Lisa's intensity around food preparation itself is also quite striking. Lisa is a working mother. She teaches language arts and science in a grammar school in a neighboring town. Given her job, it cannot be easy for her to prepare all of her children's meals.

When I questioned her about this, she said, "I feel I have an obliga-tion to be the best mother I can be." Lisa linked her rigorous habits of meal preparation to her Italian ethnic identity and the importance of family. "We have pasta on Sundays. That's when the whole (extended) family gets

25. Interview #25.

together," she adds. Lisa's food preparation, her religious practice, and her construction of her ethnicity are all quite deliberate. "You have to work at being a Catholic," she says, "It's not easy." Lisa works at being Italian, too. She did not grow up in a family that was nearly as "traditional" as the one she is dedicated to creating. For example, Lisa learned to speak Italian—which she does fluently—at age 21, when she got married, so that she could communicate with her in-laws. She also told me that she chose to marry a man of Italian descent. "I consciously did it to carry on the Italian heritage," she claims.[26] She and her husband also choose to do business with Italians when possible. Their children's orthodontist is Italian, as are their favorite grocers. Lisa goes on at great length about the delicacies that she purchases at the Italian market. I gain the impression that close family ties, strong ethnic identity, and committed Catholic faith are of a piece for Lisa. Food is the substance that holds them all together.

The work of Micaela di Leonardo, an anthropologist who studied Italians in northern California, is helpful as we think about Lisa's story. Di Leonardo's 1984 study adroitly deconstructs the myth of the Italian family, laying clear the ways that gender is inscribed in popular constructions of Italian ethnicity.[27] In particular, she shows how the work involved in maintaining ethnic kinship networks—such as cooking traditional foods for extended family gatherings and caring for elderly relatives—almost always falls disproportionately to women. Di Leonardo points out that the labor of maintaining ethnic identity is really an extension of the regular work of kinship—including organizing holiday gatherings, sending cards, giving presents, and preparing meals—that usually falls disproportionately to women, whether they identify themselves as ethnic or not.[28] Ethnic constructions of womanhood tend to add to women's kinship labor, especially in the area of cooking. In her study, di Leonardo found a great variety in women's patterns of taking on, rejecting, or compromising with the mass media image of the ideal Italian woman who cooks for and serves her family.[29]

26. Interview #25.

27. di Leonardo, *Varieties of Ethnic Experience.*

28. Ibid., 228.

29. "The Italian-American women in this study have embraced, modified, and rejected this dominant image of ethnic life. These women, like all American women, live in a society that is simultaneously class-stratified and patriarchal. They deal variously with class and gender divisions. Ethnicity is a further filter on this process; but for women in particular,

Lisa's story demonstrates the role of choice in ethnic identity in a striking way. She is a woman who has embraced the dominant popular image of the good Italian wife and mother. She did not inherit this as a "cultural characteristic," nor did she model herself after her own mother, a successful real estate agent who did not go to church. Lisa has chosen this ethnic and religious identity and her zealous habits of food preparation for her own reasons. We could speculate about what these reasons might be, but we cannot explain it simply as "culture." Lisa chooses this family-centered way of life, in which she finds joy and fulfillment. She chooses skills and styles available in what Anne Swidler might call a cultural "tool kit," in order to fashion a meaningful and satisfying life.[30]

Lisa's ethnic identity, which she maintains so scrupulously through preparing meals and hosting large-scale gatherings at her home, imposes burdens on her. For example, Lisa has raised her children with almost no reliance on baby-sitters, in deference to what she perceives to be "the Italian way." She does all the childcare herself. She also regularly visits her godmother in a nursing home, and has already promised her in-laws that they will never have to go to a nursing home, because Lisa and her husband are planning to take them into their home when the time comes. Another example of the labor burden of ethnic maintenance has to do with entertaining. Lisa says that she prefers to throw large parties at home, rather than in restaurants, because it gives more of a "family feeling." While Lisa's commitment to ethnic maintenance is no doubt made easier by her family's affluence, nevertheless, Lisa's ideal requires that she do much of the kinship labor herself. The burdens of domestic and kinship labor that Lisa very enthusiastically embraces are considerable.

The other women in Lisa's circle experience burdens, too, though they do not choose the same model that Lisa does. Lisa's two good friends who are also teachers, Josephine and Joanna, employ two alternative approaches. Josephine, whom we met in chapter 2, was brought to this country as a baby. In her immigrant family of origin, she is the best English speaker and the only one who went to college. She therefore assumes the role that usually falls to second-generation children—that of interpreting for parents, and handling all of the family's financial and legal matters.

---

just (as) for the population as a whole, there are varieties of ethnic experience." di Leonardo, *Varieties of Ethnic Experience*, 229. For two other treatments of the role of choice in ethnic identity, see Waters, *Ethnic Options*; and Leonard, *Making Ethnic Choices*.

30. Swidler, "Culture in Action," 273–86.

Josephine is married to a man she met in Sicily, and who then immigrated to this country. Early on in her marriage, for a period of seven years, Josephine's husband's brother moved in with them, causing Josephine's domestic duties to expand. Josephine and her husband have two teenage children now, and live comfortably. Josephine is extremely active in the devotions at Mary Star, where she serves as the vice-president of the Trapetto Club, a "small" society of one hundred or so members devoted to the Madonna del Ponte—Our Lady of the Bridge. Josephine teaches high school Spanish, which she sees as an extension of her ethnic identity as a European. She is also dedicated to teaching youth as much as possible about Italian culture, and even took a high school group on a tour of Italy a few years ago.

When I went to her home to interview Josephine on a Saturday afternoon, I noticed several large plates of brownies and cakes on her immaculate kitchen counter. She had baked these for an outing of the Trapetto Club, scheduled for the following day. Large bouquets of flowers were also lined up in her living room for the event. I was impressed by the amount of work that Josephine's participation in the devotions entails. Her preparation of food for these events, as well as her actual participation in them, consumes numerous hours. Josephine has thought a great deal about Italian culture, change, and women's roles. Though she is proud of her education and her profession, and claims she can draw from both Italian and American cultures, she also indicates an awareness of the additional strain that this cultural negotiation places on her. She sometimes wonders about the wisdom of taking on what amounts to double the work of the other women in her family, through her bi-cultural identity. "They're just happy with their own little small circle of life," she says of these women. "They don't worry about the environment. The more you know, the more you worry."[31]

Josephine is glad to have some of what she calls "American values." She says that she and her husband make decisions together. She appreciates what she sees as increased power in the context of her marriage. But she worries about the breakdown of the American family, and admits that dinner time around her house is often "up in the air." Though she prays every night, her family's attendance at Mass is "up and down" because she is so busy. When someone in her family needs help, she says, "Because the

31. Interview #16.

guilt is so heavy, I drop everything and go."[32] Josephine's constructions of her cultural identity as being American in one way and Italian in another give her some wiggle room—she says she can take the best from each culture. She is not as dogmatic about meal preparation or church attendance as her friend Lisa is. But Josephine's prominent role in her extended family and her vigorous participation in the devotional societies add considerable burdens of time, energy, and labor to her life. She is aware of the strain. As she put it in an interview with a different researcher, "Trying to be a modern wife in traditional society is hard."[33]

The third friend in this trio of teachers is Joanna, the daughter of Susan and Rocco, mentioned earlier in this chapter. Joanna is a third-generation woman whose parents are Italian and Sicilian. She is fiercely proud of what she calls her "heritage," in spite of the jokes that people inevitably make linking Sicilians to organized crime.[34] Joanna celebrates her Italian and Sicilian heritage through foodways, and by having a large elaborate extended family gathering in her home every Christmas Eve. She also credits her parents' Italian values for the emphasis she places on children and family. For example, Joanna is married to a non-Italian, "a real WASP," in her words. She feels his mother was always a little bit prejudiced against her for being Italian. This is clearly painful for Joanna to acknowledge. Nevertheless, now that her mother-in-law is elderly and needs frequent care, Joanna and her husband—more than any of his three siblings—have taken it upon themselves to stay nearby geographically and to provide as much care for her as they can. Joanna calls this commitment "Italian values."[35]

Joanna is the woman I quoted in chapter 1 who asked me whether I had "the guilt." She acknowledges that she feels guilty about one thing: not raising her sons in the church. This is because, unlike her friends, Joanna stopped going to church at Mary Star when she was seventeen. An excellent

32. Ibid.

33. Turley, "Development of Italian Women's Identity."

34. Josephine's sixteen-year-old son was nearby during the interview, so we asked him what he would say if some one asked him about his ethnic identity. He replied by noting that on the SAT forms, they don't have a box for Italians or Sicilians, so he checks "white." On the school soccer field, where kids regularly form teams based on ethnic and racial identity, he also doesn't quite fit. "There's a Mexican team and an Italian team," he said. "But I told them I'm not Italian, I'm Sicilian. So they put me on the white team," he laughed. Interview #21.

35. Interview #21.

high-school student, trained in science, she had begun questioning many things about her faith. But what really pushed the scales over for Joanna was a sermon that a priest preached on Mother's Day. She explained,

> I would really listen to the sermons and they'd make me angry. Every Sunday it'd make me angry. I was seventeen. It was Mother's Day. Father Logan got up there and started talkin' about the Virgin Mary; on and on about her being a virgin. On Mother's Day! I looked at my mother and said, "Do you realize he's calling you a whore?" She said, "Don't listen, honey. Just don't listen." That was it. I never went to Mass again.[36]

Joanna's comments reveal one of her mother's coping strategies that could be called resistance. Is this how she herself has been coping with sermons that offend, by just not listening? Does she feel the freedom to ignore church teachings with which she disagrees? And has she communicated this capacity to resist to her daughter, Joanna? Joanna said she couldn't stand "the hypocrisy, the insensitivity, the ignorance!" of the priest. She perceived his words as an affront to women. When she decided to leave the church, Joanna said her mother was "hurt, but not devastated." I wonder if her mother might have also been a little bit proud.

Joanna has rejected the institutional Catholic Church, but she told me that she still considers herself a Catholic, as much as she considers herself Italian. She says it's a way of thinking, a way of being that has stuck with her. Her guilt comes from knowing that she has something to fall back on, while her children do not. She says of this, "When I'm in need, I lean on prayer. When I've done everything I can logically do. I don't practice organized religion, but I resort to prayer when I have a health problem. It's hypocritical, but it's part of my being."[37] It is a part of her being that Joanna values, and finds comfort in. Her guilt comes from feeling that her sons won't have access to that source of comfort in the same way that she does.

Joanna tells me that she did make some attempts to bring her sons up in the church. She said, "When your kids are born, you get all those mother hormones." Those "hormones" apparently led Joanna to have her boys baptized. Or maybe she was hedging her bets on her scientific constructions of the universe: she also put crucifixes in her babies' rooms, and pinned red ribbons with baby medals on their layette suits for the

36. Ibid.
37. Ibid.

first three months of life—"to ward off jealousy or whatever it is."[38] Later, Joanna gave Mary Star another try, on behalf of her sons. She took them to C.C.D. (Confraternity of Christian Doctrine) classes. In fact, she sat in with them for four years when they took these classes, to see what they were being taught. But she never returned to the church.

These three women demonstrate the variety of ethnic and religious experience, even within my small sample. Joanna, more than the others, has consciously rejected the "insensitive" Catholic constructions of Mary as the ideal woman. But she does construct her identity as an Italian woman who values family above all else, a view that requires considerable kinship labor to maintain. Joanna seems less caught in the complexities of negotiating her cultural ideals, and somewhat less burdened by extra work. Still, there is that guilt.

While these three friends have arrived at different compromises in the degree to which they accept, revise, or reject the dominant construction of the good Italian Catholic woman, none of them strike me as being hoodwinked into a groveling conformity. They all exhibit some forms of resistance to official church teachings. And they all exercise some freedom in regard to their ethnic and religious practices. Because these women all went to college and entered teaching professions, they actually do have a broader range of choices open to them than their mothers did. They are also all more financially comfortable than their mothers were. Nevertheless, all of these women work hard at being "good mothers" to their own children and actively involve themselves in helping members of their extended families as well. And of course, they cook. These women are artists of ethnic maintenance and improvisation, who live out their ideals with commitment, skill, and enthusiasm. Less easy to measure are the costs, in terms of time, energy, and stress, that such deeply rooted and demanding ideals exact.

San Pietro Dinner Dance

The importance of food, ethnic constructions of gender roles, and even some of the conflict that the community experiences in relation to devotional practices were all in evidence at a fundraising dinner held in the Mary Star auditorium. This event contrasts rather sharply with the Saint Joseph's Table Feast that I described at the beginning of this chapter. Held

38. Interview #21.

in the same space a mere month later, and involving many of the same people, this event reveals both change and resistance in attitudes toward food, wealth, and gender roles.

I had no idea of what I was getting into when I decided to go to this dinner. It was unlike any event I had ever experienced, especially in the category of church fund-raising suppers. I was surprised, at first, by the turnout. I had thought that it might be slim, given the thirty-dollar per-person ticket price. I needn't have worried. I arrived to find a large crowd of extremely well-dressed people milling outside near the door. The Italian band, again led by Tony De Bruno, was already in full swing when I arrived. A busy cash bar was in operation, selling mixed drinks. The bar was set up directly under a banner featuring the words "San Pietro Society" and a picture of the saint, holding the familiar keys to the kingdom. I wondered if anyone else present saw any irony in this arrangement of a cash bar under the fisherman-saint.

My co-researcher for the evening, Josephine, was already inside, scrambling along with perhaps four hundred others for a place at a table near family and friends. The room was lavishly decorated. Fabric tablecloths covered the twenty long tables on either side of the room, and a huge centerpiece rested on each one. The centerpieces were ceramic models of fishing boats, with a lone fisherman in each one. The pieces were all hand-painted by a local artist, and each one was slightly different. These objects were on sale, for one hundred and fifty dollars each.

The large, noisy crowd soon began to form a line near the *hors d'oeuvres* table. The table featured huge platters of *bruschette*, olives, marinated mushrooms, fresh tomatoes, sliced cheeses, salami, ham, and two forms of squid—a cold salad and fried *calamari*. Amidst the noise and confusion, I saw many people that I knew, and was greeted with fond recognition and warm embraces. Eventually, Josephine and I found our way through the line and then to our places at a table. I asked Josephine how many people in the room spoke Italian. She guessed 99.9%. It occurred to me that the size and vitality of the Italian-speaking population in San Pedro is rather unusual in North America these days.[39] I listened to the music of the

---

39. Estimates indicate that there are about 45,000 Americans of Italian descent in San Pedro. Luisa Del Guidice of the Italian Oral History Institute comments that the small stream of continuing immigration constitutes something of a "brain drain" in Italy. Interestingly, she notes that there is also some return migration going on. Personal e-mail correspondence, February 8, 2001.

various dialects that I heard spoken throughout the evening, doing my best to keep up with the conversation.

There is undoubtedly conflict in this large and lively group, and some of it came to the surface in the conversation around my table at the dinner-dance. It started with a critique of the centerpieces. I was told that simple centerpieces would have been better, so that more money could go to the church. "The San Pietro Society wants to show off," was the refrain of some members of the more modest Saint Joseph Society. People then scanned the evening's program, and pointed out that nearly every item on the elaborate menu—from shrimp to steaks to tiramisu—had been donated. They estimated that the San Pietro Society would clear upwards of twelve thousand dollars on the dinner, not counting the money from the sale of drinks or raffle tickets. But when the pastor arrived to offer his blessing before the meal, he was presented with a check for five thousand dollars for the church's ongoing financial campaign to build a new high school. The pastor accepted the money graciously, but my tablemates sneered. "Why do they not give more? They keep the money for a long time," said one woman, who expressed the opinion that the San Pietro Society is entirely too fancy, and not dedicated enough to the church. This is a point of contention that I heard discussed many times. Several other individuals expressed hurt feelings over the leadership of this young society, its lavish style, and its independent banking habits.

I wondered if these were class issues, or if the tensions were possibly related to generational styles. It is interesting to note that humility is still invested with social capital for some. Others, I think, are proud of their wealth, and happy for a chance to display and celebrate it. The issue of regional differences also occurred to me. For example, could this stress be a remnant of older tensions between the Sicilian immigrants and those from Ischia? Yet there appear to be no firm lines of division between the members these groups. Many of the same people attend all of these functions. Many also prefer not to take sides in this debate, but just to enjoy the festivities. In any case, the drama of the evening soon drowned out the conflict, at least at my table.

Suddenly, with a musical flourish to introduce them, about a dozen women servers, dressed in identical flowing royal blue evening gowns, streamed down the center of the auditorium. They were each holding two fish-shaped bottles of wine high in the air, one red and one white. People responded audibly to the excitement of their entrance. The women hastened to place the bottles on each table, as some applauded and others hummed their approval. The feast had begun, and these women were at the center of it, seeming to enjoy the fanfare and their central role. But I was surprised to see that these women continued to serve the entire dinner throughout the evening. Though they used serving carts to help them, I felt concerned because some of the women were older, and I knew that at least one of them had recently been ill. I could see how hard they were working, and wondered at the fact that no one was helping the older women hand off the huge platters of steaming pasta. When the folks at the tables clamored for more food, the women ran, in their royal blue high heels, to refill the platters.

I winced at this display of female servitude. I knew that men had helped cook the dinner as they had otherwise helped plan and carry off the event. I knew there were men working in the kitchen. But women only performed this serving ritual. Their flowing dresses called attention to the female form. It seemed clear to me that this feature of the ritual was enacting and displaying painfully patriarchal divisions of labor.

I asked the pastor about this later. Did he think that these rituals helped to reinforce prescribed gender roles? He replied rather curtly that the men do more of the cooking than the women do at Mary Star. Of course, this answer does not address the role of women as servers. Also, I was not convinced that the pastor's assessment was entirely accurate. (Was he counting the cookie-baking?) His comments suggest that the men at Mary Star do routinely take on at least some of the labor of food preparation. Nevertheless, this ritualized public event was enacting and celebrating a traditional gender ideal of women serving men.

This evening expressed a joy in feasting and friendship that I find quite remarkable. The eating and drinking, dancing and conversation went on well into the night. The people engaged in feisty discussions and continued to comment on the food, the decor, and program throughout the evening. In spite of their disagreements, or maybe because of them, people were having a great time. Among friends and family, they were free to argue and critique each other's styles. But the general tenor of the evening was jovial and warm. The people were celebrating their faith, their language, their success, and their contested styles. They were also raising money for their church, and they were doing this all through the medium of food—food that was elaborately prepared, bountifully served, and heartily consumed. In their peculiarly Italian, immigrant, and Catholic ways, they were breaking bread together.

In the epilogue to her ground-breaking book about the religious meaning of food in the later Middle Ages, Caroline Walker Bynum suggests, "Perhaps we should not turn our backs so resolutely as we have recently done on . . . food and the female body as positive, complex, and resonant symbols of love and generosity."[40] It seems to me that food functions as a resonant symbol of love and generosity in the devotional practices in San Pedro. While these practices do enact traditional gender roles, the devout women here also exhibit resistance, variation, and innovation as they use food to construct their ethnic and religious identities.

Food, the substance without which human beings cannot live, is invested with sacred value in this place. Through large-scale feasts such as Saint Joseph's Table, or fund-raising dinner dances, the goodness of food and the human body are enshrined. Through regular hospitality practices, and through extensive food provision ministries, the devout and their descendants sustain themselves and others, body and soul. As in the braided loaves of sesame bread on Saint Joseph's table, the significance of food, family, survival, ethnic identity, and Catholic faith are interwoven. This community's shared practices proclaim that food is good, that life is good, and that God is always present at the table.

40. Bynum, *Holy Feast and Holy Fast*, 301.

PART TWO

PRACTICE, TRANSFORMATION, AND
RELIGIOUS IMAGINATION

5

Holding On, Letting Go, and Being Held

> The worth of a religious life depends ultimately not on what can be
> conceived but on what can be embodied.
>
> —Margaret Miles, *Practicing Christianity*

> Nor is it necessary to be theologically self-conscious to be reli-
> giously sophisticated.
>
> —Clifford Geertz, *The Interpretation of Cultures*

IN Part Two of this book, we shift our approach toward more a more explicit theological reflection upon practice, transformation, and religious
imagination. Broadly speaking, the case study reveals ways in which the
devout and their descendants hold on to their devotions, let go of them,
and/or find themselves feeling "held" by religious bonds that they had
long forgotten. Through a turn to a more interpretative reflection, we can
unlock some of the religious sophistication, situated values, and practical
wisdom of the devout. Where is God in these practices? My aim is not
to idealize the devout or their ways, nor to judge them, but to encounter
them as religious human beings, people of Christian faith, who are making their way with skill, wisdom, and wit as well as with blind spots and
blunders. Like many religious practices, the devotions reveal life-giving
and transformative potential, as well as limiting and harmful possibilities.

The religious ties and binds of Italian and Sicilian immigrants in
San Pedro suggest a dynamic interplay among immigration, identity, and
religious imagination. The practical knowledges embedded in devotional
practice in this setting are situated and specific; they only make sense
in context. At the same time, there are pastoral theological issues and
dynamics bound into these faith practices that have their analogues in

diverse communities and congregations. Reflecting on this case study can enliven and enlarge our own religious imaginations, and hopefully inform and enhance pastoral practices in other settings. I particularly hope that insights from this case study can be helpful to those in ministry who seek to engage in pastoral relationships with members of various cultural and immigrant groups.

So how do religious ties and binds *work* in the context of our historical circumstances, psychological narratives, and social interactions? All religious life involves inherited traditions, images, institutions, and language. These give substance, shape, and form to our religious experiences. Yet we also contribute to the traditions, images, structures, practices, and metaphors that comprise religious life. Every time we practice faith, we are also actively constructing it. We are changing traditions even when we think we are just handing them on. Knowingly or unknowingly, subtly or substantially, we shape our religious practices, changing them even as they are forming or transforming us.

The title of pastoral theologian Elaine Graham's book, *Transforming Practice*, has at least two meanings. One of them has to do with the power of practice to transform and shape human beings. This first meaning is similar to Alaisdair MacIntyre's definition of practice as " . . . coherent and cooperative human activity through which goods internal to that activity are realized in the course of trying to achieve excellence in that activity . . ."[1] Faithful practices can instill virtue, according to MacIntyre. Engaging in such practices can change us and remake us.

The other meaning of Graham's title alludes to the power of human beings to creatively transform their practices. We are shaped by, and shapers of religious practice. Practice and *habitus* reveal the embodied values of a group.[2] In light of these things, our next task is to look more carefully at the practices described here, in order to unearth, understand, and interpret the theologies they proclaim. Let me begin by explaining the concepts of "practice" and *habitus* in a bit more detail and illustrating them in the local setting.

---

1. MacIntyre, *After Virtue*, 175.

2. Graham depends here on Pierre Bourdieu's concept of *habitus* as both "handed down and re-interpreted anew for every generation." Graham, *Transforming Practice*, 95.

Practice

What is practice, anyway? Practice, according to sociologist Pierre Bourdieu, is structured behavior that follows certain rules or patterns.[3] It is purposeful activity performed by persons who are "both the subjects of agency and the objects of history."[4] Along these lines, Graham writes, "Members of society contribute to the active construction of the social order; but they are simultaneously situated in a world of pre-existing structures, representations, and conventions."[5]

The devotional practices that I have described in San Pedro include numerous examples of the way this works. We can find many purposeful activities that follow certain rules or patterns. Take the practice of looking at religious art and artifacts, described in chapter 2. This activity is purposeful in that the devout choose to direct their gaze toward any one of a myriad of saints while praying, or to restrict it, as some do, to a particular representation of Mary or to the crucifix in the church sanctuary. The donation of works of art such as the large marble statue of Mary holding a purse seiner also illustrates purpose and agency—in this case, the agency of the laity in shaping the visual environment of the public worship space. The agency and power exercised in the practice of donating artifacts should not be under-estimated. As we have seen, this enormous image, viewed regularly as the object of devotion, has had a profound impact upon the identity and faith of worshippers in this setting. While many outsiders may think of Catholic churches as top-down structures, run by a clerical hierarchy through he authority of local priests, here is an example of the agency of the laity in bringing this grand image of Mary to the visual center of the sacred space. This may be seen as the exertion of the financial power and theological influence of the donor; it may also be viewed as a subversive expression of popular faith triumphing over "official" Catholic theologies that now downplay Marian devotion. The relatively small crucifix, relegated to a spot off to the right side of the chancel, is dwarfed by Mary's size and location. The feminine face of God, long suppressed as secondary in Catholic teaching and repressed completely in traditional Protestant formulations, stands boldly in the center. This statue not only

---

3. Bourdieu, *Outline of a Theory of Practice*.
4. Graham, *Transforming Practice*, 98.
5. Ibid.

expresses something of the theological impulses of the donor, it has also been wordlessly shaping theological sensibilities of the parish ever since.[6]

In homes as well, we saw evidence of purposeful decisions regarding the choice and number of religious images displayed. In some homes, these images were plentiful, as in the case of the woman who described her home by saying, "Everywhere you turn you see God." In other homes the use of images was more discreet, confined to a holy card on a bedroom mirror or a single brass crucifix at the back door of the home. People also chose the particular images they wanted placed in their line of vision, such as a patron saint from their town in Italy, or a portrait of Mary hanging over the bed. In the later generations, the combination of items from diverse religious traditions, such as the Native American dream catcher with portraits of guardian angels, demonstrates the range of purposeful and innovative ways in which visual piety may be practiced. In these cases, devotional piety is probably undergoing more profound change.[7] In selecting artwork and artifacts for their churches and homes, individuals influence the make-up of both ecclesiastic and domestic spaces, thus contributing to the ongoing construction of social reality.

At the same time, all of these persons and all of their choices are also "situated in a world of pre-existing structures, representations, and conventions."[8] At this level, the practice or habit of visual piety is not entirely chosen. This practice has a given quality because the habit of looking at pictures of Mary or the saints has been so regular and ordinary in this setting. The practice is so prevalent that it can be considered a formative influence on children from the time of their birth, reinforced in home and church and school, as well as through gift-giving for key life-cycle celebrations, such as Confirmations, graduations, or weddings. In these settings, especially for children, it is not possible to escape seeing or "being seen" by these representations. The emotional import of these religious images and their conservative power are underscored by their association with beloved parents or grandparents, with natal lands, and with the sacralized

6. Geographer Neil Smith writes: "The production of space also implies the production of meaning, concepts and consciousness of space which are inseparably linked to its physical production." Cited in Chidester and Linenthal, *American Sacred Space*, 12.

7. Chidester and Linenthal write, "The strategy of hybridization, found in practices of mixing, fusing, or transgressing conventional spatial relations, presents 'the possibility of shifting *the very terms of the system itself.*'" *American Sacred Space*, 19, citing Stallybrass and White, *Politics and Poetics of Transgression*, 58.

8. Graham, *Transforming Practice*, 98.

new land. The pre-existing structures of devotional Catholic worldviews are re-enforced well through visual piety.

The devout and their children and grandchildren may hold onto items such as rosaries, relics, or holy cards, or let go of them. They may keep the items long after they have consciously discarded the worldviews that the artifacts recall. Nevertheless, the appeal and attraction of religious images may well remain with the descendants of the devout. Some persons brought up in this environment will sometimes feel "held" by memories, ideas, and impressions of the holy that have a deep, unchanging quality. Third-generation Sarah is a good example. When she speaks of her current experience of religious compassion, she associates that feeling with her childhood experience of regularly seeing Mary Star's Pietà-like statue of Mary holding Jesus in her arms. Though Sarah rarely attends this church now, she spontaneously prays for people when she feels this kind of compassion. Though Sarah's faith is clearly altered in significant ways, to designate her a "non-practicing" Catholic would almost certainly be to misname her. Her skilled practice of visual piety remains with her, shaping her even as she dramatically reshapes it.

Habitus

When religious practices such as visual piety or ritual processions become regular or habitual, they constitute features of the *habitus*. With Graham, I find Bourdieu's definition of the *habitus* the most helpful: "The *habitus*—embodied history, internalized as a second nature and so forgotten as history—is the active presence of the whole past of which it is the product."[9] Again, when we think of the pervasive presence of images of the saints in homes and in church, and comments that the devout made such as, "It's just the way it was—I didn't think about it," we can get a good sense of the *habitus* in this setting. The *habitus* also encompasses other aspects of the sense-worlds of Italian Catholics in San Pedro: the sights of fishing boats along the shore, and views of the shoreline itself (Figure 41 and Figure 42), reminiscent for some of Naples or nearby islands; the smells of fish or pasta cooking; the sounds of Italian dialects being spoken or favorite hymns to Mary being sung. When these familiar sights and sounds are bound up with religious practices, they help to convey and reinforce religious bonds

9. Bourdieu, *Logic of Practice*, 56, cited in Graham, *Transforming Practice*, 103.

through bodily memories, shared social experiences, and stories told about these experiences.

But the *habitus* is not fixed or final. Building on Bourdieu, Graham writes, "*Habitus* is thus conceived as the residuum of past actions, a deposit of past knowledge and practice, but which is always available as the raw material for creative agency or 'regulated improvisations.'"[10] Devotional practices in this setting show themselves to be both the residuum of past actions, yet always changing, changing even in the process of reproduction. The devotion to Saint Joseph is a good example of both the conservative and open-ended features of the *habitus*. The leaders of Saint Joseph's Society emphasize that their ritual feast is a "tradition," firmly rooted in the oldest Sicilian ritual. At the same time, the current San Pedro feast also incorporates certain "regulated improvisations." The fancy lights surrounding the saint are one example of a contemporary improvisation, possibly influenced by the proximity of Hollywood, and the common experience of sighting these strings of small lights around town in Los Angeles and other Southern Californian cities. These lights are regularly used as decorations of both interior and exterior spaces. The lights are visible to the public on storefronts, in restaurants, on palm trees. In this case, we might say that the ritual has absorbed a stylistic feature of the *habitus* of the Southern California. The religious tradition has been changed in such a way as to make it more appealing to local tastes. This is not to claim that the change was intentional or calculated. But the change demonstrates the way in which religious rituals, even traditional processions brought over from the "old country" and laden with conservative meanings, do shift when they are performed.

The Italian band that plays both Italian and American national anthems is another example of regulated improvisation. Both of these anthems are, of course, infused with emotional significance to the immigrants. The translocative quality of the immigrants' religion, the way in which faith functions as bridge between the old land and the new, is particularly evident in this use of music. American nationalistic sentiments have been easily grafted into the religious "tradition," giving it more emotional power. This innovation is made with ease, perhaps because these sentiments "fit" so well with the conservative nature of the ritual. Melodies and lyrics stir old memories and recall a sense of rootedness that

10. Ibid., 109.

encompasses the immigrant saga, affirming the consequential choice to come here, leaving birthplaces and loved ones behind. At the same time hearing and singing the anthems re-asserts remembered values such as loyalty, order, and obedience. A simple, but also complex sense of self and its relation to social and geographic space and place are invoked and expressed in the use of these anthems in the ritual. The activities of playing, hearing, and singing not one national anthem but two, in the context of a feast day ritual in the auditorium of this important church, both sacralize an enormous change—moving from there to here—and help to re-inscribe significant memories of former times and places into current identities. The ritual thus helps forge, renew, or invigorate personal and shared memories of the past, creating a strong sense of coherence in lives that have been irreparably fragmented.

Perhaps because of the human need for coherence in the face of contingency, the *habitus*, though not fixed, is sturdy. Bourdieu calls it the "durably installed generative principle of regulated improvisations."[11] Traditional values, such as the love of country, or the authority of the priest, are enshrined in the Saint Joseph ritual, revealing and reinforcing a hierarchical social order. At the same time, many participants in this ritual are individuals who have made enormous changes in their own lives by leaving home, defying the power of the familiar in favor of some vision of a better life. Among the participants are also those who at times challenge or disregard the authority of the priest and by extension, the church. Thus the people embody the paradox of union and separation that Winnicott said marks all of our lives: we are bound and we are free. The *habitus* and its conventions are constantly being challenged and resisted, but the residuum of past knowledge is weighty. In this case, the power of social structure coexists in tension with the individual and collective human agency of the immigrants and their descendants. The ritual asserts the emotionally powerful ties that bind these persons to their families, their friends, their church, and their origins in other times and places.

Transformation

So how does change take place? What makes transformation possible? If the residuum of the past, the *habitus*, is so weighty, how can we move beyond it? If improvisations are regulated, and structures of knowledge are so

11. Bourdieu, *Outline of a Theory of Practice*, 57.

durably installed, it is perhaps no wonder that resistance to social change is so common and formidable. Yet in biblical faith, there is great impetus for social change and spiritual transformation. The prophetic tradition of the Hebrew scriptures is one that calls people forth from bondage, and into lives of freedom and promise. The Christian gospel, also, challenges the status quo of political injustice and social marginalization. Theological reflection on these scriptures always entails an emphasis on how faith is lived and practiced in the world. Pastoral theology is concerned with transformation, involving personal and communal empowerment and holistic striving for a more just social order.

Still, we wonder, how can we help inspire change? According to Graham and other pastoral theologians who embrace an approach called "theology-in-action," we—meaning communities of faith—can effect change by identifying the religious values embedded in practices, and by taking part in new practices through which the community might re-order its life.[12] Importantly for Graham, "engagement in new practices gives rise to new knowledge."[13] Transformation depends not only on new ideas, or even on the determination of faithful people to "practice what you preach." It also works the other way around. Altering religious practices can create the capacity for spiritual and social change.

This concept is not new—it goes back to Aristotle. But in numerous seminaries and sermons, the idea of "applied theology" still holds sway. The assumption is that thought precedes and determines actions. Seminary students are still often taught that theology should precede (if not dictate) pastoral care. But Aristotle saw, and Thomas Aquinas appropriated for Christians, a different kind of logic at work in human living. The Aristotelian concept of practical knowledge or *phronēsis* is key. Elaine Graham helps unpack this concept, which "locates truth in enacted or performative knowledge."[14] Transformation can happen in relationship to two kinds of enacted or performative knowledge: first, in the acquiring of a new technical skill or bodily knowledge (such as playing the lyre or building something), hence the phrase, "practice makes perfect." Second, in realms of the spiritual or emotional, such as when one reads a poem or listens to a story, new insights can emerge that may transform future

---

12. Graham et al., *Theological Reflection: Methods*, 170–99.

13. Graham, *Transforming Practices*, 99.

14. Ibid., 7.

experience. Authors of Christian devotional manuals throughout the ages have long known that engagement in religious practices can give way to new insights, new faith.[15] We are transformed when we take new actions and "live into" new realties.

In the San Pedro case study, an illustration of such transformation is found in the story of Matthew (chapters 2 and 4), whose discovery of the writings of the Dalai Lama in high school led him to engage in the new practice of Buddhist meditation. This practice subsequently disclosed new realms of meaning, expanding his view of God and inspiring a different understanding of his Catholic practices as well. But note that even in this case, the *habitus* is "durably installed." While Matthew's world-view and devotional practices have expanded enormously, he still experiences them as tied to the strong faith and identity that he absorbed from his parents and grandparents. His practice of visual piety has been altered, but not replaced, by Buddhist practices, as the large complex altar in his living room demonstrates (Figures 27–29). The Dalai Lama is pictured there with Thomas Merton, whose writings Matthew first learned of through his grandmother. The durable quality of Matthew's *habitus* can also be seen in his commitment to a religious feeding ministry, though the fact that he instituted this program at Trinity Church rather than Mary Star, the church he grew up in, is another example of regulated improvisation.

What is important to notice here, from a pastoral theological point of view, is that it is Matthew's strong (in his words, "inescapable") ties to the *habitus* of his youth that help make his adult innovations so compelling. This recalls Winnicott's comment, noted in chapter 2, "In any cultural field, it is not possible to be original except on the basis of tradition."[16] The ability to be, in Graham's words, "creative, subversive, inspirational or prophetic,"[17] does not come to human beings from outside of our personal and social historical situations but through engagement with them.

Practical Wisdom in San Pedro

The task of contextual pastoral theology is to excavate, articulate, and interpret the accumulated and evolving wisdom of a faith community as it is expressed through practice. Elaine Graham suggests that we imagine

15. See Margaret Miles, *Practicing Christianity*.

16. Winnicott, *Playing and Reality*, 99.

17. Graham, *Transforming Practice*, 109.

Christian practices as "bearers of the living principles of hope and obligation."[18] As I understand her, Graham is calling for critical reflection and interpretation of the community's situated knowledge of God. This is an interpretative rather than a prescriptive task.

So we must ask, in critical a phenomenology of practice, questions such as: How are "healing and redemption experienced and/or prefigured through these practices?" Are these excavated values "appropriate for the complexity and diversity of human experience" in this setting? What are the "effects and traces of God" that the devotional practices suggest?[19] What aspects of the devotions lead to (disclose) transformation? What is foreclosed by these practices and shared values?

In my view, the transcendent power of the holy is always found embedded in cultural particularity. There is no unmediated knowledge of God. Therefore we cannot impose one final view of God on a particular community. Stephen Ward writes, ". . . the divine will reveal itself in ways which interact with human powers of imagination, reflection, and conceptual understanding. Therefore we will not expect one clear, decisive, certain revelation."[20] In our work of excavation and theological reflection, we are looking for "effects and traces" of the transcendent. We are looking for ways of being that glorify God and birth life-giving bonds of connection between and among us. These ways will always be fallible and our viewpoints partial. Nevertheless, we look for glimmers of transformation and hope. We look for creative forms of pastoral practice in one setting that can inform and enlarge our visions of ministry elsewhere.

Graham speaks of excavating values enshrined in practices. I hesitate to adopt the term "values," given past trends in immigration history that saw cultural values as fixed attributes of various ethnic and national groups.[21] For lack of a better term, however, I will refer to "situated values" or values arising from practice.[22] These situated values are significant themes, like musical notes sounded over and over again throughout my study. They are not universally agreed-on principles, but contested and evolving, dynamic values, born of history, habit, and choice. Three of the

18. Ibid., 111.

19. Ibid., 207–9.

20. Ward, *Vision to Pursue*, 121, cited in Graham, *Transforming Practice*, 207.

21. Steinberg, *Ethnic Myth*. The "culture of poverty" thesis is a case in point (82–127).

22. This term comes from the work of Donna Haraway. See Haraway, *Simians, Cyborgs, and Women*.

situated values that ring out to me from this case study are connection, multiplicity, and celebration. I will turn to a pastoral theological exploration of each in chapters 6, 7, and 8, respectively.

There is a strong, if not overwhelming sense of interpersonal connection between the devout as well as a strong spiritual sense of connection between the people and their religious figures: Mary, Jesus, the Saints, and angels. As we saw in chapter 2, there is a common sense of the divine presence, which is made real through visible and tangible religious representations. The connections between people are also highly valued: the practices of care and mutual aid, the closeness of families and friends, the regular gatherings and frequent conversations. What do we make of all of this togetherness? In what ways has it been empowering and sustaining for people here, and in what ways does it continue to be life-giving? Does the strong sense of connection ever become burdensome or stifling? How may similar dynamics of connection and the dual yearnings for union and separation be tended in diverse faith communities? In chapter 6 we will explore the biblical commandment to love God and neighbor through religious practices that encompass both union and separation.

The striking multiplicity of the angels and saints and their representations that are venerated in San Pedro led me to thinking about divine and human multiplicity. We will reflect on multiplicity as a value that reveals something about God. Mary Star of the Sea Church, as a multicultural congregation, "holds" diverse ethnic groups in dynamic inter-relationships that one woman referred to as a "*minestrone*." Is there a relationship between divine multiplicity and human multiculturalism? What can we learn from this case study about cultural heritage, identity, distance and belonging? As people of many faiths seek to live into more intentional multi-cultural and multi-faith relationships, we would do well to reflect upon the importance of human distinctions, and the inevitable tensions that arise when we try to embrace both unity and diversity. Practical strategies for ministry with multicultural and migrant groups are suggested.

Chapter 8 unearths another significant value in this setting: that of celebration. But how exactly is this a theological value? Protestants, especially, may wonder about aspects of the devotions that seem excessive. After studying the devotions and trying to wrest meaning from them, I have come to view the celebration of life (including its material aspects) as related to the doctrines of creation and incarnation. Lived religion, in the form of celebration, proclaims that life is good, that bodies are good, and that the Holy dwells here, in our earthly habitation.

As Margaret Miles' words noted in the epigraph to this chapter declare, "The worth of a religious life depends ultimately not on what can be conceived but on what can be embodied."[23] In the remaining chapters, I will sketch out some ways in which the embodied wisdom gleaned in the San Pedro case study might enliven our imaginations and help us as we consider what might be embodied through pastoral practice.

23. Miles, *Practicing Christianity*, 85.

6

Connection: Love as Union and Separation

> Blessed be the tie that binds our hearts in Christian Love.
> The fellowship of kindred minds is like to that above.
>
> —John Fawcett, 1872

IN the gospel according to Matthew, a Pharisee asked Jesus which commandment in the law was the greatest. "He answered, 'You shall love the Lord your God with all your heart, with all your soul, and with all your mind.' This is the greatest and first commandment. And a second is like it: 'You shall love your neighbor as yourself.' On these two commandments hang all the law and the prophets."[1] For Jews, Catholics, and Protestants, the love of God and neighbor has been widely considered the core of religious moral obligation.

While the commandment to love God and neighbor involves a great deal more than personal kindness or caring, nevertheless, actual interpersonal engagement—in the form of right or just relationships—is one important practical expression of the Great Commandment. Love at the local level matters. In Christian theology, this love is not limited to the faith community; it is understood as love that radiates outward toward all "neighbors" in extravagant hospitality. However, mutual care and concern among the faithful, "the tie that binds our hearts in Christian love," according to the English Baptist John Fawcett's lyrics, "the fellowship of kindred minds" within the congregation, is still a highly valued good in contemporary congregations.[2]

---

1. Matt 22:34–40; Deut 6:5; Lev 19:18.
2. Wuthnow, *Producing the Sacred*, 44; Bellah et al., *Habits of the Heart*, 228.

The "ties that bind" at Mary Star of the Sea involve a theological value that is similar, but a little bit different from what Protestants might call "fellowship." The most accurate term that I can come up with for this is "connection," a sense of relatedness between and among people and God. In fact, a sense of spiritual and interpersonal connection was the most ubiquitous feature of the devotional practices that I studied. Using a spatial metaphor familiar to many Protestants, we could say that this sense of connection extends vertically, between the devout and the supernatural world, as well as horizontally, between and among members of the local Catholic community. The large investment of time, money, and energy spent on relationships between the devout and God, Mary, the angels, and the saints demonstrates the importance of the devout's supernatural connections. The significance of interpersonal connections is similarly evident in the intense and regular familial and social interchanges that the devotional practices entail.

We have seen how the habit of maintaining such close spiritual and interpersonal connections is linked, at least for some of the devout, to the historical exigencies of immigration and the fishing occupation, and the attending heightened needs for emotional, spiritual, and practical support. We have also seen how religious art and artifacts, both in form and in function, emphasize and promulgate this value. The sharing of food, at regular family meals, hospitable coffee breaks, large-scale saints' day feasts, fund-raising dinners, as well as in pastoral food provision programs, also expresses and re-enforces interpersonal and cultural connectedness. The labor and expense involved in these activities indicates the importance of the value of connection in this community. This value of connection is evident in the lives of the men as well as the women whom I interviewed.

In this chapter, we will interpret this "situated value" of connection, and explore its ramifications in the lives of the devout, considering both the life-giving aspects of this embedded theology and its hazards or limitations.[3] Reflecting on how this value works in the case study sparks our thinking about the value of connection in other contexts of care.

3. Doehring, *Practice of Pastoral Care*, 112–18. Doehring explains her use of the terms "embedded" and "deliberative theology."

Connection—Possibilities and Pitfalls

In the case study, the stories of Joy and Sarah suggest the rich promise of connection as a religious value. Joy is the immigrant fisherman's wife, described in chapter 3, whose close ties to the saints and to her friends and relatives helped her navigate the difficult experiences of her husband's two accidents at sea, and her own brushes with life-threatening illness. Joy's way of living "in connection" has afforded her considerable social support as well as spiritual peace. Because the practice of her devotional faith as she understands it requires Joy to help other immigrants as much as she can, her strong social network is continuously renewed. One benefit of Joy's practice of connection is the reciprocity of care that she experiences within her religious circle of friends. She reports that when she was hospitalized with cancer, her room was filled with cards and flowers. She was moved as she described this memory, and convinced that the care and prayers she received from her circle of friends in the congregation helped her get well.

Joy's prayer-life, too, supplies a sense of connection and care. Through regular prayer and Bible reading, aided by numerous religious images, Joy has found a way to manage and endure a great deal of uncertainty and fear. Beyond endurance or survival, she seems to have hewn out of her years of devotion a trustful disposition. This may have been a feature of her disposition early on, but more apparent to me is the sense that this is something Joy has practiced. She seems to have internalized, taken into her personality, the grace that she experiences in relationship to God, Mary, and the saints. The practice of kindness and the reciprocity of care that Joy experiences help provide her with an emotional, social, and spiritual "holding environment" during times of uncertainty and crisis.

The strength of spiritual and interpersonal connections is also evident in the story of Sarah, the third-generation woman who is recovering from domestic abuse. Sarah's story also demonstrates change and innovation. She does not attend Mass regularly or hold as tightly to the devotional practices in the way that Joy does. Nevertheless, she bears witness to the help that she draws from a strong sense of connection to God and to her family of origin. Sarah credits her connection to God with her survival of her overdose when she relates, "Something inside me told me to tell my ex-husband what I'd done."[4] When Sarah was finally able to leave her abusive spouse, she came home to a neighborhood filled with relatives and friends who cared about her. She is grateful. Sarah also uses her various religious artifacts as well as prayer and meditation in order to continue to nurture her sense of spiritual connection.[5] For Sarah, a youngest child who grew up with strong ties to her large family, her sense of connection has become a kind of practical knowledge, a resource that she has been able to draw upon both during her ordeal and in her ongoing healing work.

To hold up connection as a positive and life-giving pastoral value in this setting does not require us to idealize this feature of the *habitus* or to ignore its ambiguity. Indeed, many of those interviewed alluded to various problems with the strong emphasis that is placed on relationships in this setting. The imperative toward marriage is one of the questionable implications that the ideology of strong religious, familial, and social connections can take on. We might ask whether the value placed on marriage as an almost inviolable connection contributed to or influenced Sarah's experience of domestic abuse. Did this value lead her to rush into marriage? Alternatively, did feelings of discomfort within her tightly knit church or neighborhood exert internal pressure upon her decision to wed an "outsider" whom she met at a Protestant church youth group? Did the high value placed on marriage contribute to her decision to stay in the abusive marriage longer than she might have? It is hard to know the answer to these questions, though Sarah did volunteer that when she confided her situation of abuse to a priest, he assured her that in light of the abuse, she would be eligible to have her marriage annulled by the Church.[6]

It is also important to ask the question about who is excluded from the strong bonds of connection that are so valued in this setting. What happens to those who remain single in this kind of community? I could not tell much about this from my limited sample. Similarly, not much was said to me about gay or lesbian bonds of love and affection. There were only two comments made to me, both pejorative. One man casually made a joke, sarcastically suggesting that he was gay. The other comment was made at the San Pietro fund-raising dinner, where there was much dancing going on. One woman at my table, who knew I was a researcher,

---

4. Interview #29.

5. We have already noted that a sense of connection is one of the two most important experiences in the recovery process. Herman, *Trauma and Recovery*, 133–54.

6. Interview #29.

pointed to two women who were dancing together, and said, "I don't want you to think that they're gay, just because they're dancing together." From these comments, along with a general silence on the matter of sexual orientation, I gained the impression that the topic was taboo. Perhaps I participated in this taboo, by not questioning these responses further. We could view this as an example of the way in which the bonds of connection function to conserve traditional relational norms and deny or foreclose conversation about relationships that do not fit the religiously and culturally endorsed ideal.

An area of exclusion that several people did discuss with me related to non-Catholics. One second-generation woman experienced profound disconnection when she chose to marry a previously divorced man. This was more than forty years ago, prior to Vatican II. The woman was excommunicated and not allowed to marry in the church. She remembers how much it hurt her father, a deeply religious man, who could not see his daughter married in the church he loved.[7] The woman also lost out on regular interpersonal connections to the church community. These connections might have benefited her in later years, when she endured a period of emotional stress. Of course, the Catholic Church has since shifted on this point, allowing more annulments, remarriages, and "intermarriages" with non-Catholics now.

Yet a legitimate problem remains for both Catholics and Protestants regarding the fellowship of "kindred minds." What happens to the fellowship of Christian love when one changes one's mind, or when one falls in love with someone of a different religious mind, or someone who falls outside the group's theologically endorsed boundaries? A too–strong value placed on unity can tend to discourage difference and quiet social critique; unity can become uniformity.

So much close connection also raises a question in regard to what happens to those who want out, or to those who find such strong connection stifling. Unfortunately, because my research sample is tilted toward the devout, I missed out on hearing many stories of the disaffected. While I tried to gain interviews with children and grandchildren of the devout, stressing that I wanted to talk to folks whether they were religious or not, I heard only a few such stories. I suspect that some individuals declined out of guilt or embarrassment, thinking they were not religious enough for

---

7. Interview #4.

my study. In this, my positioning myself as one who was interested in the devotions may have played a role in excluding dissonant voices. Those who declined interviews might have offered revealing insights. Perhaps they wanted to keep their dissent quiet, rather than go on record disagreeing with their parents or grandparents or with the church.

From a clinical perspective, many family therapists might view the strong sense of connection and obligation within these families and religious societies as being unhealthy. In the jargon of family therapy, the favorite word for this is "enmeshed." The devout could very well be judged enmeshed or even "fused" in their relationships with Mary, the saints, the church, their families, and friends. In family systems theory, "fusion" signifies a too-close connection between people, a sense of togetherness that becomes "stuck together." This stuck-together quality can hamper individual freedom and development. Life in a "fused" system can lead to conformity and to a suspicious posture towards outsiders. Enmeshment or fusion can be seen in families or in larger relational systems such as congregations.[8]

Of course, the enmeshed diagnosis is now itself controversial. Some see it as a culturally biased label that privileges individualism and pathologizes non-Western societies that stress group cohesion. Feminist family theorists point out that both women and members of diverse cultural and ethnic groups have sometimes been pejoratively cast as too deeply mired in relationships and thus not fully mature.[9] When "mature" is equated with "autonomous," we have good cause for suspicion.[10] In my view, interdependence rather than autonomy is a hallmark of maturity. Furthermore, theologically, the love of God and neighbor requires us to live in relationships.

Notwithstanding these critiques, it is still important to ask questions about the pitfalls of extremely close familial and religious ties. When and how do the ties that bind our hearts in filial piety become overly restrictive? When does the habit of close connection that carries a sense of intense obligation to regular interaction with family and friends as well as ethnic maintenance become too burdensome? When do religious ties become binds?

8. For more on the terms, "enmeshment" and "fusion," see Nichols and Schwartz, *Family Therapy*, 591–92; For an explanation of how these dynamics can play out in congregations, see Richardson, *Creating a Healthier Church*, 80–89.

9. Luepnitz, *Family Interpreted*, 14–15.

10. McGoldrick et al., *Women in Families*, 10; Falicov, "Cultural Meaning," 38–39.

These questions are not limited to those who practice Italian Catholic devotions in San Pedro. To put them in a broader context, we can ask, when does a robust and committed religious community life absorb individuals' time and energy to the point of their spiritual, emotional, or physical detriment? While the care and support of a congregation can be a tremendous resource, the obligation to tend to this connection to the exclusion of all else is problematic. Over-functioning leaders—both clergy and lay—can model an unhealthy involvement in the work of the congregation, which often includes committee meetings, work projects, and ministries. We often hear of "burn out" among both clergy and volunteers, because over time, this level of involvement tends to wear people down, emotionally and physically. This over-functioning can also lead to the avoidance or neglect of other relationships, including those with family and friends.

While community and commitment are intensely prized theological values in many settings, people also need a sense of balance. How can we hear the "still, small voice" of God if we have no time apart? As family systems theory has suggested, we long for both individuality and togetherness. We need both separateness and union. In order to practice love holistically, we need to strike a balance between the two.

Yet the ways in which diverse groups of people strike this balance will vary wildly. It is no wiser to judge the devout as too enmeshed or fused than it is to judge North American religion as too ruggedly individualistic.[11] It is always easier to see the speck in our sister's eye than it is to see the log in our own (Matt 7:3). This tendency can also play out theologically and denominationally. For example, consider the ways in which evangelical and orthodox congregations have been characterized as constricting and authoritarian, valuing sameness and conformity to doctrine more than freedom of thought. On the other hand, more progressive groups such as the United Church of Christ and the Unitarian Universalist Association, who prize diversity and social activism, may be judged as too vague and amorphous, devoid of theological clarity and commitment. These judgments inevitably turn out to be stereotypes that do not do justice to the variety and complexity of cultural interactions. There is no one right way to strike the balance between union and separation in the practice of love as embodied connection.

---

11. See Bellah et al., *Habits of the Heart*, 232–37 for a well-known critique of "radical religious individualism."

Connection on Balance

In San Pedro, immigrants' stories of poverty, illness, and hardship suggest that the practice of obligatory mutual support arose in the context of the struggle to survive. In light of this, it is not surprising that familial and social connections would become valued over time in this setting. Bourdieu might consider this is another case of necessity becoming a virtue.[12] In the situation of extreme poverty, strong familial and social connections are extremely helpful to numerous current immigrant groups as well. Mutual aid societies spring up because the practical and social support they offer is a crucial resource for immigrants who face uncertain chances. But does this virtue, over time, continue to serve well?

Many of the folks I interviewed, though acknowledging some ambivalence, seemed to suggest that for them, it does. I was particularly surprised by the strong spiritual and social connections that I observed among the men in this community. These connections are evident in the relatively high level of male participation in religious rituals, societies, and retreats. For example, I witnessed the participation of surprisingly large numbers of men at Sunday Mass (the pastor estimated a sixty-forty ratio of women to men), at fundraising dinners, church rituals and feasts, and in religious societies. Some of these societies, such as the Knights of Columbus, have entirely male memberships. The local chapter of the Italian Catholic Federation (ICF) includes both men and women, but men have dominated its leadership for many years. Though I found fewer men than women who were willing to be interviewed, those who did talk with me spoke enthusiastically about their spiritual, familial, and social connections.

I interviewed one immigrant who is a twenty-year past president of the ICF. He proudly showed me several plaques honoring him for his service, which are displayed on a hallway wall in his home. "Sal" is an immigrant from Ischia. He is retired now, age seventy-three, well known and liked among his peers. Sitting with his wife and me around their kitchen table, Sal was warm, open, and poignant. He spoke in a way that I would describe as simultaneously casual and intimate. "Religion," he said, "is like a good cup of coffee. If you don't have it, you miss it."[13]

Over a good cup of coffee, he told me more. Having grown up on a vineyard, Sal made his living grafting fruit trees. He immigrated first

12. Bourdieu, *Distinction*, 189.

13. Interview #6.

to Canada, where he earned enough money to bring his first wife here to San Pedro in 1953. After only a few years in this country, his wife died of cancer, leaving Sal with three children. He was devastated emotionally and financially, going "in debt down to my shoes" to pay for her funeral. He and his children moved in with a brother during the worst part of the crisis. His devotions increased during this period. Some years later, in 1969, he met and married his present wife, Ella, who was a widow with four children of her own. The two families came together in a way that both adults are proud of. Sal says of finding Ella, "It was a relief for me and a blessing for my kids." He adds with tears in his eyes, "God was good to me. My first wife was very, very good. And the second one is even better." "Thank you," Ella adds quietly, looking surprised.

Sal's spiritual connections are also important to him. Saint John-Joseph of the Cross, the patron Saint of Ischia and the ICF, is one recipient of his prayers. The saint's statue resides in one of the couple's home shrines. "The saints are our lawyers," Sal offers. "They intercede for us. They have more connection with God. They are closer to him."[14] But Sal seems fairly well connected himself. It is his habit to spend approximately two and one-half hours praying in the sanctuary of Mary Star church prior to attending Mass each morning. He says of this, "It's the best time I spend in the whole day. Then I have breakfast, and then I take my walk." Sal's religious practice is clearly a priority in his life, as well as something he enjoys.

Sal's interview reveals the extent and depth of his devotion. In the course of our time together, he recites and sings, in Italian, some of his regular prayers to Saint John-Joseph. These prayers emphasize the saint's patronage of all the children of Ischia, wherever they may be.[15] Sal speaks at length about prayer, its meaning and help in his life, and about the

14. Ibid.

15. A portion of the "Responsorio" that Sal sings reads in translation:

"Reign with God in heaven, O Saint John-Joseph
Our fellow citizen, Pride and boast of Ischia...
O illustrious Isclano and saint, Let your blessing fall
On our native land which bestows honors on you
O our great Patron
From our bodies and from our souls
Keep away all evils
Guide, sustain, and save,
Those who sail the seas . . ."

"Responsorio," 8.

mysteries of the rosary—joyful, sorrowful, and glorious. In the course of our conversation, he seems to take on each of these moods in turn. Finally, he gives his own rendition of the golden rule: "Be human. Grow as a human. Treat you fellow man justa like youself [treat your fellow man just like yourself]."[16] Sal's spiritual connections bring him back to the love of God and neighbor.

Sal's interpersonal connections are important to him. He does not seem stifled by them, but enlivened, enriched, and grateful. In their book *The Healing Connection*,[17] Wellesley Stone Center theorists articulate a vision of psychological maturity that is based on growth-fostering relationships. In their relational theory, "the goal of development is not forming a separated self or finding gratification, but something else altogether—the ability to participate actively in relationships that foster the well-being of everyone involved."[18] Sal's devotional life seems to inspire him toward achieving a kind of growth-in-connection that these authors would applaud.

Immigrants such as Sal remember times of poverty that fueled the need for close connections. Now that many of them are enjoying times of relative ease, they still hold on to their social and spiritual connections. Through religious societies such as ICF, they continuously renew relationships in a social circle of devout immigrants. Beyond this, though, they also practice charitable activities that connect them to a larger ethnic and religious community. Participation in ICF, for example, links the devout to a nationwide Italian Catholic population. This organization raises funds to support various cultural and charitable causes, such as scholarships for students in Italian Studies programs, and medical research and treatment of Thalassemia, a genetic form of anemia that affects persons of Mediterranean descent.[19] These activities and these causes keep Sal connected on many levels.

We might appreciate Sal's religious practices as "translocative," in that by venerating Saint John-Joseph, his "fellow Isclano," he can imaginatively cross back and forth over the sea to the island where he was born. In fact, Sal also flies across the ocean to Ischia to visit his homeland and honor the

---

16. Interview #6.

17. Miller and Stiver, *Healing Connection*.

18. Ibid., 22.

19. "About Italian Catholic," *Bollettino*, 3. The reader may also wish to view the ICF website, "Italian Catholic Federation."

Saint with some regularity. When I visited Ischia myself in 2004, some of Sal's friends showed me his old home and praised him for his devotion. He is known and remembered there. On the other hand, through his involvement with ICF, an American Catholic organization, Sal reconstitutes himself, to some degree, as a pan-Italian American, and not just an Isclano. Through his connections and charitable activities associated with ICF, Sal's network of belonging and his opportunities for faithful service have expanded.

Judith Jordan, another Stone Center theorist, writes: "Our perspective appreciates that people experience a sense of personal history, and coherence; . . . we see context, the ongoing relational interplay between self and other, as primary to real growth and vitality."[20] The devotional practices that Sal and other immigrants and their children participate in seem to help them maintain a sense of personal history and coherence through "ongoing relational interplay" in spiritual, geographic, cultural, and interpersonal fields. Meeting with Sal, I get a sense of his personal integrity. His strong connections do not seem to squelch his individuality, but rather it appears that the coherence he experiences in these various connections gives him life.

I wonder whether many American Protestants, particularly descendants of European immigrants, miss out on the kind of cultural and religious coherence that Sal and others in this setting seem to enjoy. Protestant denominations, I think, provide some of this kind of cultural cohesion for their members. Yet as denominationalism wanes, and people moving into new communities increasing church-shop across denominational lines, this source of cohesive cultural connection is likely to be eroded. In some cases, cultural cohesion then becomes limited to a particular congregation, which may or may not be strongly connected to the wider church.

Pastoral practices that recognize the value of cohesive cultural experiences and emphasize sharing historical narratives can assist the faithful in the ongoing process of forging religious identity. It may not be so important that people tell similar stories about their family origins, but that they practice telling and hearing their diverse cultural stories in a faith community.[21] This is a way of embodying the value of connection that also honors individual distinction.

20. Miller and Stiver, *Healing Connection*, 56.
21. Belenky et al., *Tradition that Has No Name*, 258–92.

Connection and Social Ministries

Love as connection to one's neighbor also informs the pastoral ministries of the devout. This is evident in their responsiveness to the needs of the poorest citizens of San Pedro. The food provision ministries of the various Catholic churches (described in chapter 4) are a good example of this. The memory of poverty and hunger, enshrined in rituals such as Saint Joseph's Table, fosters a sense of commonality and connection between the devout and local neighbors who are struggling to subsist. Because the feast vividly enacts the narrative of drought and famine and the miraculous aid of Saint Joseph, it invokes visceral memories and images (real and imagined) of struggling parents, grandparents, friends and neighbors, both here in San Pedro and back in Sicilian and Italian homelands. The sense of historical continuity and ethnic identity that is forged and re-forged in these rituals incorporates an obligation to provide food for the hungry, especially those in our midst.

These efforts are extensive and apparently effective means of offering sustenance. From a pastoral-theological standpoint, though, we could and perhaps should question religious food ministries that do not go beyond charitable hunger relief to the harder work of social advocacy or organizing. Do such programs inadvertently re-enforce social inequities, rather than work to abolish the root causes of poverty? Are these grocery deliveries and sandwich-making ministries merely stopgap measures that help maintain capitalism and its requisite underclass? These are important questions to ask in regard to any social ministry endeavor. It is true that hunger relief work alone does not challenge the broader causes of poverty. Such programs may be, in the language of Methodists, "acts of compassion," but they are not, ultimately, "acts of justice."[22]

Nevertheless, these ministries address needs for food that are critical and emergent. As new immigrants from the Philippines and Mexico continue to make their homes in San Pedro, recent welfare reform legislation makes it difficult if not impossible for them to receive government aid. In this context, food distribution programs are critical. While it can be argued that social reform is also needed, at the same time, the faithful cannot ignore their neighbors' urgent needs for basic provisions.[23]

22. See Watson, *Covenant Discipleship*.

23. A related question that I did not explore in my interviews, is whether or not the folks involved in these relief ministries are also active in political advocacy.

The devout who recall their own family stories of struggle sense the urgency of current immigrants' financial needs. They respond out of compassion. The significant value that I want to lift up in this setting is the sense of connection to and identification with the hungry that fuels these ministries. This is not charity from a distance, accomplished by writing a check. Rather, what I witnessed here was human interaction. Rocco, from chapter 4, experienced a physical sensation that he interpreted as the Holy Spirit alerting him to the needs of the homeless standing on the corner of 19th and Pacific Avenue. This sense of connection comes from the habit of involvement and friendship with the folks who live here. This connection is complex and imperfect—recall Rocco's earlier comments about "druggies and winos"—revealing his frustrations and perhaps a degree of social distancing. But the connection he experiences is also based on Rocco's own memory and experience of a traumatic brush with death. He has said that he is sure that God is calling him to do this work. Rocco confided that he would have liked to be ordained as a deacon in the Catholic Church, but he could not pursue this because he lacks a college degree. Instead, he fulfills his intense sense of being called—chosen and saved from that boating accident at age fourteen—through relationships of care and connection to people whose lives are on the line.

I do not wish to suggest that Rocco or the feeding ministries at these local churches are ideal. All persons and all ministries are complex and problematic to some degree. When religious persons and communities try to "live into" the commandment to love your neighbor, we often come up against the tendency to objectify the neighbor. I am not sure that this can be entirely overcome. As a colleague recently remarked to me while we were visiting a shelter program for homeless women in Chicago, "Altruism is always contingent." Another colleague agreed, adding, "You can't resist without also being complicit."[24] In order to push beyond objectification of one's neighbor and complicity in oppression, we need to remember ourselves as fully human, embodied creatures. In my view, ministry grounded in self-knowledge—including the awareness of one's own physicality—is more likely to create life-giving connections, connections that help to overcome the social boundaries we erect.

Philosophical theologian Paula Cooey suggests that the human body, in all of its particularity and all of its ambiguity, can be viewed theologi-

24. Personal conversation, June 19, 2005.

cally as a common condition that we all share. She writes, "The body simultaneously presents our individual particularity and our common human conditions of vulnerability and finitude."[25] Here is a key point: our bodies remind us that we are all both unique and alike at the same time. We are both the same and different. It seems to me that life-giving social ministries are those that respond to the genuine needs of those who are marginalized while at the same time recognizing our common human vulnerabilities. Though social ministries will always be marked by limitations and contradictions (the recipients of altruism can tell us more about these), ministry focused on relieving human suffering in this world helps remind us of our own profoundly contingent condition.

The "body lived," as Cooey calls it, is messy and complex. We have (or are) our particular gendered bodies, existing in sentience and sensuality. Our bodies are the site of both religious practice and imagination. We cannot get away from our bodies. Furthermore, theologically, it is good that we don't pretend to escape our bodily condition by concentrating on visions of otherworldly rewards. The body lived, felt, experienced, in all of its frailty and all of its capacity for pleasure, constantly reminds us of the ethical demand for justice and compassion in this world.[26] Thus, our capacity to feel, to be aware of both pain and pleasure, serves to remind us of our dependent human condition that we might otherwise try to deny. When we can live in more conscious awareness of our bodies, we can be awakened by the cries of others in need. We can sense the positive good in working for more just social arrangements.

According to Cooey, an emphasis on the body lived in all of its complexity also helps us undercut dualistic thinking.[27] Dualistic thinking sees the culturally different as "other," and otherness is often read in physical terms: skin color, gender, able-bodied-ness, etc. Pastoral theologians know that when we devalue our own bodily-ness, by attempting too much self-control or denial of emotion, we are not able to fully respond to our own or others' pain. When are emotionally distanced from our own bodily-ness, we do not have sentient moral and spiritual responsiveness in relationship to others.

25. Cooey, *Religious Imagination and the Body*, 128–29.

26. Ibid., 36–37.

27. Ibid., 30.

An emphasis on connected, embodied human love is, in my view, central to life-giving pastoral practice. Through the body we substantiate love; through sensation we project and imagine others' realities. Our projections—like Rocco's—will always be flawed. But when ministry is informed by self-awareness, our intuitions and projections will come closer to actual love. We will be more open to transforming moments, moments when the distance between human beings is not dissolved, but imaginatively bridged, and the bodily needs of another can be felt, stirring us from our recline, awakening us into compassionate understanding and responsive service. Connected, embodied ministries restore our visceral awareness of our own needs, and simultaneously create a place to stand in honest and more level interaction with so-called others.

It seems paradoxical to me that the connections the devout enjoy with supernatural images so often lead to food-provision ministries in this world. The devotions appear at first to be otherworldly, focused on an imagined pantheon of heavenly beings. Yet the saints are also encountered as human beings whose lives modeled the love of God and neighbor. The devotional practices involve prayer for material human needs and continually draw the devout back into concrete and tangible forms of care. The visual, geographic, gustatory, and memorial elements that comprise the devotional worlds keep the devout's feet firmly planted on earth even as they tend their connections to God, the saints, and each other.

Dependence and Empowerment

The value of connection as it is enacted in the devotional practices studied here raises some additional questions. I have noted examples of stories in which strong spiritual and interpersonal connections have been experienced as healing, supportive, oriented toward psycho-spiritual growth, and conducive to engagement in caring Christian ministry. I have also suggested some of the problematic dimensions of ties that may be practiced in a way that is too binding, in that they may be experienced as either stifling or exclusionary, so as to delineate social boundaries and discourage difference. Perhaps the most serious remaining pastoral theological question I have about such close religious connections is whether they tilt toward meeting defensive needs such as safety and survival, rather than encouraging growth, empowerment, and transformation. To what extent do the devotions promote dependence on the saints or on the church, at the expense of the devout's own development, agency, and subjectivity? Another way of putting this is to ask whether the devotions are more helpful than harmful to the full potential of the people who practice them.

Robert Orsi artfully describes a similar tension in his historical study of American Catholic women's devotion to Saint Jude, the patron saint of hopeless causes. In analyzing the impact of the devotional practices in that context, he writes, "The ambiguity of the devotions lies in this point exactly, whether the practices foster growth in the devout," or the qualities of passivity and dependence, in Orsi's words, "capitulation, resignation, and self-delusion."[28] Orsi finds some truth in the latter assessment. For American women struggling to work through difficult situations in the context of cultural limitations, "Jude," he writes, "turns out to be Judas after all."[29] At the same time, Orsi finally points to the ambiguity of this judgment when he describes his overall impressions of the actual women who participate in the devotion, women he has interviewed and observed for countless hours. He finds that even those women who give Jude the credit for much of what they themselves have done, speaking the language of humility and dependence, do not embody or live out a passive orientation to life.[30] Orsi concludes, "The challenge here is to consider how it could be that intimacy and dependence . . . could apparently be the ground of action, choice, autonomy, and healing . . ."[31] The juxtaposition of these apparently contradictory dynamics is indeed intriguing.

I find a similar challenge when I try to probe and interpret the value of connection in the devotional practices in San Pedro. Does this connection really boil down to a kind of dependence that ultimately harms more than it heals? In this setting there are many women, in particular, who profess a great sense of humility, especially in relation to Mary and the saints. I think of Anna (chapter 4), who shies away from taking public credit for her organizing role in Saint Joseph's Table feasts, even while asserting herself mightily in practice. "I'm not the president," she demurs.

---

28. Orsi, *Thank You, Saint Jude*, 193.

29. Ibid., 196.

30. One woman, for example, was an 89-year-old writing from the *independent care* floor of the nursing home about how Jude keeps her going, although she tries to help herself first. Orsi, *Thank You Saint Jude*, 197–98.

31. Orsi goes on to explore not only the ambiguity of the graces that the devotion yields to women, but also the possibility that the very dependence and intimacy that devotion fosters might actually be related to its transformative aspects. *Thank You, Saint Jude*, 201.

"I run it. I tell people what to do."[32] And then there is Susan, who would bless all of the family's new cars with holy water. But according to Susan's daughter, when her mom ran out of holy water, she would simply bless more tap water herself "in the name of Jesus." "Why not?" Susan said to me. "We're saints too."[33] This self-confidence is quite striking.

I wonder if some of this confidence actually comes from a life-long practice of devotion, giving Susan a kind of cumulative confidence in her own practical wisdom. She knows how to give a blessing "in the name of Jesus." More importantly, she knows that she is worthy to give a blessing. She has studied the saints' lives and practiced emulating their goodness. She identifies with the saints, and girds herself with their power. Perhaps because of her close familiarity with the saints, and their legends of humble lives combined with their beatified status, Susan can manage the ambiguity of being both humble and strong. When she perceived that her children needed it, she consecrated the water.

Is there a link between the comfort and security inherent in close spiritual and interpersonal connections and the subversive energy —such as Anna and Susan's—that moves beyond passivity, humility or conformity? Could it be that when the devout's defensive needs are met, whether through connections to Mary or the saints or through the support of a closely connected family or social group, they gain the freedom to improvise, resist, or subvert?

I wondered what the current pastor of Mary Star, Monsignor Patrick Gallagher, would think about these things. I asked him what he thought the devotions meant, and whether they were more a source of comfort or transformation. His reply was both quick and telling:

> We obviously put Jesus first. The saints are models that lead us to him. And greatest model of all is his mother. Jesus must be first. He is the Son of God and He is God. Our religion eventually calls us to transformation. The life of Jesus invokes and calls us to a deeper union with our Lord. In times of crisis, yes, the saints are a comfort. But we need both. We have a need to grow and mature in the faith and in life.[34]

32. Interview #7.

33. Interview #21. "And we are all children of God," Susan added later. Written communication, November 2003.

34. Informational interview #06.

The pastor's careful answer expresses the official post-Vatican II Catholic interpretation of the role of the saints as models (not mediators) that lead us to Jesus. This includes a reminder that Jesus is "first," needed here because not all of the devout exactly see it—or practice it—that way. But along with the pastor's theologically correct answer, which he offered hastily and a bit defensively, I think, came a very sensitive interpretation of the need for both comfort and transformation, and even a hint that there might be a connection between the two.

It seems to me that the emphasis on connection in these devotions is indeed a comfort to many in this setting where there is so much history of crisis, loss, and change. These experiences have been woven into the immigrants' religious and ethnic identity, and passed on in varying degrees to their children and grandchildren. It is therefore not surprising that strong habits of spiritual and social connection would persist and continue to be cherished. But will these connections foster security to the detriment of growth? Father Gallagher, an immigrant himself, patiently works the balance. He sees continuity between his pastoral goals of comfort and transformation.

I suspect that there is a link between the experience of connection and safety on the one hand, and action and choice on the other. I think that it is the intimacy and security of close connections in devotional practices that foster the courage and creativity needed in order to face enormous changes. Just as the emotionally secure child is more likely to dare to strike out on her own, the spiritually secure devout—the religious virtuoso—is more inclined to innovate. Subjective capacities are nurtured through practices that involve close and caring relationships. Maturity is not achieved by the rending of interpersonal ties, but by living with them and through them, sometimes holding on, sometimes letting go, sometimes finding oneself held by a larger reality.

Union and Separation

This whole discussion about the value of connection harks back to Winnicott's work on the paradoxical tension between union and separation. Life-giving human and religious connections seem to require both of these paradoxically interrelated experiences, held in some kind of balance. Strong bonds of union that meet our human needs are the rich soil in which seeds of creativity and innovation can grow. Actual caring relationship provide a "facilitating environment" in which the true self can be reached, experienced and nourished.[35] Without this, the soul is not seen or recognized, and eventually becomes hidden.[36] Spiritual growth requires both strong and authentic community, and the capacity to be alone, as noted in chapter 2.

It may seem to some that I am equating spiritual growth to psychological and emotional maturity. It is not my intention to collapse these two dimensions into each other, though I believe that they are interrelated. I suspect that it is the "true self" in us that calls out to God, the larger reality. It is in reaching and nourishing this soul that religious practices have the greatest potential for supporting genuinely faithful, transformative forms of praxis.

What is involved in the flowering of the kind of faith that can not only help hold us together during a storm but also help push us toward growth and transformation? Simply put, we learn to love by being loved and practicing love. Connection, when it is "good enough," will include such things as "reliability, attentiveness, responsiveness, memory, and durability."[37] We need to gather together. We gain vigor through belonging to genuine communities. We also gain confidence and courage through participation in shared ministries inspired by corporate visions of the public good.[38]

We also need to withdraw to the wilderness. We need access to illusion, to free-floating experiential states in order to "reach" or restore the soul. Winnicott grouped religious experiences together with other cultural endeavors, such as music and art, and saw them as a kind of adult "play" or portal to the experiential realm. Religionists of diverse faiths know that prayer or meditation can lead to the opening up of an in-between space, somewhere between life as we know it and life as we wish it could be.

For this kind of prayer life we need separation, space. Separation helps us find space in which to experience an original and unique relationship with the larger reality. Sacred spaces such as sanctuaries can hold memories through material symbols of the holy that link us to loved ones, ancestors, religious heroes, or saints. In such spaces we can find the courage to be

35. Greenberg and Mitchell, *Object Relations in Psychoanalytic Theory*, 201.

36. Palmer, *A Hidden Wholeness*. Palmer speaks uses the language of "the soul" to describe an often hidden center of identity.

37. Winnicott, *Maturational Processes*, 201.

38. Galindo, "What Makes?" 1.

alone before the mystery of all that there is. In sacred space or in sacred (alone) time, such as in prayer, we can imagine ways to negotiate the ties and binds of external life, or we can let go of imagining and float. In this space we can hear "the still small voice" of our souls, living and breathing and having our being in God.

The "situated value" of connection in the San Pedro case study discloses a lively and robust practice of the love of God and neighbor. The value of loyalty and commitment, which some say is missing in congregations, seems amply enshrined in this setting. The case study also reveals the potential harm or limitations that can result when unity is so highly prized. Ties can become binds.

This interpretation suggests the pastoral wisdom of seeking a balance between union and separation, and attempting to hold these two elements of love together in practice. Even Robert Bellah et al. (authors who would decry my emphasis on psychology), reach a similar conclusion. They say that finally, ". . . individuality and society are not opposites but require each other."[39] Connection is a complex but crucial religious value, one that can empower the faithful in the practice of love toward God and neighbor.

39. Bellah et al., *Habits of the Heart*, 246–47.

7

Engaging Multiplicity

A catholic personality is a personality enriched by otherness, a personality which is what it is only because multiple others have been reflected in it in a particular way . . . The Spirit unlatches the doors of my heart saying: "You are not only you; others belong to you too."

—Miroslav Volf, *Exclusion and Embrace*

It's like a minestrone. We're a minestrone. We all mixa together.

—"Anna"

In the course of my research in San Pedro, the ever-expanding nature of the pantheon of saints, angels, and various manifestations of the Madonna that people venerated often surprised me. The list of supernatural figures grew to include more and more names, some familiar to me—such as Our Lady of Fatima, Saint Teresa, Saint Lucy, Padre Pio, and Mother Cabrina—and some more obscure such as Santo Vito, the keeper of the dogs, Saint Dymphia, who is said to be "good for" peace of mind and for preventing mental illness, San Genaro, San Trifone, Maria Del Lume, Patrona di Porticello, San Pasquale, protector of the deaf (now removed from the Vatican's official list of saints), and the Madonna de Porto Salvo, Our Lady of the Wharf. Among the figures are many patron saints of particular localities—for example, Saint John Joseph of the Cross and Saint Restituta represent one side of the beautiful island of Ischia, off the coast of Naples, while other saints are the patrons for people living further around the island. Then there are the more "universal" objects of devotion, such as the Sacred Heart of Jesus, known to Catholics around the world. What can we make of this panoply of holy figures and images? How can we engage the theological value of multiplicity that is at play here, so that we might be, in Miraslav Volf's phrase, "enriched by otherness?"[1]

"Anna," one of the devout, offered a tantalizing take on the subject. A second-generation immigrant from Sicily, Anna is primarily devoted to Saint Joseph. A large statue of the Saint occupies a prime spot in her backyard garden. Anna spoke at great length about the many diverse ethnic groups at her church, and their corresponding devotions to the patron saints of their natal lands. She told me that she was always willing to help out with the other groups' devotions, assuring me that she prays to the Madonna as well as to Saint Joseph. When Anna showed me a picture of the Madonna del Ponte—Our Lady of the Bridge—the patron Saint of Trapetto, Sicily, who is known for performing many miracles, I expressed my amazement over the sheer number of saints that I was hearing about. In a flourish of theological clarity, Anna intoned, "It's like a minestrone. *We're* a minestrone. We all mixa together."[2]

Minestrone as Metaphor

Minestrone? I had to pause over this striking and apt metaphor. It is a good example of the competence of ordinary people in imaginatively interpreting their own religious lives. To begin with, Anna's use of a food metaphor expresses a complex idea in a simple and direct way that appeals to gustatory sensations. The metaphor of minestrone suggests that the saints are varied, but mixed, just as the diverse groups of people in the church are varied and mixing. Anna seemed proud of this cultural mixing, as did another devout whom I asked about this. "Here we have the unity!"[3] she claimed with a smile.

Minestrone as a metaphor for cultural mixing suggests a particular kind of unity, a unity that includes diversity. Minestrone, though also a soup, differs from the notorious image of the melting pot, into which the national origins and cultural identities of diverse American immigrants were supposed to disappear in the years following World War Two. In minestrone, the various vegetables do not merge or melt—they are not pureed. In good minestrone, flavors tend to mingle and gradually influence each other. They become, over time, something different from what

1. Volf, *Exclusion and Embrace*, 51.
2. Interview #7.
3. Interview #11.

they were at first. This mingling of flavors reminds me of what American religious historian Catherine Albanese calls "contact and combination."[4] Cultural and religious mingling is clearly a subtext in the larger story of religious history in America, though it is perhaps more obvious in the historically multi-ethnic congregation of Mary Star of the Sea.

Anna's comments caused me to wonder about what's actually been happening for the devout over time as they practice devotions to a multiplicity of saints in this multi-ethnic parish. What is wrought through all of this interchange, this supernatural and human contact and combination? I think that at least some of the devout at Mary Star of the Sea have been praying to a God who is, in certain respects, multiple and varied. Of course, the pastor and others would argue that the saints are not God, but mere models of faithful lives that help point people toward God. This is the theologically correct post-Vatican II position of the Roman Catholic Church. However, I do not think that this point would be argued so vigorously here if the saints were not so vitally important to the devout.

Official theologies notwithstanding, for some folks, Mary and the saints do seem to function, not as divinities themselves, but as *very close relatives*. In the practice of engaging spiritually with so many supernatural figures, the devout are experiencing multiplicity close to the heart of their spirituality. And, Anna suggests, this minestrone of saints is reflected or mirrored in the intercultural congregation of Mary Star. Anna's metaphor employs a logic that goes something like this: since God is accessed in or through Saint Joseph as well as through the Madonna, both of whom I know and revere, then perhaps God may be accessed as well in or through Our Lady of Guadalupe, whom the woman in the pew next to me knows and reveres. We—this woman and I—are similar; we can mingle together.

As a pastoral theologian, I believe that there is theological wisdom in this kind of spiritual multiplicity and its analogue in human diversity. The multifarious Madonnas and saints seem to render the devout's everyday imaginative experiences of God larger, more complex and compelling. Similarly, the capacity to love one's neighbor is potentially expanded via the inclusion or appreciation of one's neighbor's saints. This chapter is an attempt to "play" with this local wisdom, reflect on it theologically, and see whether we can imagine analogous insights and strategies for pastoral ministry in other settings.

4. Albanese, "Exchanging Selves, Exchanging Souls," 200–226.

Critiques and Challenges

Many Christians will contest the idea of multiplicity as a theological value. To Protestants especially, the multiplicity of saints may seem theologically confusing and cluttered at best, or polytheistic and idolatrous at worst. Along with an almost visceral rejection of the use of visual images—addressed in chapter 2—there are at least two sets of theological objections to the veneration of saints that are likely to be raised. Both of these relate back to the Love Commandment, (taken up in the last chapter), the commandment to love God with your whole heart and soul and mind, and your neighbor as yourself. The first set of objections has to do with the love of God, and the second with love of neighbor.

First, consider the commandment to love God above all else. When the devout venerate Mary and the saints, it could be argued that they are in danger of missing the unity and transcendence of God. The multiplicity of saints and their quasi-divine images that mirror national origins might be perceived as unorthodox and idolatrous, and likely to interfere with the love of God. The second main set of objections likely to be raised has to do with love of neighbor. It asks whether diverse cultural images of Mary and the saints aren't likely to reinforce ethnic and racial divisions, rather than nurturing intercultural connection. In a world that desperately needs peace and unity, do we really want to encourage the maintenance of ethnic identity?

In response to these objections, it must first be pointed out that the meanings and roles of the saints in San Pedro are complex, elastic, and shifting. Like all religious symbols, the saints take on a life of their own. They do not mean one thing to all people, or even to the same people, for very long. Nevertheless, as I noted in chapter 2, I do think that the representations of the saints play a mirroring role for the faithful. That is, the devout can see a little bit of themselves in the faces of the Italian statues and dark-haired portraits of the saints. We have seen how, emotionally and spiritually, this can be a positive experience that supports identity formation. Building on Kohut's insights, I think it is fair to say that at times we all long for ideal figures with whom we can identify, and it helps when these figures resemble us in some way. Theologically, if we believe that we are created in God's image, then this longing for "essential likeness" need not be seen as problematic.

Jaroslav Pelikan's beautiful volume, *Jesus Through the Centuries*, is only one example of many works that display the grand diversity of images of Jesus that artists and theologians have conjured up throughout the history of the church.[5] Christians have routinely imagined that God in some way resembles them, whether in character, theology, or appearance. Members of dominant social groups have not always been aware of this tendency, until their dominant assumptions are challenged. For example, consider the enormous popularity of Warner Sallman's "Head of Christ" portrait from 1940, reported in David Morgan's 1993 landmark study. The image of the serene, bearded, white Jesus portrays a savior who is, in Morgan's words, "instantly recognized" by American Protestants and Catholics.[6] One respondent to Morgan said of this portrait that it was "an exact likeness of Our Lord Jesus Christ."[7] This very particular image of a serene, white, long-haired Jesus did not seem to disturb Protestants, who wrote of using this portrait while they prayed in ways that very much resemble the devout's use of holy images.[8]

It is only when dominant images of the divine are challenged, say, by the image of a black Jesus, or by the use of a feminine pronoun in reference to the deity, that many white Christians have tended to become disturbed and to issue renewed calls for theological orthodoxy. Therefore I find it disingenuous to claim that it is the *particularity* of multiple religious images that constitutes *the* theological problem with ethnic saints. What is disturbing to some is seeing the particularity of non-dominant groups mirrored or lifted up in religious images or language.

Considering multiplicity as a theological value may be a useful practice for Western Christians who have often had difficulty "seeing" our own cultural biases in our theologies. Theological multiplicity can function as a reminder that all theologies are only words about God, and not God Godself. Multiple images of the divine can also relativize any one image or concept, helping to de-center the faithful, and offering much-needed perspective. The value of theological multiplicity, however troubling it may be, lies in its power to suggest a larger reality—more complex and encompassing—than any one image can evoke by itself. In other words, if the idea of a multiplicity of religious images (that mirror a broad swath

5. Pelikan, *Jesus Through the Centuries*.

6. Morgan, *Visual Piety*, 1.

7. Ibid., 34.

8. Ibid., 28–58.

of human diversity) disturbs our sense of theological certainty, this dissonance may be good for us.[9]

Now, some will object that neither the multiplicity of God-images nor their cultural particularity is the main theological problem. To some, the saints *themselves* are the problem, and that problem is idolatry. This is a long-standing Protestant objection to the veneration of Mary and the Saints. If these figures are the primary focus of religious devotion, are they not idols that come before God?

This concern, while theologically salient on the surface, misses the deeper point of what is transpiring in the devotional lives of the faithful. For the devout whom I interviewed, God is all in all. The saints do not compete with God. God is God. In fact, it may be the extreme reverence that is reserved for God alone that makes the saints so appealing to the devout. Many of the devout, who think of themselves as humble people, feel that Mary and the saints are more approachable, accessible, than God is. The devout worship God, but they *visit* with Mary and the saints. The saints are human figures, with whom the people can identify. They are also holy figures, and perceived as powerful; but the saints are connected to God. God is found in them and through them; God is all in all. The devout revere Christ, and offering blessings "in the name of Jesus." But they often choose to "hang out" with the saints. Is this idolatry?

In *The Heart of Christianity*, Marcus Borg takes up a discussion of the Great Commandment. He claims that this command requires faith primarily in the sense of faithfulness, fidelity, or loyalty to God and neighbor. In Borg's reading of the biblical texts, the opposite of faithfulness is idolatry. He writes, "Faith as *fidelitas* does not mean faithfulness to *statements* about God, whether biblical, creedal, or doctrinal. Rather, it means faithfulness to the God to whom the Bible and creeds and doctrines point."[10]

When I think about the way the devout actually practice their devotions, it seems to me that they are really practicing fidelity to God, if not to orthodox theology. The saints and their images help facilitate a radical focus on the divine, a loyalty that can challenge idols such as wealth or human status. Recall the case of Josephine, described in chapter 2, who used her devotions to help her cope with cancer. Reflecting on this period later, after her recovery, she said, "It made me a better person. My faith was able to

9. See Armstrong, *Spiral Staircase*, 304.

10. Borg, *The Heart of Christianity*, 32–33.

get me through it. . . . You realize that affluence is not the most important thing."[11] Josephine's devotional life helped her cope with a serious illness; it also helps her re-order her life, and challenge the idol of affluence.

Of course, we cannot infer that all of the devout use their devotions in precisely this way. Yet, in a general sense, I think it is fair to say that the devotional practices in this setting function to help people stay focused on God, by constantly reminding them of the presence of God in their mundane lives. The devotion to Mary and the saints may seem idolatrous at first, especially to those who are accustomed to a different religious aesthetic and an emphasis on orthodox theological constructions. On closer examination, I hope that readers can see the ways in which the devotions support the *fidelity* of the devout. In their *lived religion,* many of the devout exhibit the fruits of radical faithfulness—love and loyalty to God and neighbor.

Is there the potential for idolatry in the devotional practices? I think that there is. Yet there is the potential for idolatry in all religious practices. I do not think that the test of idolatry is in whether or not the devout imagine that the saints help them out with their prayer requests. We all rely on finite means and materials and beings when we try to gain access to the infinite. When devotional practices help people orient their lives toward the love of God and neighbor, they become practices of fidelity. To borrow from the words of Jesus in the Sermon on the Mount, "You will know them by their fruits."[12]

The second set of problems that readers may raise in regard to multiplicity as a theological value has to do with love of neighbor. This is the concern that sacralizing ethnic distinctions may lead to increased bigotry as well as civil and international strife. Surely we know from history and from the current world scene that reifying ethnic distinctions, claiming that they are fixed and final attributes of the divine, is dangerous. Diverse fundamentalist groups in this country and around the world promulgate ethnic, national, or cultural hatreds in the name of particular gods.[13]

Miroslav Volf, speaking out of his Balkan heritage and experience, claims that the human will for identity is formidable and can fuel social conflicts around the world.[14] When we start to believe that God is on

11. Interview #16.

12. Matt 7:16.

13. See Kimball, *When Religion Becomes Evil.*

14. Volf, *Exclusion and Embrace,* 17.

our side only, and not on the others' side as well, we lose touch with divine transcendence, the larger reality. When the holy becomes too closely aligned with our internal images or our particular social causes, we run the risk of unleashing powerful symbolic forces that disregard the humanity of the perceived "other." History is sadly replete with examples of this, from the crusades to Nazi Germany, from Rwanda to the Balkans, and now from the World Trade Center and the Pentagon to Abu Ghraib and Guantanamo Bay, and to Sudan as well.

Asserting the superiority of one group over another, and using God to support the lie, devastates human dignity. The historical case of black slavery in North America is a potent example of this. When some Christian clergy and congregations defended the institution of slavery, asserting that it was a biblically sanctioned positive good, they claimed that blacks were by nature inferior and incapable of governing themselves.[15] This belief in black inferiority is at the heart of white supremacy; it is an idea that persists and continues to stymie African Americans' full acceptance and equal opportunity in America. The legacy of slavery and the idolatry of skin color remain with us in the form of prejudice, discrimination, and racism. The insidious ideology of white supremacy and black inferiority keeps black Americans on what historical theologian Beverly Mitchell calls "a quest for human dignity," a quest that she notes is still "unfulfilled."[16]

The damage done by associating God too closely with any one ethnic group or skin color is palpable. And yet, people do form images of God.[17] Attempts to avoid anthropomorphic images altogether have not always been met with enthusiasm, in Christian congregations, for example. The staying power of God-images, whether helpful or harmful, is also notable. Attempts to alter existing God images, such as by using inclusive language in hymnals, have often encountered resistance.

When leaders and members of a multi-racial Presbyterian church outside of Atlanta tried to redress racism by changing the skin color of Jesus from white to brown in one of their stained glass windows, they achieved some public recognition and felt proud of themselves for a while. But a year or so later, one of the pastors reports, the window came up for more honest reflection and critique among African American church members. It was noted that the figure of Jesus wasn't really black, only the skin tone

15. Mitchell, *Black Abolitionism*, 25.

16. Ibid., 148–54.

17. See Rizzuto, *Birth of the Living God*.

had been changed. One church member pointed to the long, straight hair and claimed that the image really depicted a white Jesus with dark skin.[18] This story demonstrates the difficulty of trying to alter God images; it also demonstrates the difficulty of trying to challenge racism in the context of a church building that was designed with a white Jesus in mind.

Any anthropomorphic images of the divine will necessarily be particular; they therefore will be limited in their capacity to point to the holy in whose image we claim to be created. But we cannot completely get away from particular images, nor, from a pastoral point of view, I would argue, should we. It is better, I think, to add to the repertoire rather than to attempt to take away cherished religious images that contain and reflect people's self-understandings. This is where theological multiplicity can help us curb or diminish (but not do away with altogether) our divisive and self-aggrandizing tendencies. If we proffer multiple religious images, and insist always on including alternative images, we have a better chance at staying humble, and keeping our theological and nationalistic narcissism in check.

In the ethnically inflected devotions at Mary Star of the Sea, the saints have been employed in the historical and ongoing work of forging cultural identity in the context of immigration. This has, to varying degrees throughout the years, involved ethnic boundary maintenance. Yet the multiplicity of saints mitigates the tendency toward cultural dominance of any one group in this setting. While on the one hand, so many distinct saints and images and religious societies do foster and maintain ethnic differences, on the other hand, the multiplicity of saints implicitly challenges and limits the identification of God with any one group. The ever-expanding panorama of diverse religious images suggests a larger vision of God as one who is present in each and every saint, and, it follows, in each and every person.

While the value of theological multiplicity has its hazards, it nevertheless can give way to gracious and generous understandings of the religious and cultural other. An appreciation for cultural diversity can follow from a pluralism of holy images. It cannot be claimed that Anna's perceived link between divine multiplicity and human diversity is unanimously shared in the community at Mary Star. However, in the cases of several of the long-time devout in this setting, I found a developing interest in inter-cultural

18. See Stroupe and Fleming, *While We Run this Race*, 90, 152–53.

relationships, relationships in which individual differences are allowed to stand and to flourish.

Anna helps out with other groups' devotions not only because she enjoys them, but also because their Madonnas and saints and traditions are familiar, similar to her own experiences of the saints. The other groups' customs, such as the Filipino May Day rosary recital, are both familiar and distinct. They are familiar both because they are similar in some ways to the Italian traditions, and also because the diverse devotions are performed in close spatial proximity to each other. The distinct rituals are all performed somewhere within or near the sacred space of the church; therefore members of the congregation see diverse rituals, whether by intention or by chance, on a regular basis. They also see and hear their priests blessing the diverse symbols, rituals, and groups. Contact and combination have brought these distinct religious groups and practices together. The theological unity that is preached and practiced in the parish supports mutual inter-connections between and among members of diverse groups. Their flavors mingle.

This did not happen overnight. The long history of multiple saints and multi-cultural co-existence has helped habituate the devout to the presence of human diversity in this religious community. Since its beginning in 1889, when a French priest was called to minister to a diverse group of immigrant fisherman and their families, Mary Star has been a multi-ethnic congregation. Each of the immigrant groups, including many regional subgroups, brought with them traditions of devotion to their own particular saints. Through the years, the clergy have encouraged the proliferation of numerous distinct ethnic societies that have now become a key part of the organizational structure of the church. Pastors have also made space in the church's sanctuary for artifacts from diverse immigrants' natal lands. The ethnic diversity of the parish has also been mirrored and reinforced by a diverse staff of multilingual priests, offering Mass in many languages.

This might not have happened at Mary Star of the Sea. Historically, Monsignor George Scott was the church's most influential pastor. He was also the only American-born pastor, and in his time, he expressed his hope for Americanization—that the parish would become one in both language and system. Though Scott was a wildly successful leader, in terms of church growth and vitality, his goal of Americanization as assimilation never completely took hold at Mary Star. Instead, this has remained an immigrant church, and the number of various ethnic societies within the church has continued to grow; it was thirty-two by last count. As the church continues to incorporate new groups of immigrants, additional societies are continuously formed.

By creating and maintaining elaborate devotional practices at Mary Star, both the people and their pastors have made space for ethnic boundary maintenance. Currently at Mary Star, this dynamic is especially critical for the growing Mexican and Mexican American population, and for the arriving Filipinos. This is not to say that the particular groups do not compete with each other; they do. Nor is the congregation free from racism or cultural bias, as we shall see. However, a degree of unity, a flavor of minestrone, is detectable here. As more ethnic groups have appeared at Mary Star, the *habitus* has been able to absorb them (and, in some cases, their saints) into a structure that can expand to make space (literal and cultural) for new devotions.

It is in a sense paradoxical that the strategy of honoring distinctions in ethnic identity has resulted in a kind of unity in the parish. Though George Scott's vision of amalgamated unity never fully took hold, another vision of unity can be said to be brewing. Monsignor Gallagher, pastor since 1985, has through his sermons and weekly bulletins taken on the topics of prejudice, tolerance, and discrimination.[19] He has called for Christian unity, even as he has continued to encourage the proliferation of new societies. Gallagher, an immigrant from Ireland himself, seems to understand the enormous struggle that immigration can entail. By encouraging groups to pursue their treasured devotional traditions, involving food, dress, language, and celebrations, he has helped to facilitate an important form of communal pastoral care for immigrants: giving them space in which to locate themselves symbolically, spatially, socially.

These multiple "spaces" allow for devotions to take place alongside of each other, just as images of diverse saints in the sanctuary occupy separate altars alongside each other. The saints' statues are like neighbors. The devout "visit" one and then go "next door" to see another, or just bow briefly in passing. In the practice of sharing and negotiating the use of sacred space and time, in the form of the devotional calendar, the devout from various groups come into regular contact with each other and each other's saints. The presence of multi-ethnic saints and societies has gradually given

19. See, for example, Gallagher, "Pastor's Corner—Discrimination."

way to more relaxed boundaries between and among ethnic groups over time. "Here we have the unity," said one of my informants. She is an Italian immigrant married to a Croatian immigrant. The inter-ethnic marriages in the community represent a hard-won kind of unity, or perhaps a better adjective would be "slow-cooked." This unity has not developed easily or quickly. Some would say it hasn't developed enough at all, given that groups still routinely gather to pray, sing, or raise money separately a good deal of the time. But at 11:00 a.m. on Sunday mornings at Mary Star, there is often an upbeat, diverse, and intermingling crowd of worshipers. Many in the pews seem to be making connections, not only with God or Mary or the saints, but also with each other.

Of course the church is not free of ethnic or racial or other forms of interpersonal bias. For one thing, the pastor would not be preaching about these issues if he did not perceive them as problems. In my research, I was initially impressed more by a sense of unity than by any indications of prejudice or divisiveness. However, I eventually began to hear some grumbling. I heard two critical comments about how the Latino population has run down the old neighborhoods, and one disturbing racial epithet describing an African American. In the case of the last, the man I was interviewing realized from looking at my face that he had made a mistake. He asked me to erase the tape. I imagine that most people were probably trying to be on their best behavior during these interviews. If they did have conscious biases, they were not going to knowingly express them when my tape-recorder was rolling.

Some peoples' comments expressed bias in an indirect way: "Some people say the Filipinos are taking over the church. That's what they're saying!"[20] These tensions, in part, have to do with the fear of having to share resources and power. Note the emphasis on "taking over the church." Resistance to newcomers comes up here, as it does in many American congregations, in part because people do not want their own cultural space or their power in the group to be threatened or diminished. As Volf puts it, "More often than not, we exclude because in a world of scarce resources and contested power, we want to secure possessions and wrest power from others."[21]

---

20. Interview #24.
21. Volf, *Exclusion and Embrace*, 78.

As we saw in chapter 3, scarce resources and contested power have been part of Mary Star's history as a congregation that included diverse and competing groups of people, many of whom were quite desperate to make a living. As well, a complex mix of issues and contests of ethnic and racial identity have played out in the history of the congregation,[22] as is evident in the production of a minstrel show in 1948. As European immigrants in San Pedro began to gain acceptance and economic security in a land that was slow to recognize them as full citizens, their racial identity shifted and they began to be considered white. As was the case for many "new immigrants," their success and acceptance involved forms of assimilation that may still leave them feeling excluded. However ambivalent some individuals in this setting may be about their own assimilation, the devout's current efforts to maintain ethnic identity reveal the degree to which they have a choice about their ethnicity—a privilege that non-whites do not enjoy. As in many congregations, there is still much work to be done here in coming to terms with white privilege and the ongoing injustice of racial discrimination. I like to imagine that someone will bring a black Madonna into the sanctuary one day, and that a religious society will grow up around her.

Still, I contend that at least for some folks in this setting, the practice of devotions has already begun to challenge ethnic and racial biases and to open up larger visions of God's love for all people. The diversity of saints, both human and supernatural, offers the devout a bit of transcendence or at least symbolic distance from themselves. Just as the devout are accustomed to turning to different saints for different needs—Saint Anthony for lost items, Saint Jude for lost causes—they are also accustomed to seeing a diversity of ethnic celebrations, seeing people with varied skin tones—now including African Americans and African American clergy as well, hearing the Mass in a variety of languages, and smelling and tasting a variety of ethnic foods. All of these activities take place in the sacred space of the church, where they have been brewing together over the years.

On balance, it may be more accurate to say that multiplicity—or minestrone—is still *simmering* at Mary Star. It is simmering with unresolved tensions, and simmering with hopeful possibilities for connection and community as well. Broadly speaking, all human contact and combination produce a certain amount of tension and anxiety. This tension

22. Orsi, *Religious Boundaries*, 335.

or stress sometimes results in a desire to exclude whatever or whoever is perceived as threatening or new. The tendency to exclude is often linked to the need to know and express one's own identity—to say that this is "me," and that is "not me," in Harry Stack Sullivan's formulation.[23]

Theologian Miroslav Volf names exclusion as "sin"—a sin of false purity—and explores three different ways in which human beings manifest this sin. First, exclusion can mean cutting off the bonds of connection, treating the other as the enemy we try to eliminate. A second form exclusion can take is assimilation, where we attempt to erase difference or in effect tell the other to give up his or her identity, and become like us. This is domination. The third form of exclusion is abandonment or indifference, the tendency to "cross to the other side" and ignore others.[24]

Perhaps all of these forms of exclusion have been practiced in some way in Mary Star's history, and there is no doubt that some of these strategies persist among some individuals today. Yet in a church that has always been a home for diverse people, with a sanctuary that displays numerous representations of the holy, the sin of exclusion has been out in the open for some time, and subject to theological challenge. Cultural particularity and intercultural connections are continuously nurtured, resisted, and renegotiated in this space.

"Enriched by Otherness"

The experience of interacting with divine and human multiplicity at Mary Star has helped foster, for some, what Volf calls "a catholic personality." Described in the epigraph to this chapter, this is a personality that is "enriched by otherness." This is an identity that is larger and more complex for knowing the other, a heart that recognizes the other in itself. This kind of intrapersonal ambiguity is generally difficult for us to tolerate. One commentator suggests that it is hard for us even to say the word "different" without thinking to ourselves, "better or worse?"[25] Difference is often experienced as threatening to one's own identity. Among threatened and unsure beings, who are often focused on boundary maintenance—getting clear about what is "me" and what is "not me"—it is fair to ask whether the catholic personality that Volf speaks of is even possible.

23. See Sullivan, *Interpersonal Theory of Psychiatry*.
24. Volf, *Exclusion and Embrace*, 75; Luke 10:31.
25. The author cannot confidently identify the source of this quotation.

Reflecting on his own experience, Volf theorizes that a complex cultural and religious identity requires both distance and belonging:

> Belonging without distance destroys. I affirm my exclusive identity as a Croatian and want to either shape everyone in my own image or eliminate them from my world. But distance without belonging isolates: I deny my identity as a Croatian and draw back from my own culture . . . (I) become trapped in the snares of counter-dependence. Distance creates spaces in us to receive the other.[26]

We need belonging in order to build identity. But we also need internal distance or perspective in order to recognize that we are more than members of a particular group. God is larger than any group; we need distance to perceive it. We need both distance and belonging in order to create the spaces in us into which we can receive the "other."

Implications for Pastoral Practice

The dynamics of cultural interaction and engagement operate at different levels—the intra-personal/spiritual level, and the interpersonal level, and the intercultural level—at the same time. For those engaging in ministries with recent immigrants and other diverse or marginalized persons and groups, it becomes clear that the goal of inclusiveness is not sufficient. Many congregations that attempt to be multicultural do not understand what intercultural or interracial engagement really entails. Merely including immigrants or cultural outsiders—letting them in the door—does not necessarily lead to empowering relationships. As Volf points out, if inclusion is practiced as an invitation to assimilation, if it means, "change yourself to become just like us," it is really a disguised form of exclusion. By contrast, the love of neighbor involves entering into relationships, mixing and mingling in such a way that we can validate and learn from each other, without the requiring anyone to hide or erase differences. This requires practicing engagement, mutual give and take, and experiencing ongoing opportunities to get accustomed to difference.

The love of neighbor is expressed in communal pastoral practices that embody mutuality or reciprocity. Such practices would offer newcomers opportunities for both giving and taking, so that they are not reduced to the status of "charities," but find a place to share their gifts and make

---

26. Volf, *Exclusion and Embrace*, 50.

their mark even while receiving care and encouragement from the "host" community. Congregations that invite "outsiders" in need to be prepared to change and to be changed, enlarged by new relationships.

Ministries to migrants must also honor the newcomers' needs for a balance between social distance and belonging. Those who are engaged in the hard work of relocating spatially and culturally need time to make their way on their own terms, even while experiencing opportunities to forge new connections and to give and receive care. Engagement that is more than mere assimilation is forged over time. It grows and develops, as people make room in the building and room in their lives for each other. Members of host congregations receiving newcomers will also need supportive care, so that their identities or "hearts" can be enlarged, stretched, rather than shut down by fear.

Edward Said wrote that all cultures are "hybrid and encumbered, or entangled and overlapping with what used to be regarded as extraneous elements."[27] When we interact with newcomers whose habits, looks, or languages are unfamiliar, we are challenged to accept or reject the "entangled" parts of our selves. It is always tempting to try to find a way to flee this complexity. The persistence of racial segregation in the majority of American congregations demonstrates this well. The stress of cultural complexity and change must be acknowledged, discussed, and managed. Honest sharing of diverse stories, fears, and hopes can help a congregation grow into deeper, more authentic relationships.

When the "old guard" in a congregation is feeling displaced or devalued by all the attention going to new persons or groups, preaching unity is not likely to be enough to create unity. Those who feel threatened or displaced also need to be recognized and valued—they need to be seen for who they are. In the midst of congregational transformations, they need to know that their most precious traditions will be still honored: their favorite hymns, for example, may still be sung; their past contributions will still be remembered, their stories told. All of the people in congregations can benefit from seeing a little bit of themselves in the sacred symbols employed. The diversity of the congregation can be mirrored in the leadership, the arts, and liturgies employed. Congregations must find ways to make space for the particular contributions, gifts, and tastes of evolving and diverse sectors of people.

27. Said, *Culture and Imperialism*, 317, in Volf, *Exclusion and Embrace*, 52.

Racial identity theorists such as Beverly Tatum have pointed out the benefits of ethnic and racial boundary maintenance at key stages in the process of racial identity formation. Tatum's popular book, *Why Are All The Black Kids Sitting Together in the Cafeteria?* notes the psychological and social benefits of practicing boundary-maintenance for blacks in relation to secondary school success.[28] She found in her research that when students had time apart in all-black student meetings, they improved their school success and they were more likely to engage in social interactions with non-blacks as well. Tatum stresses that the "psychological safety" of discussing race-related stress in one's own group is a necessary part of the developmental process of forging racial or ethnic identity. Creating safe space for separate gatherings of those in marginalized groups seems to be a wise strategy. The Women's Theological Center, a Boston-based organization, for over twenty years has been doing anti-racism training in separate settings for women of color and for whites, in order to provide safe space for the deep spiritual resistance needed for this work.

While safe spaces for boundary maintenance may offer crucial support to particular groups, boundary maintenance as a goal is ultimately insufficient. As Volf points out, we need both belonging and distance in order to cultivate the complex identities that can make room for another. We need cultural interaction and dialogue. Sharing physical and cultural space is perhaps one way in which we can begin to nurture genuine inter-connections.

Congregations can be intentional about making space for human multiplicity of many sorts (ethnicity, class, age, skin-color, sexual orientation, physical dis/ability, to name some examples). Religious diversity, too, can be honored in sacred space. When Beverly Tatum was dean of the religious life at Mount Holyoke College, students of non-Christian faiths complained that their worship practices could not fit into the existing sanctuary and chapel, which were both clearly built for Christian wor-

---

28. Tatum cites in particular the example of METCO (Metropolitan Council for Educational Opportunity), an organization that introduced a program known as Student Efficacy Training (SET) to assist black students who were bussed to a predominantly white suburban school in Eastern Massachusetts. Black students met together each day for a class period, where they were encouraged to discuss their experiences related to race openly with each other, with the support of school staff. Students who participated in this program dramatically improved their grades and reported more positive school experience. Tatum, *Why Are All the Black Kids?* 71–74.

ship.[29] Tatum met with students over a period of time in order to come up with a way to honor the distinct practices of Muslims, Buddhists, Hindus, and Jews. They decided to remodel the smaller chapel into an inter-faith worship space. This meant removing the pews, a decision that was controversial, especially among the alumnae whose families had donated them. But finally it was done, and the physical space was transformed to a space that includes religious symbols from each of these faith traditions. Many of the items are movable, such as Hindu icons enclosed in a movable cabinet, which are displayed when in use, and stored during other services. Tatum calls the chapel, "a powerful symbol of the social transformation we seek in a pluralistic society."[30]

Of course, others may view the chapel differently. Some may see the creation of inter-faith worship space as going too far—in fact, a capitulation to market forces that demand more religious options for students, and as such an abandonment of the radical particularity of Christ. Others may view the inter-faith sharing of the worship space as a practice that does not go far enough, one that is insufficient as a means of inter-faith communications and connection, because diverse religionists and their symbols are not brought together in the chapel, but rather take turns, and thus do not necessarily engage each other in dialogue and relationships.

Multiplicity is indeed a challenging religious value. Still, I think that both the Mary Star of the Sea case study and the Mount Holyoke College chapel example lean in the direction of hope. The creative use of sacred space can help a community engage human multiplicity, rather than obstruct or deny it. When we consider the vast variety of images and symbols that diverse people use to evoke or honor the divine, we are reminded that God is both within and beyond our imaginations.

Engaging symbolic and human multiplicity through pastoral and religious practices, can, over time, transform us. We may find ourselves to be complex, our souls "hybrid and encumbered with what used to be regarded as extraneous elements."[31] When we engage each other in all of our cultural complexity, we may find that our theologies and worldviews, tastes and preferences, gifts and needs mingle and become transformed. We may find our hearts enlarged by otherness.

---

29. Tatum, *Why Are All the Black Kids?*, 216.

30. Ibid., 217.

31. Said, *Culture and Imperialism*, 317, in Volf, *Exclusion and Embrace*, 52.

8

Celebration and Incarnation

> To really receive a work of art, we need to go to it and let it look at us as much as we look at it, from all angles and in all its parts, its part-objects, which gradually we put together into a whole, to find that it, in turn, is putting us together into a whole.
>
> —Ann Ulanov, *Finding Space*

> I came that they may have life, and have it abundantly.
>
> John 10:10

THE doctrine of the incarnation is the bold conviction that the word has become flesh, and dwelt among us: the sacred has mingled with the mundane. The celebrative, abundant, and expansive aspects of the devotions bespeak faith in a God who is here, with us, in fullness and glory. Celebration is a theological value lived in the devotions at Mary Star of the Sea.

We can see this lavish energy enshrined in the striking central altar, in the towering representation of the Madonna, standing in the sea and cradling the community's livelihood. We can see plenty in the large stained-glass window that colorfully depicts the "abundant catch" of the disciples, whose fishing nets are overflowing. We can see bountiful grace in the brimming food on Saint Joseph's Table. We can see human life embraced and made sacred in the elaborate celebrations of the life-cycle marking Baptisms, First Communions, Confirmations, graduations, weddings, and funerals. God's overflowing, abundant provision is celebrated in all of these.

The theme of celebration and incarnation that is evident in large displays and festivals is echoed in many smaller practices and gestures that bring meaning and moment to everyday interactions. I can recall the bouquet of flowers purchased for the saint, the intricate flavors of home-baked cookies, as well as the joyful celebration of meals and coffee breaks with families and friends. A sense of celebration was also shared in my interviews, in the form of humor or energetic, deep, and often delighted sharing. I remember enjoying this abundant energy immensely during the actual research. I was surprised and moved to experience it again when replaying the tapes later.

The community's celebration of beauty is visible in the array of sacred art displayed both at Mary Star church and in the homes of the devout; it is evident in the range of colors and media employed, in paintings, mosaics, fabrics, and stained glass. The size and complexity of the various statues and artifacts, as well as the large sums of money that have been invested in them, are also indications of the enthusiasm that motivated their purchase. A penchant for celebration has also marked the devout's participation in the fishing industry, evident in the history of Fishermen's Fiestas and Blessings of the Fleet. Elaborate flowers, lights, and decorations, as well as colorful clothing and abundant consumption of ethnic foods, are the hallmarks of these events. Food itself is infused with religious meaning, prepared with care and often served with a bountiful flourish. The devotional practices are characterized by habits of plenty or even excess: plentiful food, flowers, emotions, singing and dancing; plentiful generosity and sharing, a lavish sense of the fullness of life.

To view lavish celebration as a situated theological value may indeed seem odd, if not downright disconcerting, to some Christians. The idea of abundant celebration goes against certain philosophical and religious conceptions of modesty. An ethos of restraint or self-control is more familiar to many mainline, middle-class congregations. From Aristotle's call for "moderation in all things," to Cicero's cardinal virtue of temperance, to the asceticism and monasticism of early (and some current) Christian groups, to the more contemporary dictums such as "Live simply, so that others might simply live," we learn the value of restraint. Restraint in emotion, restraint in consuming food, sexual restraint, and (some forms of) financial restraint are implicitly or explicitly taught in many American churches, both Protestant and Catholic.[1] Though the Gospel of John reports Jesus saying, "I came that they might have life, and have it abundantly," abun-

---

1. This emphasis on restraint is often a class-inflected religious virtue, with gendered and racial implications as well. See Bourdieu, *Distinction*.

dance and celebration are not typically cited as themes for Christian living, in the way that, for example, "forgiveness" is. The abundance of God is not often celebrated or consciously practiced.[2]

In lifting up the theological significance of celebration, it is not my intention to deny the moral value of self-control or temperance in a well-lived life. Nor am I promoting a so-called "prosperity gospel."[3] I am also aware of several theological critiques of consumerism and economic injustice that implicate human indulgence; these are enormously important conversations.[4] Further, it has now become clear to people around the world that our excessive consumption of energy generated by the burning of fossil fuels has resulted in climate change and concomitant forms of damage to Earth's ecosystem. Given the harm that we have wrought on the environment, it is imperative that human beings practice restraint in energy consumption, and that we take on the challenge of restoring and preserving the planet's ecological balance.[5]

The value of celebration that I note in the practice of the devotions does not condone wastefulness, but rather elevates the importance of generosity. Celebration here involves a willingness to enjoy, rather than hoard, our daily bread. Bread, like the manna in the wilderness, is received as the gift of God that is enough to sustain us for this day. The extensive food-sharing ministries described in chapter 4 exhibit this kind of generosity—literal loaves and fishes are distributed every day. This practice proclaims faith that God will provide: there will be enough and often something left over. We can partake of and share what we have today.

Celebration as a theological value accents the goodness of life, and embraces the present moment in time and space. In the New Testament we can find evidence of such an expansive, subversive, and celebrative tendency in the life of Jesus of Nazareth himself. The gospels of Matthew and Luke quote Jesus saying, ". . . the Son of Man has come eating and drinking, and you say, 'Look, a glutton and a drunkard, a friend of tax

2. Neither celebration nor abundance is among the "practices of faith," for example, in recent theological volumes on Christian practice. See, for example, Bass, *Practicing Our Faith.* The one exception in this volume is Sharon Parks' essay on "Household Economics," where she speaks of "abundance and enoughness" in the context of living into a more just distribution of goods.

3. Van Biema and Chu, "Does God Want You to Be Rich?"

4. See Moe-Lobeda, *Healing a Broken World*; Poling, *Render Unto God*; Couture, *Seeing Children, Seeing God*; and Ballard and Couture, *Globalisation and Difference.*

5. See Ruether, *Gaia and God*; and McFague, *Life Abundant.*

collectors and sinners!'"[6] Jesus apparently aroused suspicion because he appeared to be enjoying himself, partaking freely of food and drink, entering into camaraderie with the outcast.

The capacity to embrace life in its materiality and temporality—to enjoy, treasure, and celebrate with friends and neighbors—need not involve wastefulness or consumerism. To me, the theological value of celebration pertains to being present and awake, attentive to the beauty and goodness of life. This value is akin to what Buddhists might call "mindfulness."[7] This is a capacity to feel wonder, to experience both pain and pleasure, to enter into the fullness of life in this present moment.

Celebration as a realization of the incarnation is both a critical inward spiritual capacity and a vital social practice. Celebration involves the wisdom to receive the blessings of human community. Abundant life is marked by the capacity and the will to stop what we're doing, and, in words of the parable, "come to the banquet."[8]

This capacity to celebrate life with gusto and soak it all in is an art form among the devout. This skill is historically rooted in family stories of economic struggle, immigration, and fishing. It was the struggle for survival that brought many immigrants to this country to begin with. The extremes of the fishing life and its attendant risks, losses, and fears also contributed to the intensity and vigor of the prayers of the people. Because of the uncertainties related to fishing fortunes, accidents, and illnesses, the immigrants that I interviewed, their children, and their grandchildren have absorbed a frightening knowledge of the tenuous and contingent nature of life. I think that it is this embodied knowledge that fuels the community practices of celebration.

It may even be that a version of the fishermen's "live for today" bravado (described in chapter 3) has been retained in the devotional practices. Currently, many of the devout immigrants and their children are in their retirement years, enjoying more wealth and leisure time than they expected. They are grateful to God and their saints both for their survival and for their surprising material ease. At the same time, the devout find that their saints "hold" memories of loved ones lost, of the fear and worry of difficult times, of the knowledge that nothing can be taken for granted.

6. Luke 7:34; Matt 11:19.

7. Hahn, *Blooming of a Lotus*, vii–ix.

8. Matt 22:9.

These are things that people both want to remember and want to forget. So it makes sense that at least some of the people celebrate the devotions a little bit like fishermen going into a bar after a long time away at sea. On saints' days, the devout do not just decorate their saints' shrines; they adorn them with flowers and fabrics and votive candles. The people do not just pray; they perpetually adore. They do not just eat; they put on an elaborate feast with music and dancing and extraordinary dishes, and open the doors to anyone who will come. They then share the leftovers with the neighbors the next day.

This penchant for celebration might also be thought of as vitality. I hesitate to use this word, as it brings up stereotypes of the so-called "primitive vitality" that cultural anthropologists used to use when describing those people they viewed as racially and culturally "other." It has been pointed out that this kind of stereotyping may function as a projection of scholars' unacknowledged or repressed fantasies and needs. When immigrants, urbanites, indigenous peoples, or people of color are seen as exotic or hypersexual or entertaining, they serve to "hold" the disclaimed aspects of the viewer. Whether such stereotypes idealize people or denigrate them, they still keep the "other" firmly at a distance.[9] I hesitate to use the term vitality because I do not wish to engage in this kind of romanticism, whereby the devout and their "popular" Catholic practices become a stand-in for the spiritual energy or enthusiasm that some of us may long for or lack.

I lift up vitality, rather, because I think it is an important dimension of all human life. Pastoral theologian Kathleen Greider defines vitality as ". . . essential aliveness and life-affirmation, . . . human agency that manifests in passion and capacity to endure."[10] Certainly this celebrative energy is characteristic of the devotions, which proclaim "essential aliveness and life-affirmation." Perhaps this is because in practicing them, the devout recall and reaffirm so much of their history and identity. Without even thinking about it, the devout through their practices ground themselves in memories of endurance, hope, and survival. Religious practices that are so firmly rooted in history and identity have the capacity to spark energy and vitality when they are creatively adapted to life in the present.

9. See Orsi, "Introduction: Crossing the City Line," 7–13 in *Gods of the City*; and di Leonardo, *Exotics at Home.*

10. Greider, *Reckoning with Aggression*, 9.

The memory of the past is, in the words of social historian Paul Connerton, "sedimented, or amassed, in the body."[11] The devotions keep the lively past fresh for the devout, in part because they require skilled physical postures that hold bodily memories. In the skilled practice of visual piety, for example, the devout can approach—go toward—the holy presence, bringing with them whatever current needs, hopes, or fears they may have.

This movement toward the saints can be viewed as what Greider calls the "life force . . . part of the impulse to survive and thrive."[12] This is an expression of our human aggressive impulse. In Greider's view, the aggressive impulse can either be expressed negatively, as violence, or positively, as vitality or passion for living. Perhaps the vitality of these devotional practices derives from the great sense of freedom that they offer. There is a freedom to confide in the saints, to express intimate emotions such as hope and fear and even anger. Through the devotions, people can go toward their saints with the intensity of grief and the bold desire to survive and thrive. The saints, because they are understood as eternal in the heavens, are not harmed by human emotions or expressions of aggression. One can go toward them in a way that might be thought too intimate or familiar if one were approaching God directly. The saints can take the onslaught of petitions, grief, guilt, or fear. In the transitional space of prayer to one's particular patrons, such emotions may be processed, engaged, met, and/or transformed into creative energy and actions.[13] In response, Mary and the saints calmly gaze at the devout; they not only endure, they smile.

I think that the devotions remain robust in this setting also because they are malleable. Artistic renderings of supernatural figures express variety, invite improvisation. We have seen how the large-scale feasts embody both durability and change. But even daily rituals—such as bringing flowers to the saint—present small opportunities for the devout to shape and reshape her or his physical environment. By going to church, where sacred art surrounds her, or by going to the florist or the garden to find flowers for the saint, the devout alters and enriches her environment, filling it with

11. Connerton, *How Societies Remember*, 72.

12. Greider, *Reckoning with Aggression*, 35.

13. Winnicott links adult creativity and a sense of aliveness to the ability to experience through playing or formlessness a foray into the transitional realm. It is through such experiences that a sense of self develops that is genuine, more than mere compliance. *Playing and Reality*, 64–65.

fragrance or friendship. We have seen how time spent in the sanctuary alone (in the presence of God) can be a centering, grounding experience. As well, habitual personal involvement in the material maintenance of sacred space tends to create a deeper commitment.

The devotions involve social interaction. This interaction can at times be burdensome, as we saw in chapter 4, when it absorbs the time and energy of women (and men) whose lives are already too full. But this social interaction can also be seen as life enhancing, especially for widows and retirees who report that they enjoy the opportunity to participate, shape, "have a hand in" the devotional activities. Consider the case of the continuous devotions held around the clock in the perpetual adoration chapel at the entrance to Mary Star. Parishioners sign up for their hours to pray there. One person cannot leave until the next person arrives. The presence of each person is noticed, valued. Each person is counted upon to fulfill their obligation by getting up and showing up. In this, the devotions tap into and nourish a sense of purpose in the devout as they age, rather than allow it to wither.

The story of Maria (chapter 2) illustrates the creativity to which the devotions give rise. Maria could be described as a religious virtuoso, not just because of the time she invests in devotional practices but also because of the energy she exudes in her practices of faith. I noticed this in at least three arenas: in her praying and Bible reading; in her domestic arts of baking and sewing; and in her comments about her faith. When Maria reads the Bible, she feels that God is communicating with her, and helping her to interpret it to her friends. She does this with gusto, with "feeling," to use her word. She prays with feeling to the Madonna Rosa Mistica, to Jesus, and to diverse saints. Maria also exhibits creativity in her baking and sewing. She showed me some traditional Italian costumes that she had recently made for a devotional feast (Figure 43). The fabrics used were bright and crisp. Some of the white fabric was embellished with eyelet and embroidery, giving it the intimation of a liturgical vestment. Such vibrant colors and contrasts announce a vivid and creative faith.

In many ways, Maria is a humble woman. Yet in displaying these boldly beautiful articles she had created, she also seems quite fulfilled. Finally, Maria's thoughtful comments about her life and faith suggested a subversive thread. She told me that she had been sitting near the Monsignor himself at recent church dinner. She watched as he was served his meal first. She said, "I told him I would like to be born a man, so I can go to priest [so I can become a priest]. Then I can get served first."[14] She makes this comment sweetly, with no hint of malice. Nevertheless, her comment reveals her awareness of and resistance to her inferior status as a woman: she has experienced a religious call to preach; and she is aware of the privileges of the clerical office, privileges that she won't enjoy in this life. Aware of all of this and not shy about protesting, she makes her own fine vestment and goes to the banquet.

Sometimes I wonder whether the celebrative energy of the devout in San Pedro isn't affected by or related to the physical presence of the Pacific Ocean. Many folks told me that they love the ocean and often go down by the marina to walk, to think, or to meditate. Several of the folks I interviewed can actually see spectacular views of the water from their homes. The beauty of the water and a sense of the wonder and mystery of the sea, were frequently remarked upon. Many people also suggested that views of the coastline remind them of their hometowns along the Southern coast of Italy, or of life on one of the islands. For example, one man noted that the distant shape of Catalina Island viewed from San Pedro is similar to that of Ischia from the vantage point of the coast of Naples. I saw these resemblances myself when I traveled to Ischia: the steep cliff coastlines and the rock formations in relief against the sky, the sweeping blue waters (Figure 44). Now that many of the immigrants and their children travel back and forth to these other coasts with some frequency, their combined memories of clear blue water and the immense power of the seas here as well as there refresh these visual memories. The ocean is, of course, also a reminder of fishing livelihoods, adventures, and accidents. For some, the sight of the water may still recall their actual voyages to America. Some claim that the ocean is experienced as a spiritual presence. This ocean inspires a sense of danger, power, and majesty. It is a potent life force with which to reckon.

I started to wonder whether living in such close proximity to the Pacific Ocean has contributed to the expansive quality of the community, its generosity of spirit. This quality is evident in the large-scale celebrations that I have described as leaning toward excess. But it is more than that. One woman whom I interviewed told the story of recently attending the second wedding of her daughter's ex-husband. The couple had had a bitter divorce but had kept their interactions civil, in the interest of their children. "Donna," the woman I interviewed, wasn't sure whether she should

14. Interview #18.

attend this wedding.[15] But her former son-in-law begged her to come, so she went, and enjoyed a place of honor there. Even more surprisingly, the man invited his ex-wife, who also chose to come; she even stood to offer kind words to the new couple. When Donna told me this story, I was amazed. Where did this woman get such an expansive spirit, one that could make room for new people and new arrangements, without having to blame or disown or distance herself from anyone?

Later that evening, I waited while Donna took a break from our interview so she that could put her husband to bed. Her husband had suffered a debilitating stroke approximately two years earlier, and Donna had been caring for him in their home ever since. Since his bed is now in the living room, I could not help but overhear as Donna sang him to sleep. "Have I told you lately that I love you?" she sang, in a quiet voice full of kindness and affection. I was moved by this tenderness. Whether it is due to the loving gaze of Mary, or the inspiration of the water, or pure coincidence, a smooth and expansive kind of love seems evident here.

Pastoral Theological Implications

What can we learn from the theological value of celebration, and the expansive, vital abundance that it proclaims? In this case study, I found that religious vitality was often rooted in the aesthetic and embodied dimensions of the practice of the devotions—in art and activity, in skilled actions. Pastoral theologians can find energy for transformative change by focusing on faith practices that incorporate aesthetic sensibilities and skills. The theological significance of art and architecture is certainly an example of one area that is ripe for exploration in many diverse religious settings.

Catherine Kapikian, in her book, *Art in Service of the Sacred*, makes a case for reclaiming the spiritual power of visual art in Protestant congregations. She, too, makes the connection between the language of incarnation and the material forms that can help to mediate the meaning of the word through aesthetic experience.[16] She understands that the capacity to see is a vital religious skill, one that she claims is "in need of thoughtful reinvigoration.[17]

15. Interview #3.
16. Kapikian, *Art in Service of the Sacred*, 36.
17. Ibid., 41.

Kapikian takes up the issue of the religious mistrust of the sensual, which she relates to the hierarchical body/spirit split that can prevent us from understanding even the scriptural assertion that "beauty is of God."[18] Kapikian and other artist–theologians are helping to break down this split, not only through their teaching but also through their work with numerous congregations that are seeking transformation of their worship spaces.

Interestingly, Kapikian involves the ordinary faithful, and not just the artistically gifted, in her practice of creating art for congregations. She sees the central importance of religious imagination in the life of faith, and like Winnicott, points to the role of creativity in maturity. Kapikian explains:

> What does a leap of faith require? Does spiritual maturity reside in the person who is unaccustomed to transcending limits, a hallmark of the creative act? Can aspirations for wholeness of personhood be realized in an environment weak in opportunities giving wings to imagination?[19]

Ministry that would empower people to bold transformation cannot ignore the evocative power of the arts to "give wings to the imagination."

In Protestant settings, embodied and aesthetic religious experience will often already be deeply familiar through the field of music. Both in singing hymns and in listening to them, the body, the senses, and the aesthetic sensibilities of the faithful are called forth.[20] This is a practice and an experience of religion that moves people into the transitional realm, the space in between our inner worlds and the larger external reality. As the musician and homiletician, Don Saliers, points out, the words of worship depend radically upon that which is not verbal for their depth and meaning.[21]

The importance of music and lyrics can also be grasped by considering the intensity of arguments that are generated when new hymnbooks are introduced in mainline Protestant congregations. Or, consider the debates about styles of music—traditional, praise, blended, etcetera—which congregations routinely engage in. All of this energy and investment indicates that music is a vein of vitality in congregational life. Religious leaders

18. Ibid., 34–35.
19. Kapikian, *Art in Service of the Sacred*, 23.
20. Slough, "Let Every Tongue," 175–206. Also see Hess, "Practices in a New Key."
21. Saliers, "What Languages Shall We Borrow?"

might have more patience with these controversies, if their theological importance were more fully appreciated. Rather than seeing battles over hymns as petty or personal power grabs, wise leaders can decide to view them as rich opportunities for theological dialogue. Hymns themselves can be seen as forms of celebration, instances of incarnation, strains of the glory of God.

Sacramental Imagination

Ann Ulanov writes, "To really receive a work of art, we need to go to it and let it look at us as much as we look at it, from all angles and in all its parts, its part-objects, which gradually we put together into a whole, to find that it, in turn, is putting us together into a whole."[22] The three situated values that I have identified in the practice of these living devotions—connection, multiplicity, and celebration—represent angles and parts of the picture of devotional piety that we have been looking at. When we put them all together, they add up to something larger, something that I would call a sacramental view of life.

The Catholic sociologist and novelist Andrew Greeley writes about "the sacramental imagination," or "the enchanted imagination" of Catholics.[23] Greeley argues for a special Catholic imagination, one that emphasizes the presence of God in mundane life. He claims that Catholic writers tend to stress presence of God in the world, while Protestant writers more often speak of God's absence. Or, to put it another way, Catholics emphasize the immanence of God, while Protestants emphasize divine transcendence.[24] While I do not agree with Greeley's entire line of argument, my explorations of the devotional practices lend credence to the idea of a sacramental approach to life that is distinctly Catholic.

Certainly an emphasis on presence is borne out in these pages, especially in regard to visual piety. The Baltimore Catechism includes the question, "Where is God?" The answer, "God is everywhere," is visually clear in this devotional Catholic community. The message of holy presence can be read in church art and architecture, in the devout's bed stand photos, backyard shrines, classroom corners, or refrigerator magnets. Religious

22. Ulanov, *Finding Space*, 65.

23. Greeley, *Catholic Imagination*. Greeley builds upon the work of David Tracy. See Tracy, *Analogical Imagination*.

24. Greeley, *Catholic Imagination*, 5.

imagination, in this setting, involves visual skill and aesthetic sensibilities, shaped from childhood and reinforced at regular Mass, at annual religious feasts, and at key moments of ritual celebration across the lifespan.

Whether or not a religious community displays religious representations, visual surroundings in homes and sacred spaces are influential in forming religious identity. Art, architecture, and landscapes all play a role in the formation of human beings, our concepts of God, of ourselves, and of our relationships to each other and all of creation. The presence *or* absence of religious images in our lives says something about us and to us every day.

"Incorporated Conviction"

The work of Paul Connerton also speaks to a distinctly Catholic experience of faith. He roots this distinction primarily in Catholic liturgy. Connerton, a theorist of social memory, notes that Catholic liturgy is "not propositional statement but sacred action." Sacred actions "convey conviction by incorporating it. . . . Not the pulpit but the altar is the privileged site. In the pulpit the sacred narrative receives a commentary. At the altar the substance of the narrative is communicated in physical signs that contain it."[25] The "substance of the narrative," the presence of Christ, is communicated to Catholics in a particularly visceral way through the sacrament of Holy Communion.

The devout are accustomed to experiencing the presence of Christ in the actual wafer they receive weekly or even daily in the sacrament of Holy Communion. In this ritual, spiritual and material realms are regularly intermingled. Catholics' embodied knowledge of this experience is explicitly underscored in the doctrine of transubstantiation, which holds that the elements of bread and wine actually become the body and blood of Jesus through the sacrament of Holy Eucharist. It is not difficult to understand how a sacramental view of life can follow from this regular ritual experience, combined with the teaching of this venerable doctrine.

A sacramental worldview is exemplified in the comments of a couple I interviewed, both members of the third immigrant generation. Each of the two had experienced the painful break-up of a previous marriage, and they had only recently married each other.[26] The couple told me of

25. Connerton, *How Societies Remember*, 70.

26. The couple did not describe the circumstances of their divorces and/or annulments.

their profound sense of God's grace in their union, and in the blending of their new family. They are both active at Trinity Church, where the woman is active in the ministry of music, and the man helps serve Holy Communion, a task he approaches with great intensity and heart. In the course of our interview, after they had spoken at length of their love, their religious practices, and the intimacy of their shared faith and ethnic heritage, the man placed his hand down firmly on the dining room table. He said, "This is the altar. This is where everything happens. This is where we break bread!"[27] At this, his wife embraced him, and began to weep gently. This couple experiences the presence of Christ in breaking bread together, at home at their table. They bring what could be called a "sacramental imagination" or an "incorporated conviction" to their relationship. Indeed, I could see how both the brokenness and the healing of their lives are expressed in the dual "incorporating practices" of participating in the Eucharist at church and sharing food and love as they sit down around their own dining room table.

Conclusion

The situated values of connection, multiplicity, and celebration suggest some of the embodied practical wisdom that arises from the devotions in San Pedro. These values are not exactly ontological statements, nor are they fixed cultural characteristics of the immigrants. Rather, they are ways to name "the effects and traces of God"[28] that can be glimpsed in these local religious practices during this brief snapshot in time. These are values of "hope and obligation" in this place.[29] These values shift and allow for innovation as they are continuously reconstituted in practice, even as they also exhibit signs of being durable, reliable reminders of a sacramental way of life.

In this community, the values of connection, multiplicity, and the celebration of life are communicated both through speech and through action. Explicit theologies provide the background music for rituals, ministries, and liturgies that enact living mysteries with fanfare and flourish. The devout's Catholic *habitus* in San Pedro is continuously renovated

---

However, it is clear that they currently enjoy full participation in the church.

27. Interview #28.

28. Graham, *Transforming Practice*, 207.

29. Ibid., 206.

through innovative practices that depict, influence, and shape perceptions of the divine, as well as constructions of self and other.

Likewise in homes, the sacred and the mundane inhabit devotional shrines, bumping up against each other in apparent confusion. One woman's bedroom slippers, folded neatly on her bedside table, rest against a picture of her deceased mother, a picture that is itself draped with rosary beads (Figure 19). There is a kind of jarring admixture of the spiritual and the material in home shrines, a blurring and blending. It is understandable to me that Protestants might gasp at the ease with which statues can sometimes stand in for the saints they represent, or at the way in which images of Mary or the one of the saints can seem to upstage the cross. I can appreciate the concern that a sense of divine transcendence might be lost in all the clutter.

Yet I hope that this narrative also demonstrates some of the merits of a sacramental imagination and a sacramental way of life. I hope that readers can better appreciate the pastoral value of devotional practices that relax the barriers between heaven and earth. When the sacred can be treated in such mundane and familiar ways, can human life itself become more sacred, more dear? My unprovable conclusion is that the transcendent power of God is not lost in this setting; it is accessed. It is accessed through experiences of art and land and sea, and through bonds of affection and attachment to female as well as male representations of the holy. It is accessed through memory and hope. In this sacramental way of life, the devout mark the miracle of daily sustenance and survival, with prayer and dedication, with food and festivity, and with courageous attempts to live passionately in the face of fear, loss, and change.

The immigrants, their children and grandchildren, to varying degrees, hold onto their religious practices, or let go, or reject them. Some individuals experience themselves as held by religious bonds that they thought they had broken long ago. Others find themselves remembering loved ones, saints, or sensations with affection. In the vital and rich practice of devotions, worlds of meaning transpire. Like ripples in the ocean, effects and traces reverberate across the generations. Everywhere you turn you see God.

Appendix A

Definitions and Research Procedures

Definitions

Devotional Practices

CATHOLIC devotional practices have traditionally been defined as forms of prayer to Mary, Jesus, the angels, or the saints. Devotional practices include such activities as prayer, singing, touching holy water, medals, or relics, gazing at holy images or cards, saying the rosary, fasting, lighting candles, keeping novenas (continuous prayer marathons), and celebrating feast days of the saints with ritual processions, traditional foods, and special clothing. For the purposes of this study, I began by looking at these kinds of explicitly pious and Catholic activities in this setting, and asking people what they meant to them. I explored, in as much detail as possible, the material cultural dimensions of the devotions. This led me to consider activities that might not be considered religious practices at all, such as one man's role in organizing the practical details of a feast day celebration, involving such tasks as writing letters to government officials in order to obtain city permits for the procession in the street. Raising money for the church, money often donated in the name of a particular patron saint, is another example of an activity that is not explicitly pious, but is nevertheless crucial to maintaining the devotional practices. Caring for statues by dusting them or decorating them with lights or flowers, donating and preparing food for the Saint Joseph's Table feast, sewing traditional garments and selecting people to play parts in sacred dramas—these are all substantial and time-consuming activities that express the devotion of the people.

Italian Immigrants

While San Pedro is a multi-ethnic community and Mary Star is a multi-ethnic church, I chose to focus my study on Italian and Sicilian immigrants, for several reasons. Practically speaking, my own Italian heritage and language skills both motivated me and helped me gain access to this population. I wanted to be able to explore the ways in which immigration from Italy and later generations' constructions of ethnicity influenced religious practices and vice-versa. Interconnections between and among individuals from various ethnic groups are examined here, but not as extensively as they could be. The central axis of comparison is generational.

I chose San Pedro, California as the location of my study in part because there is an unusually large concentration of people of Italian and Sicilian immigrants and their descendants living there. Italians in San Pedro come from all over Italy, but the two largest groups come from the islands of Ischia and Sicily. Ischia is a small island in the Bay of Naples, near Capri. Another large group of immigrants comes from Sicily. These folks often refer to themselves as Italian, speaking in such a way as to indicate that they view Sicily as a region of Italy. In my writing, I have tried to use the language that the people themselves use to describe themselves. These two groups are well represented in this study, but persons from other parts of Italy are included as well. I refer to the persons who are the subject of my research as Italian immigrants and their descendants. I have intentionally tried to refrain from giving them identities such as "Italian American." Instead, I tried to invite people talk about their ethnic identity in their own words.

Three Generations

I set out looking for thirty persons to interview, persons who I hoped would be evenly spread over three immigrant generations—that is, ten Italian immigrants, ten members of the second generation (the first generation born here), and ten members of the third generation. I expected to have a difficult time finding immigrants—and rushed to interview the oldest persons first, for fear this generation would die out before I could get to them. I soon learned that I would have no shortage of immigrants to interview, because Italian immigration has been a continuing phenomenon in San Pedro. Though the numbers of new immigrants have dwindled significantly in recent years, the relatively young age of many immigrants here is unusual. I also interviewed several second-generation young women who had intentionally gone back to Italy or Sicily to marry, and brought their husbands with them back to San Pedro. The age range of the immigrants I did find was a good deal wider than expected.

While I anticipated that inter-ethnic marriage would complicate my sample in the later generations, I did not anticipate the messiness of defining the generations. Most research deems persons who immigrated under the age of twelve or fourteen members of the "one and a half" generation, because they usually learn English quickly and perform roles that are in many ways analogous to members of the second generation—translating for their parents, filing government forms, and bearing the brunt of the conflicts involved in processes of assimilation or cultural interaction. I then wasn't sure how to classify their children. A "two and a half" designation seemed to signify less. Also, I found persons whose parents were of different generations, so I started coding them with fractions such as two-thirds generation, meaning second generation via the maternal side, and third generation paternal. One of my interviewees is from the fourth generation.

Research Procedures

I employed three research methods: participant observation, qualitative interviewing, and the examination of historical documents. During the course of a year, I traveled to San Pedro from my home in Riverside regularly to observe, interview, participate, scan documents at the local public library and the San Pedro Bay Historical Society, sit in church, and/or walk the beach. I met and spoke with several persons in the community, including the pastor and other members of the pastoral staff of Mary Star Parish, several Episcopal clergy persons in the area, some restaurant owners and patrons, and the staff at the San Pedro Bay Historical Society. I also acquired copies of two small research projects previously conducted in San Pedro by the Italian Oral History Institute at the University of California Los Angeles.

The thirty-one taped interviews with immigrants and their descendants constitute the centerpiece of the research. The interviews lasted anywhere from one to three hours, the average being about two hours. They were semi-structured. The questions I started with are included in Appendix B. I used the questions in order to lead into a few general areas of inquiry. The main areas that I explored included the family's immigration story, past and current devotional practices, ties to the fishing industry, and the meaning that all of this had for the person I was interviewing. If a person seemed to focus on a particular religious celebration or event or issue, I would try to follow his or her lead, even if it meant that we did not cover all of the questions.

All of the thirty-one interviewees signed release forms giving me permission to make audio tape recordings of the interviews. I noted on these forms that I would not use interviewees' real names in any writing or publications related to this research. In some cases, where the persons interviewed did not read English, I obtained verbal permissions, which are recorded on the tapes.

Because the tapes do include names, I have kept them confidential and stored them in a locked safe. While most of the persons I interviewed did not express any particular concern about anonymity, and a few expressly gave me permission to use their real names, I decided to be consistent and used pseudonyms throughout. In writing this book, I altered or omitted some of the most sensitive personal details shared in the interviews.

The persons I interviewed ranged from ages twenty-four to ninety-one. They were mostly bi-lingual; only five of the interviews were conducted partly in Italian. Most of the interviews were conducted in peoples' homes, at kitchen or dining room tables, often overlooking the sea. In some cases, I met family members or friends, who sometimes contributed to the conversation. While most interviews were conducted individually, some were done with couples, and one in the context of a dinner party. I was frequently the recipient of great hospitality on these visits. Italian coffee and homemade cookies—often with a plate to take home—were generously offered. About half of the time, I managed to plan ahead enough to bring a small gift—such as a loaf of bread or a coffee cake—as an expression of thanks and as a way of participating in the exchange of hospitality.

My research partners were gracious in allowing me to photograph their religious art, artifacts, altars, and shrines. Some individuals asked me to take their pictures. I have avoided using names in the captions accompanying the figures used in this dissertation in order to err on the side of caution and protection of anonymity. I also took photographs of the sanctuary at Mary Star, some of which include worshippers and participants in devotional events. Finally, there are some photographs included that I took in public places in San Pedro. All photographs referenced here and found at http://www.MaryMoschella.net/LivingDevotions are my own.

Appendix B

Interview Questionnaire

A. These are some of the questions used for semi-structured taped interviews with immigrants and some members of the second generation. These forms were not distributed as questionnaires. They were used in order to initiate open-ended conversations.

1. Name:_____

      Mention: your name is important to help me trace family connections. It will not, however, be used in any articles or books that may result from this research.

2. Age:_____Male_____ Female_____

3. Describe your education and occupation.

4. Where do you live now?_____ Where were you born?
_____

5. Briefly describe the people in your family tree, including parents and grandparents, spouse, children and grandchildren. Include names, ages, places of birth, occupations, and any outstanding features.

6. Describe your own experience of immigration, or recall stories of immigration told to you by parents or grandparents. Include dates.

7. What did your neighborhood in the homeland look like? How does it compare or contrast to San Pedro?

8. Describe your church and devotions in the homeland.
9. Describe your current practice of religion.

10. Are there any particular saints to whom you pray? Which are most important to you and why?

> San Giovan Giuseppe della Croce
> St. Joseph
> St. Ann
> Our Lady of Guadeloupe
> Our Lady of the Assumption
> Our Lady of Perpetual Help
> Padre Pio
> St. Jude
> St. Anthony
> Other

11. Describe the appearance, character traits, and history of the saint or saints to whom you most frequently pray.

12. Do you have home altars? In what rooms?

> Describe these altars, how you created them, and where the statues came from.

13. Describe your devotional practices at home and in church:

> How frequently do you pray?
> What or whom do you pray for?
> Do you bring flowers to the saint?
> Light candles?
> Fast?
> Offer money?
> Use rosary beads?
> Holy cards?
> Hymns?
> In what language do you pray?
> In what position is your body?
> What are you looking at?

14. How do you feel when you pray?

How have your prayers been answered?

15. If you are an immigrant, when you came to this country, did your devotion increase? decrease? remain the same?

16. Did any of the saints help you adjust to life in this country? If so, how?

17. In what ways do your devotions remind you of your homeland?

18. In what ways do your devotions remind you of your family?

19. How old were you when you first learned these devotions?

20. How do you feel about the saint(s) to whom you pray? Describe the relationship in as much detail as possible.

21. What does the saint do for/to you?

22. What does the saint require of you?

23. Do you share your devotional experiences or practices with anyone?
    friends
    priests
    family members?

24. Do you belong to any religious societies? Please specify which ones and describe your participation.
    St. Ann's Society
    ICF
    St. Joseph's Table
    Velike Gospe Society
    Hermandad Catolica Hispanoamericana Club
    Croatian Catholic Family Guild
    Other

25. How do you feel about the devotional practices and feast days of other ethnic saints at Mary Star? Do your or your children or grandchildren participate in any of them?

26. Do you think of yourself as being Italian? How do your parents, children, and/or grandchildren describe their ethnicity?

27. Have you tried to pass on your devotions to your children? Do your children or grandchildren practice these devotions? If so, are they as fervent as you are?

28. Does the Mary Star church building, or any particular statue, image, or relic, hold special meaning for you?

29. Do you participate in any special feast day celebrations, masses, novenas, or processions? Please describe them in detail, including special foods, customs, clothing, hymns, etc. Also, specify your role and your reasons for participating.

30. Did you or your parents or grandparents participate in the fisherman's fiesta? Please describe your experiences of in detail.

31. Do you have any photographs, diaries, or written accounts of your family's devotional practices that you would be willing to show me?

32. Do you read any Catholic magazines or devotional literature?

33. Is there anything else about you, your family, or your devotional life that you want me to know?

B. Research questions used with members of the later immigrant generations. These topics were also used to prompt open-ended conversation.

Name:
Age:

Gender:
Education:
Employment:

Family tree:
Family immigration history:
What is your ethnic background?

What does your ethnic identity mean to you?

Have you visited your family's country or countries of origin? What was that like for you?

Do you speak your parents' or grandparents native language? Do your children?

Do you consider yourself Catholic?

What does being Catholic mean to you?

Did you grow up in a home with indoor or outdoor shrines to the saints, holy water containers, religious art, etc.?

If you can recall, what were your childhood impressions of such art or objects in your home? Do you recall any emotions associated with these representations?

What about your recollections of religious statues or art in the church? Any special figure that you did or do focus on while praying or attending Mass?

Did you go to Catholic school?

Describe your current religious practices, noting frequency.
  Mass
  Candles
  prayers
  confession
  Rosary
  Flowers
  novenas
  feasts

Do you pray to any saints?
  John Joseph
  Joseph
  Anthony
  Jude
  BVM
  Padre Pio
  Sacred Heart

Do you have home altars, crucifixes or shrines? Where?

For whom or what did/do you pray? Have your prayers ever been answered?

What do the saints require of you?

What do the Saints mean to you?
Do they remind you of your family?
Are they linked to your family's immigration story?

Did your family take part in the fishing industry in Italy or San Pedro? The Fisherman's Fiesta? What was that like for you?

How did you feel about the sea when you were little?

Were there many stories of fishermen lost at sea?

Did you feel growing up that Mary Star was a fishermen's church?

How did/do you feel about your parents' religion? Was it helpful, burdensome, pleasurable, boring, etc.?

Did/does their religion help or hinder them in coping with difficult life circumstances? What specifically?

How do you deal with adversity in your life?

Are there attitudes, customs, or social connections that you have kept with you related to your family's immigration history or religious practices?

Do you try to pass these on to your children (if you have any?)

Is there anything else you would like to tell me about the meaning of your faith or spirituality in your life?

Bibliography

"About the Italian Catholic Federation." *Bollettino: Monthly Newspaper of the Italian Catholic Federation*, Feb. 2000, 3.

Ainsworth, Mary D. Salter. "The Development of Infant-Mother Attachment." *In Review of Child Development Research*, Vol. 3, edited by Bettye Caldwell and Henry N. Ricciuti, 1–94. Chicago: University of Chicago Press, 1973.

Albanese, Catherine. "Exchanging Selves, Exchanging Souls: Contact, Combination, and American Religious History." *In Retelling U.S. Religious History*, edited by Thomas A. Tweed, 200–26. Berkeley: University of California Press, 1997.

Ammerman, Nancy Tatom, and Arthur Emery Farnsley. *Congregation and Community*. New Brunswick, NJ: Rutgers University Press, 1997.

"Angel's Gate Salutes . . ." Angel's Gate Council, No. 1740, Knights of Columbus, circa 1975.

Armstrong, Karen. *The Spiral Staircase: My Climb Out of Darkness*. New York: Anchor, 2004.

Atkinson, Clarissa, Constance Buchanan, and Margaret R. Miles, eds. *Immaculate and Powerful: Female Sacred Image and Social Reality*. Boston: Beacon, 1985.

Aune, Michael B., and Valerie Demarinis, eds. *Religious and Social Ritual: Interdisciplinary Explorations*. Albany: State University of New York Press, 1996.

Ballard, Paul F., and Pamela D. Couture, eds. *Globalisation and Difference: Practical Theology in a World Context*. Cardiff, UK: Cardiff Academic, 1999.

Barrett, James R., and David Roediger. "Inbetween Peoples: Race, Nationality, and the 'New Immigrant' Working Class." *Journal of American Ethnic History* 16 (Spring 1997): 3–44.

Bartlett, Arthur. "Islands of San Pedro Bay." In *Shoreline*. San Pedro, CA: San Pedro Historical Society, 1997.

Bass, Dorothy C. *Practicing Our Faith: A Way of Life for a Searching People*. San Francisco: Jossey-Bass, 1998.

Belenky, Mary Field, Lynne A. Bond, and Jacqueline S. Weinstock. *A Tradition That has No Name: Nurturing the Development of People, Families, and Communities*. New York: Basic, 1997.

Bell, Catherine. *Ritual Theory, Ritual Practice*. New York: Oxford University Press, 1992.

Bellah, Robert N., Richard Madsen, William M. Sullivan, Ann Swidler, and Steven M. Tipton. *Habits of the Heart: Individualism and Commitment in American Life*. Berkeley: University of California Press, 1985.

Birren, James E., Gary M. Kenyon, Jan-Erik Ruth, and Johannes J. F. Schroots, eds. *Aging and Biography: Explorations in Adult Development*. New York: Springer, 1996.

Bobich, Mel, and Samuel J. Palmer, Jr., eds. *Mary Star of the Sea Parish Centennial, 1889–1989*. San Pedro, CA, 1989.

Boisen, Anton. *Exploration of the Inner World*. New York: Harper Torchbooks, 1950.

Borg, Marcus. *The Heart of Christianity: Rediscovering a Life of Faith.* New York: HarperCollins, 2003.

Bourdieu, Pierre. *Distinction: A Social Critique of the Judgement of Taste.* Translated by Richard Nice. Cambridge: Harvard University Press, 1984.

———. *The Logic of Practice.* Translated by Richard Nice. Cambridge, U.K.: Polity, 1990.

———. *Outline of a Theory of Practice.* Translated by Richard Nice. Cambridge: Cambridge University Press, 1977.

Bourdieu, Pierre, and Loic J. D. Wacquant. *An Invitation to Reflexive Sociology.* Chicago: University of Chicago Press, 1992.

Bowlby, John. *Loss: Sadness and Depression.* Vol. 3, *Attachment and Loss.* New York: Basic, 1980.

"Breaking New Ground." *Mary Star of the Sea High School Capital Campaign Update* 3, no. 2, March 2000, 4.

Brown, Karen McCarthy. *Mama Lola: A Vodou Priestess in Brooklyn.* Berkeley: University of California Press, 1991.

Browning, Don S. *A Fundamental Practical Theology: Descriptive and Strategic Proposals.* Minneapolis: Fortress, 1991.

Bynum, Caroline Walker. *Holy Feast and Holy Fast: The Religious Significance of Food to Medieval Women.* Berkeley: University of California Press, 1987.

Carroll, Michael P. *Madonnas That Maim: Popular Catholicism in Italy since the Fifteenth Century.* Baltimore: Johns Hopkins University Press, 1992.

Carter, Elizabeth A., and Monica McGoldrick, eds. *The Family Life Cycle: A Frame Work for Family Therapy.* New York: Gardner, 1980.

Chidester, David, and Edward T. Linenthal. "Introduction to American Sacred Space." In *American Sacred Space,* edited by David Chidester and Edward T. Linenthal, 1–42. Bloomington: Indiana University Press, 1995.

"Church Grows to Meet Community Needs." *San Pedro News Pilot,* September 28, 1989, D14.

Ciarrocchi, Joseph W., and Robert J. Wicks. *Psychotherapy with Priests, Protestant Clergy, and Catholic Religious: A Practical Guide.* Madison, CT: Psychosocial, 2000.

Clebsch, William, and Charles Jaekle. *Pastoral Care in Historical Perspective.* Englewood Cliffs, NJ: Prentice Hall, 1983

Connerton, Paul. *How Societies Remember.* Cambridge: Cambridge University Press, 1989.

Conzen, Kathleen Neils, David A. Gerber, Ewa Morawska, George E. Pozzetta, and Rudolph J. Vecoli. "The Invention of Ethnicity: A Perspective from the U.S.A." *Journal of American Ethnic History* 12, no. 1 (1992): 3–41.

Cooey, Paula. *Religious Imagination and the Body: A Feminist Analysis.* New York: Oxford University Press, 1994.

Couture, Pamela D. *Seeing Children, Seeing God: A Practical Theology of Children and Poverty.* Nashville: Abingdon, 2000.

Couture, Pamela D., and Rodney J. Hunter, eds. *Pastoral Care an Social Conflict: Essays in Honor of Charles V. Gerkin.* Nashville: Abingdon, 1995.

Csikszentmihalyi, Mihaly, and Eugene Rochberg-Halton. *The Meaning of Things: Domestic Symbols and the Self.* Cambridge: Cambridge University Press, 1981.

Daly, Mary. *Beyond God the Father: Toward a Philosophy of Women's Liberation.* Boston: Beacon, 1973.

Davaney, Sheila Greeve. "Conclusion: Changing Conversation: Impetuses and Implications." In *Changing Conversations: Religious Reflection and Cultural Analysis*, edited by Dwight N. Hopkins and Sheila Greeve Davaney, 255–62. New York: Routledge, 1996.

———. "Mapping Theologies: An Historicist Guide to Contemporary Theology." In *Changing Conversations: Religious Reflection and Cultural Analysis*, edited by Dwight N. Hopkins and Sheila Greeve Davaney, 25–41. New York: Routledge, 1996.

———. *Pragmatic Historicism: A Theology for the Twenty-First Century.* Albany: State University of New York Press, 2000.

Davidman, Lynn. *Motherloss.* Berkeley: University of California Press, 2000.

———. "Truth, Subjectivity, and Ethnographic Research." In *Personal Knowledge and Beyond: Reshaping the Ethnography of Religion*, edited by James V. Spickard et al., 17–26. New York: New York University Press, 2002.

Davies, John. "U. S. Runs out of Money to Reimburse Fishermen." *San Pedro News Pilot*, November 18, 1980, A1, B1.

Del Guidice, Luisa. "St. Joseph's Tables." Exhibition Brochure. Italian Oral History Institute, Los Angeles: University of California, Los Angeles, March 1998.

DeMarinis, Valerie M. *Critical Caring: A Feminist Model for Pastoral Psychology.* Louisville: Westminster John Knox, 1993.

di Leonardo, Micaela. *The Varieties of Ethnic Experience: Kinship, Class, and Gender among California Italian-Americans.* Ithaca, NY: Cornell University Press, 1984.

———. *Exotics at Home: Anthropologies, Others, and American Modernity.* Chicago: University of Chicago Press, 1998.

Doehring, Carrie. *The Practice of Pastoral Care: A Postmodern Approach.* Louisville, KY: Westminster John Knox, 2006.

Dolan, Jay P. *The American Catholic Experience: A History from Colonial Times to the Present.* Garden City, NY: Doubleday, 1985.

"Ecuador Captures Eight Tuna Boats." *San Pedro News Pilot*, November 14, 1972, A1.

Espin, Orlando O. *The Faith of the People: Theological Reflections on Popular Catholicism.* Maryknoll, NY: Orbis, 1997.

Falicov, Celia Jae. "The Cultural Meaning of Family Triangles." In *Re-Visioning Family Therapy: Race, Culture, and Gender in Clinical Practice*, edited by Monica McGoldrick, 37–49. New York: Guilford, 1998.

Freud, Sigmund. *The Future of an Illusion.* Translated and edited by James Strachey. New York: W.W. Norton, 1961.

Fulmer, Melinda. "It's the End of the Line for L. A. Harbor's Chicken of the Sea Canning Operation." *Los Angeles Times,* August, 2, 2001, C1, C6.

Galindo, Israel. "What Makes a Congregation a Real Faith Community?" In *Alban Weekly* 158 (July 30, 2007). http://www.alban.org/conversation.aspx?id=4748.

Gallagher, Patrick. "Pastor's Corner—Discrimination." *Mary Star of the Sea Newsletter.* March 2000, 1.

Gaventa, Beverly Roberts, and Cynthia L. Rigby, eds. *Blessed One: Protestant Perspectives on Mary.* Louisville: Westminster John Knox, 2002.

Gebara, Ivone and Maria Clara Bingemer. *Mary: Mother of God, Mother of the Poor.* Maryknoll, NY: Orbis, 1987.

Geertz, Clifford. *The Interpretation of Cultures: Selected Essays.* New York: Basic, 1973.

Gerkin, Charles. *An Introduction to Pastoral Care.* Nashville: Abingdon, 1997.

———. *Widening the Horizon: Pastoral Responses to a Fragmented Society.* Philadelphia: Wesminster, 1986.

Goffman, Erving. *Interaction Ritual: Essays in Face-to-Face Behavior*. Garden City, NY: Anchor, 1967.

Goldenberg, Naomi. *Changing of the Gods: Feminism and the End of Traditional Religions*. Boston: Beacon, 1979.

Graham, Elaine L. *Transforming Practice: Pastoral Theology in an Age of Uncertainty*. London: Mowbray, 1996.

Graham, Elaine, Heather Walton, and Frances Ward. *Theological Reflection: Methods*. London: SCM, 2005.

Graham, Larry Kent. *Care of Persons, Care of Worlds: A Psychosystems Approach to Pastoral Care and Counseling*. Nashville: Abingdon, 1992.

Greeley, Andrew. *The Catholic Imagination*. Berkeley: University of California Press, 2000.

Greenberg, Jay R., and Stephen A. Mitchell. *Object Relations in Psychoanalytic Theory*. Cambridge: Harvard University Press, 1983.

Greider, Kathleen J. *Reckoning with Aggression: Theology, Violence, and Vitality*. Louisville: Westminster John Knox, 1997.

Greider, Kathleen J., Gloria A. Johnson, and Kristen J. Leslie. "Three Decades of Woman Writing for Our Lives." In *Feminist and Womanist Pastoral Theology*, edited by Bonnie Miller-McLemore and Brita Gill-Austern, 21–50. Nashville: Abingdon, 1999.

Grimes, Ronald L. *Ritual Criticism: Case Studies in Its Practice, Essays on Its Theory*. Columbia: University of South Carolina Press, 1990.

Gutiérrez, Gustavo. *A Theology of Liberation*. 2nd ed. Maryknoll, NY: Orbis, 1988.

Hall, David D., ed. *Lived Religion in America: Toward a History of Practice*. Princeton: Princeton University Press, 1997.

Hallisey, Charles. "In Defense of Rather Fragile and Local Achievement: Some Reflections on the Work of Gurulogomi." In *Religion and Practical Reason*, edited by David Tracy and Frank Reynolds, 121–62. Albany: State of New York Press, 1994.

Hamington, Maurice. *Hail Mary? The Struggle for Ultimate Womanhood in Catholicism*. New York: Routledge, 1995.

Hammersley, Martyn, and Paul Atkinson. *Ethnography: Principles in Practice*. 2nd ed. London: Routledge, 1995.

Hanh, Thich Nhat. *The Blooming of a Lotus: Guided Meditation for Achieving the Miracle of Mindfulness*. Translated by Annabel Laity. Boston: Beacon, 1993.

Hanson, Marcus Lee. "The Problem of the Third Generation Immigrant." Address, Augustana Historical Society, Rock Island, IL, May 15, 1937. Reprinted as *Augustana College Library Occasional Paper*, no. 16. Rock Island, IL: 1987, 13–17.

Happel, Stephen and James G. Walter. *Conversion and Discipleship*. Philadelphia: Fortress, 1986.

Haraway, Donna. *Simians, Cyborgs and Women: The Reinvention of Nature*. New York: Routledge, 1991.

Hareven, Tamara. "The Search for Generational Memory." In *Oral History: An Interdisciplinary Anthology*, edited by David K. Dunaway and Willa K. Baum, 241–56. Walnut Creek, CA: AltaMira, 1978.

Herman, Judith Lewis. *Trauma and Recovery*. New York: BasicBooks, 1992.

Hess, Lisa M. "Practices in a New Key: Human Knowing in Musical and Practical Theological Perspective." Ph.D. diss., Princeton Theological Seminary, 2001.

Hiltner, Seward. *Preface to Pastoral Theology: the Ministry and Theory of Shepherding*. Nashville: Abingdon, 1958.

"History of the Fisherman's Fiesta," Unidentified Photocopy, 9.

Holifield, E. Brooks. *A History of Pastoral Care in America: From Salvation to Self-Realization.* Nashville: Abingdon, 1983.

Hummel, Leonard M. *Clothed in Nothingness: Consolation for Suffering.* Minneapolis: Augsburg Fortress, 2003.

Hunter, Rodney J. "Religious Caregiving and Pedagogy in a Postmodern Context." *Journal of Pastoral Theology* 8 (1998): 15–27.

"Italian Catholic Federation." http://www.ICF.org (accessed July 26, 2007).

Jacobson, Matthew Frye. *Whiteness of a Different Color: European Immigrants and the Alchemy of Race.* Cambridge: Harvard University Press, 1998.

James, William. *The Varieties of Religious Experience: A Study in Human Nature.* Edited by Martin Marty. Middlesex, England: Penguin, 1982.

Jenkins, Philip. *The New Anti-Catholicism: The Last Acceptable Prejudice.* New York: Oxford University Press, 2003.

Johnson, Elizabeth A. "Mary and the Female Face of God." *Theological Studies* 50 (1989): 500–526.

———. *Truly Our Sister: A Theology of Mary in the Communion of Saints.* New York: Continuum, 2003.

Jonte-Pace, Diane, and William B. Parsons, eds. *Religion and Psychology: Mapping the Terrain. Contemporary Dialogues, Future Prospects.* London and New York: Routledge, 1991.

Junger, Sebastian. *The Perfect Storm: A True Story of Men Against the Sea.* New York: HarperTorch, 1997.

Kapikian, Catherine. *Art in Service of the Sacred.* Edited by Kathy Black. Nashville: Abingdon, 2006.

Kawasaki, Kanichi. "The Japanese Community of East San Pedro, Terminal Island, California." M.A. thesis, University of Southern California, 1931.

Kelly, Edith Summers. "The Head Cutters." In *Cannery Women, Cannery Lives: Mexican Women, Unionization, and the California Food Processing Industry, 1930–1950,* by Vicki L. Ruiz, 126. Albuquerque: University of New Mexico Press, 1987.

Kim, Ai Ra. *Women Struggling for a New Life: The Role of Religion in the Cultural Passage from Korea to America.* Albany: State University of New York Press, 1996.

Kimball, Charles. *When Religion Becomes Evil.* New York: HarperCollins, 2003.

Kohut, Heinz, and Ernest Wolf. "The Disorders of the Self and Their Treatment: An Outline." *International Journal of Psychoanalysis* 59 (1978): 413–25.

Kronman, Mick. "Breakfast at Canetti's." *National Fisherman,* July 1998, 26–27.

Lagies, M. J. "The Two Sides to the Ecuador Tunaboat Seizures." *San Pedro News Pilot,* March 15, 1975, A1.

Lartey, Emmanuel Y. *Pastoral Theology in an Intercultural World.* Cleveland, OH: Pilgrim, 2006.

Leonard, Karen Isaksen. *Making Ethnic Choices: California's Punjabi Mexican Americans.* Philadelphia: Temple University Press, 1992.

Lott, Brett. *Jewel: A Novel.* New York: Pocket, 1991.

Luepnitz, Deborah Anna. *The Family Interpreted: Feminist Theory in Clinical Practice.* New York: Basic, 1988.

MacIntyre, Alasdair. *After Virtue: A Study in Moral Theory.* Notre Dame, IN: University of Notre Dame Press, 1981.

Madison, D. Soyini. *Critical Ethnography: Method, Ethics, and Performance.* Thousand Oaks, London, and New Delhi: Sage, 2005.

Maffly-Kipp, Laurie F., Leigh E. Schmidt, and Mark Valeri, eds. *Practicing Protestants: Histories of Christian Life in America, 1630–1965.* Lived Religions. Baltimore: Johns Hopkins University Press, 2006.

Markholt, Ottilie. *Maritime Solidarity: Pacific Coast Unionism, 1929–1938.* Tacoma, WA: Pacific Coast Maritime History Committee, 1998.

May, Melanie A. *A Body Knows: A Theopoetics of Death and Resurrection.* New York: Continuum, 1995.

McDannell, Colleen. "Interpreting Things: Material Culture Studies and American Religion." *Religion* 21 (1991): 371–87.

———. *Material Christianity: Religion and Poular Culture in America.* New Haven: Yale University Press, 1995.

McFague, Sallie. *Life Abundant: Rethinking Theology and Economy for a Planet in Peril (Searching for a New Framework).* Minneapolis: Augsburg Fortress, 2000.

McGoldrick, Monica, ed. *Re-Visioning Family Therapy: Race, Culture, and Gender in Clinical Practice.* New York: Guilford, 1998.

McGoldrick, Monica, Carol M. Anderson, and Froma Walsh, eds. *Women in Families: A Framework for Family Therapy.* New York: Norton, 1989.

Meissner, W.W. *Psychoanalysis and Religious Experience.* New Haven: Yale University Press, 1984.

Merton, Robert K. *Social Theory and Social Structure.* Rev. ed. Glencoe, IL: Free, 1957.

Miles, Margaret R. *Image as Insight: Visual Understanding in Western Christianity and Secular Culture.* Boston: Beacon, 1985.

———. *Practicing Christianity: Critical Perspectives for an Embodied Spirituality.* New York: Crossroad, 1988.

Miller, Jean Baker and Irene Pierce Stiver. *The Healing Connection: How Women Form Relationships in Therapy and in Life.* Boston: Beacon, 1997.

Miller-McLemore, Bonnie J. "Feminist Theory in Pastoral Theology." In *Feminist and Womanist Pastoral Theology,* edited by Bonnie J. Miller-McLemore and Brita L. Gill-Austern, 77–94. Nashville: Abingdon, 1999.

———. "The Living Human Web: Pastoral Theology at the Turn of the Century." In *Through the Eyes of Women: Insights for Pastoral Care,* edited by Jeanne Stevenson Moessner, 9–16. Minneapolis: Fortress, 1996.

Mitchell, Beverly Eileen. *Black Abolitionism: A Quest for Human Dignity.* Maryknoll, NY: Orbis, 2005.

Mitchell, Stephen A., and Margaret J. Black. *Freud and Beyond.* New York: Basic, 1995.

Moe-Lobeda, Cynthia. *Healing a Broken World: Globalization and God.* Minneapolis: Augsburg Fortress, 2002.

Morgan, David. *Visual Piety: A History and Theory of Popular Religious Images.* Berkeley: University of California Press, 1998.

Naples, Nancy A. *Feminism and Method: Ethnography, Discourse Analysis, and Activist Research.* New York and London: Routledge, 2003.

Nichols, Michael P., and Richard C. Schwartz. *Family Therapy: Concepts and Methods.* 3rd ed. Needham Hights, MA: Allyn and Bacon, 1995.

Nouwen, Henri J. M. *With Open Hands.* Notre Dame, Ind.: Ave Maria, 1972.

Orsi, Robert A. *Between Heaven and Earth: The Religious Worlds People Make and the Scholars Who Study Them.* Princeton: Princeton University Press, 2005.

———, ed. *Gods of the City: Religion and the American Urban Landscape.* Bloomington and Indianapolis: Indiana University Press, 1999.

————. *The Madonna of 115th Street: Faith and Community in Italian Harlem, 1880-1950.* New Haven: Yale University Press, 1985.

————. "The Religious Boundaries of an Inbetween People: Street *Feste* and the Problem of the Dark-Skinned Other in Italian Harlem, 1920–1990." *American Quarterly* 44, (Sept. 1992): 313–47.

————. *Thank You, Saint Jude: Women's Devotion to the Patron Saint of Hopeless Causes.* New Haven: Yale University Press, 1996.

Pack, Susan. "3 Die, 6 Saved in Boat Sinking." *San Pedro News Pilot*, December 17, 1987, A1.

Palmer, Parker. *A Hidden Wholeness: The Journey Toward an Undivided Life.* San Francisco: Jossey-Bass, 2004.

Parks, Sharon Daloz. *Big Questions, Worthy Dreams: Mentoring Young Adults in Their Search for Meaning, Purpose, and Faith.* San Francisco: Jossey-Bass, 2000.

"Pastor Calls San Pedro 'God's Country—Special.'" *San Pedro News Pilot*, December 17, 1987, A1.

Patton, John. *Pastoral Care in Context: An Introduction to Pastoral Care.* Louisville: Wesminster John Knox, 1993.

Pelikan, Jaroslav. *Jesus Through the Centuries: His Place in the History of Culture.* New Haven: Yale University Press, 1999.

Perkins, Richard R. "The Terminal Island Japanese: Preservation of a Lost Community." M.A. thesis, California State University, Dominguez Hills, 1992.

"Pescatore Desparate—Despairing Fishermen." Episode 101 in *Listening at the Luncheonette*, PBS. Filmed at Canetti's Seafood Grotto, San Pedro, CA, 1988.

Poling, James Newton. *Render Unto God: Economic Vulnerability, Family Violence and Pastoral Theology.* St. Louis: Chalice, 2002.

Ramsay, Nancy J. "A Time of Ferment and Redefinition." In *Pastoral Care and Counseling: Redefining the Paradigms,* edited by Nancy J. Ramsay, 1–43. Nashville: Abingdon, 2004.

Recinos, Harold J. "Mission: A Latino Pastoral Theology." In *Mestizo Christianity: Theology from the Latino Perspective,* edited by Arturo J. Banuelas, 132–45. Maryknoll, NY: Orbis, 1995.

"Responsorio." Prayer Pamphlet.

Richardson, Ronald W. *Creating a Healthier Church: Family Systems Theory, Leadership, and Congregational Life.* Minneapolis: Fortress, 1996.

Rizzuto, Ana-Maria. *The Birth of the Living God: A Psychoanalytic Study.* Chicago: University of Chicago Press, 1970.

Rodriguez, Jeanette. *Our Lady of Guadalupe: Faith and Empowerment among Mexican-American Women,* Austin: University of Texas Press, 1980.

Roediger, David. *The Wages of Whiteness: Race and the Making of the American Working Class.* London: Verso, 1991.

————. *Towards the Abolition of Whiteness: Essays on Race, Politics, and Working Class History.* London and New York: Verso, 1994.

Rosaldo, Renato. *Culture and Truth: The Re-Making of Social Analysis.* Boston: Beacon, 1989.

Ruether, Rosemary Radford. *Gaia and God: An Ecofeminist Theology of Earth Healing.* San Francisco: HarperCollins, 1992.

————. *Sexism and God-Talk: Toward a Feminist Theology.* Boston: Beacon, 1983.

"S. Giovan Giuseppe Della Croce: Coroncina Al Santo." Pamphlet, n.p.

Sahagun, Louis. "Commercial Fishing Industry Is a Waning Force in L.A. Harbor." *Los Angeles Times,* June, 3, 2001, B1, B11.

Said, Edward. *Culture and Imperialism.* New York: Alfred A. Knopf, 1993.

Saint-Exupéry, Antoine de. *The Little Prince.* Translated by Richard Howard. San Diego: Harcourt, 2000.

Saliers, Don. "What Languages Shall We Borrow?" Lecture presented at Wesley Theological Seminary, March 8, 2007.

Schmidt, Leigh Eric. "Practices of Exchanges: From Market Culture to Gift Economy in the Interpretation of American Religion." In *Lived Religion in America: Toward a History of Practice,* edited by David D. Hall, 69–91. Princeton: Princeton University Press, 1997.

————. "The Easter Parade: Piety, Fashion, and Display." In *Religion and American Culture,* Vol. 4, No. 2 (Summer 1994): 135–64.

Sepeckbacher, Franz. "Apparitions of Our Lady at Montichiari." http://www.mgr.org/rosamystica.html (accessed July 14, 2007).

Slough, Rebecca J. "'Let Every Tongue, By Art Refined, Mingle Its Softest Notes with Mine': An Exploration of Hymn-Singing Events and Dimensions of Knowing." In *Religious and Social Ritual: Interdisciplinary Explorations,* edited by Michael B. Aune and Valerie DeMarinis, 175–206. Albany: State University of New York Press, 1996.

Smith, Jonathan Z. *Map is Not Territory: Studies in the History of Religions.* Chicago: University of Chicago Press, 1978.

Smith, Wilfred Cantwell. *Belief and History.* Charlottesville, VA: University of Virginia Press, 1986.

Society for Intercultural Pastoral Care and Counselling. "Mission Statement." http://www.sipcc.org (accessed July 26, 2007).

Sollors, Werner, ed. *The Invention of Ethnicity.* New York: Oxford University Press, 1989.

Spickard, James V., J. Shawn Landres, and Meredith B. McGuire, eds. *Personal Knowledge and Beyond: Reshaping the Ethnography of Religion.* New York: New York University Press, 2002.

Stallybrass, Peter, and Allon White. *The Politics and Poetics of Transgression.* Ithaca, NY: Cornell University Press, 1986.

Steinberg, Stephen. *The Ethnic Myth: Race, Ethnicity, and Class in America.* New York: Atheneum, 1981.

Stroupe, Nibs, and Inez Fleming. *While We Run This Race: Confronting the Power of Racism in a Southern Church.* Maryknoll, NY: Orbis, 1995.

Sullivan, Harry Stack. *The Interpersonal Theory of Psychiatry.* New York: Norton, 1953.

Swidler, Anne. "Culture in Action: Symbols and Strategies." *American Sociological Review* 5 (April 1986): 273–86.

Tatum, Beverly Daniel. *"Why Are All the Black Kids Sitting Together in the Cafeteria?" and Other Conversations About Race.* New York: Basic, 1997.

Taves, Ann. *The Household of Faith: Roman Catholic Devotions in Mid-Nineteenth-Century America.* Notre Dame: University of Notre Dame Press, 1986.

Thandeka. *Learning to be White: Money, Race, and God in America.* NY: Continuum, 1999.

Theodore the Studite, *On the Holy Icons.* Translated by Catharine P. Roth. Crestwood, NY: St. Vladimir's Seminary Press, 1981.

Tracy, David. *The Analogical Imagination: Christian Theology and the Culture of Pluralism.* New York: Crossroad, 1981.

Turley, Erica. "The Development of Italian Women's Identity." Unpublished Paper, June 1999.

Tweed, Thomas A. *Our Lady of Exile: Diasporic Religion at a Cuban Catholic Shrine in Miami.* NY: Oxford University Press, 1997.

———, ed. *Retelling U.S. Religious History.* Berkeley: University of California Press, 1997.

Ulanov, Ann Belford. *Finding Space: Winnicott, God, and Psychic Reality.* Louisville: Westminster John Knox, 2001.

Van Biema, David, and Jeff Chu. "Does God Want You To Be Rich?" *Time,* December 10, 2006. http://www.time.com/time/magazine/article/0,9171.1533448-2.00.html.

Vita, William S., et al. "Sixty Years in Our Parish (1889–1949)." San Pedro, CA: Mary Star of the Sea Parish, 1949.

Volf, Miroslav. *Exclusion and Embrace: A Theological Exploration of Identity, Otherness, and Reconciilation.* Nashville: Abingdon, 1996.

Ward, Keith. *A Vision to Pursue: Beyond the Crisis in Christianity.* London, SCM, 1991.

Warner, Marina. *Alone of All Her Sex: The Myth and the Cult of the Virgin Mary.* New York: Vintage, 1976.

Waters, Mary. *Ethnic Options: Choosing Identities in America.* Berkeley: University of California Press, 1990.

Watson, David Lowes. *Covenant Discipleship: Christian Formation Through Mutual Accountability.* Eugene, OR: Wipf & Stock, 2002.

Winnicott, D. W. *The Maturational Processes and the Facilitating Environment: Studies in the Theory of Emotional Development.* New York: International Universities Press, 1965.

———. *Playing and Reality.* London: Routledge, 1971.

Wulff, David M. *Psychology of Religion: Classic and Contemporary Views.* New York: Wiley, 1991.

Wuthnow, Robert. *Producing the Sacred: An Essay on Public Religion.* Chicago: University of Illinois Press, 1994.

Zangs, Mary. "Terminal Island History." In *Shoreline.* San Pedro, CA: San Pedro Historical Society, 1991.

Subject Index